L'ART DE RECEVOIR
(THE ART OF ENTERTAINING)

First Edition

Caroline Chaplin & Evelyn Pascal

HARLAND PUBLISHING LIMITED

Published by Harland Publishing
c/o Harland Simon Limited
Bond Avenue
Bletchley
Milton Keynes MK1 1TJ

First Published in 1996

ISBN 0 9517776 0 2

Printed by J W Arrowsmith Limited
Winterstoke Road
Bristol BS3 2NT

Acknowledgements

We would like to express our gratitude to R J Ashman Esq., for his support, advice and encouragement throughout the preparation of this book.

We are indebted to Helen Deas for drawing pen and ink illustrations.

We would like to thank Sam Twinings of the Twinings Tea Company.

INTRODUCTION

The essence of entertaining is to please your guests and share with them a happy occasion.

Always try to be in a relaxed and jolly frame of mind, your guests will sense this and be put at ease very quickly. Remember, laughter is infectious.

Careful forward planning is paramount. Using tried and trusted menus will ensure success. It is a simple but efficient method. This book is designed to give the reader confidence without, we hope, being too dogmatic.

Over the period it has taken us to compile this book, we have enjoyed the experience immensely. Our writing sessions frequently ran overtime, we had long chatty debates and great fun.

We do hope you find 'L'Art de Recevoir' interesting, but most of all we wish you countless happy hours of entertaining at home.

"We may live without poetry, music and art,
We may live without conscience and live without a heart,
We may live without friends, we may live without books,
But civilized man cannot live without cooks."
OWEN MERIDITH (E. R. B. LYTTON, EARL OF LYTTON)

SYMBOLS USED IN THE BOOK

Recipe Format	❀	**Easy**
	❀❀	**Intermediate**
	❀❀❀	**Advanced**
Recipe Cost	☆☆☆	**Reasonably priced**
	☆☆☆☆	**Medium priced**
	☆☆☆☆☆	**Expensive**
Red Wines	🍷	**Under £10.00**
	🍷🍷	**£10.00 to £20.00**
	🍷🍷🍷	**Over £20.00**
White Wines	🥂	**Under £10.00**
	🥂🥂	**£10.00 to £20.00**
	🥂🥂🥂	**Over £20.00**

CONTENTS

DAILY & SEASONAL MENUS

PARTIES

MENUS FROM AROUND THE WORLD

APPENDIX

INDEX

ETIQUETTE

E tiquette is important but should never be unduly rigid and hinder true enjoyment. Entertaining is an Epicurean exercise designed to make people happy.

INVITATIONS

FORMAL INVITATIONS

Formal invitations are always written in the third person and should list the following:

- The name and address of the host and hostess (and if they wish their telephone number).
- The venue, if different from their usual residence.
- The occasion.
- The time of arrival and departure.
- The dress
- RSVP with the address.
- A map is a good idea, and will be very welcome.

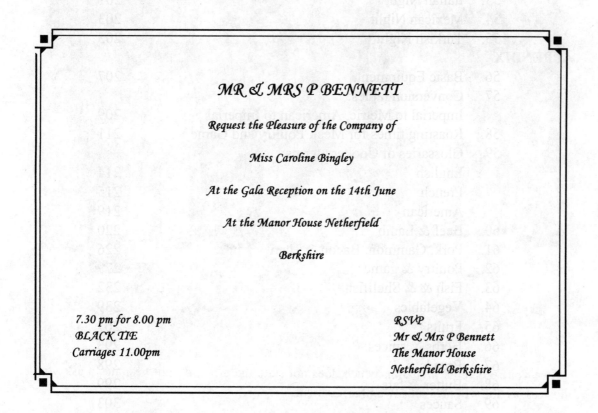

MR & MRS P BENNETT

Request the Pleasure of the Company of

Miss Caroline Bingley

At the Gala Reception on the 14th June

At the Manor House Netherfield

Berkshire

7.30 pm for 8.00 pm
BLACK TIE
Carriages 11.00pm

RSVP
Mr & Mrs P Bennett
The Manor House
Netherfield Berkshire

There are four types of dress for a formal occasion. The dress refers to the gentlemen only.

Black Tie: Black dinner jacket and trousers. The ladies should wear an evening dress, long or short.

White Tie: White tie is very formal and is worn for Royal and diplomatic occasions. Black-tailed evening suit, white waistcoat, or white stiff-fronted shirt with wing collar and white marcella bow tie.

The Ladies must wear a ballgown and long gloves. Long gloves are kept on for shaking hands and dancing and taken off for eating. However they will not be removed completely as they usually have an opening at the wrist to enable the hand to slide out. The hand part of the glove is then tucked inside the opening at the wrist. For this reason rings are worn inside the gloves, bracelets outside.

Morning Suit Grey & Black: This is the day-time equivalent of white tie, worn at weddings, Ascot, Parliament and State openings. Black or dark grey trousers with a fine stripe, a grey waistcoat and a black or dark grey-tailed morning coat.

Ladies would wear an elegant morning dress or suit with a hat.

Lounge Suit: Suit with a tie, ladies can wear either a dress or a suit.

When you receive an invitation which does not state the dress, do not hesitate to ask your hostess, as this will prevent any embarrassment.

Reply in writing using the third person (even though you might have already accepted by telephone). Repeat all the necessary details mentioned on the invitation. Do this promptly to give the hostess time to plan.

If you are a vegetarian or on a special diet it is best to inform your hostess of your circumstances in good time.

Miss Caroline Bingley has much pleasure in accepting
Mr & Mrs P. Bennett's kind invitation to the Gala Dinner
on the 14th June at the Manor House, Netherfield, at 7.30pm

INFORMAL INVITATIONS

Remember to make a note of whom you have invited particularly when dealing with large numbers of people - logical you might say, but it is easy to mix up dates or to forget one of your friends!
Printed invitations can be sent, and you may wish to indicate whether contributions are welcome (i.e. bring a bottle).

AT HOME

A perfect host will put his guests at ease by welcoming them in a relaxed, happy and chatty manner. He will then proceed with introductions, offer drinks, and endeavour to bring the guests together by breaking the ice with jovial and stimulating conversation.

Ensure the front door is adequately lit so your guests do not fumble in the dark. When the weather is unclement do not leave your visitors standing in the pouring rain. Offer to take their coats and gracefully accept any contributions.
It is tactful to let them know where to find the cloakroom (check in advance that there are ample provisions for their use).

INTRODUCTIONS

The basic rules are simple, introduce:
- The gentlemen to the ladies.
- The younger members to the older members.
- The junior members to the senior members.

If your guests have a rank the lower rank should be introduced to the higher rank.
When personages of equal status and age are being introduced there is very little dilemma.
Children are introduced to adults by their christian names, the adult is introduced to the child using the surname.
When a lady enters a room, any seated gentleman should rise to acknowledge her presence; the same applies when she leaves the table.

FORMS OF ADDRESS

Whether you are compiling a guest list for a formal or informal occasion you might need to refer to the following list. For further information we recommend "Debrett's correct form".

Duke:	His Grace the Duke of
Duchess:	Her Grace the Duchess of
Marquess:	The Most Hon. the Marquess of
Marchioness:	The Most Hon. the Marchioness of
Earl:	The Right Hon. the Earl of
Countess:	The Right Hon. the Countess of
Viscount:	The Right Hon. the (Lord) Viscount
Viscountess:	The Right Hon. the Viscountess or the Viscountess
Baron:	The Right Hon. Lord, or The Lord
Baroness:	The Right Hon. the, or The Baroness
Baronet:	Sir ....., Bart. or Bt.
Baronet's wife:	Lady .....
Knight:	Sir .....
Knight's wife:	Lady .....
Archbishop:	His Grace the Lord Archbishop of
Bishop:	The Right Rev. the Lord Bishop of
Dean:	The Very Rev. the Dean of
Clergy:	The Rev. .....
Judge:	The Hon. Mr. Justice .....
Privy Councillor:	The Right Hon. ..... M.P.
Member of Parliament:	..... Esq., M.P.
Dr. or Surgeon:	Dr. ..... or ..... Esq., MD
Commissioned Officers of H.M. Forces:	Address by rank together with decorations.

PLACE SETTINGS

To avoid confusion, decide in advance where to seat your guests. The use of place cards adds a little touch of sophistication.

Seating plan:
The host sits at the top of the table, the hostess at the other end (opposite if round table). The female guest of honour sits on the right hand side of the host, the male guest of honour sits on the hostess' right hand side.
In the instance of one host, the guest of honour will sit on his right hand side, the second guest on his left.

Alternate ladies with gentlemen, bearing in mind personalities. Remember the most important duty of any host is to make sure that his or her guests enjoy themselves. Protocol is only a guide, the clever host will adapt it wisely; for instance, husband and wife can be seated apart or together, but it could be very unkind to part sweethearts.

Thirteen can be considered an unlucky number to be seated around a table. There are many theories behind this superstition, the most probable one being 'The Last Supper' Matthew's 26, with Jesus and his disciples.

If this occurs, add another chair and place on it your favourite Teddy Bear!

SERVING FOOD & WINE

Food is served from the left and wine from the right. Female guests are served first.

Time should not hang heavily between courses, equally so it should not appear rushed. At the end of the main course it is a good idea to pause for several minutes to relax and enjoy the wine and company, before dessert or cheese.
If you find it difficult to carve make sure you do it in the kitchen out of sight, and that your electric knife is muffled, so no one is aware of the struggles going on.
It is sensible to avoid serving food that is awkward to eat, but if you do, take the trouble to prepare it adequately. For example, provide a finger bowl and napkin with prawns in their shells.

SETTING THE TABLE

Before choosing your menu make sure you have enough china, cutlery and glasses to complement each course.

Cutlery is laid on each side of the place setting, the cutlery for the first course is placed furthest away from the plate. The bread knife is either placed on the right hand side furthest away from the place setting or on the side plate.
One glass should be set for each wine to be served, plus one for water. The glass to be used for your first wine should be nearest your place setting and the water glass furthest away.
Ensure there are condiments, butter and ash trays on the table.
Floral arrangements or candles should not obstruct your guest's vision or be cumbersome, keep the table as clear as possible yet attractive.

LIGHTING

Lighting plays a part in creating the atmosphere. Harsh lighting is not to be recommended. Candles cast a delicate glow and alleviate the air of tobacco smoke but they do not provide enough light on their own; a gloomy warm room sends people to sleep. It is important that your guests can see what they are eating and who they are sitting by!

THE HOSTESS BOOK

A 'Hostess Book' is invaluable if you entertain frequently. Use a page for each occasion to record date, time, event, menu and wine and the table plan to figure the seating arrangement.

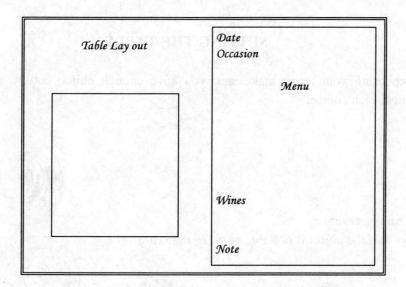

Table Lay out

Date
Occasion

Menu

Wines

Note

AWKWARD SITUATIONS

"Strange to see how a good dinner and feasting reconciles everybody."
SAMUEL PEPYS.

Occasionally a host will be presented with embarrassing situations he has been unable to foresee. These can hopefully be smoothed over diplomatically

- **Avoid discussing:**
  Religion, politics and money.
- **Food spilt over someone's clothing:**
  Treat <u>immediately</u>, offer all the help needed.
- **Guest not eating one of the courses:**
  Offer an alternative if possible, otherwise think nothing of it.
- **Late arrivals**:
  Make light of the situation, greeting the guests as though nothing had happened.
- **Making incorrect introductions:**
  Apologise gracefully.
- **Two people with conflicting views locked into a heated discussion:**
  Tactfully change the subject and break it by creating a diversion.

- Duplicating presents:
Quickly hide the object if possible or make light of it.

- Ladies wearing the same outfit:
When it is two of your guests make light of the situation. In the case of the hostess she should immediately change.

- **Recently bereaved or divorced:**
  If appropriate inform the other guests in advance.
- **Social gaffes and faux pas:**
  Either subtly change the subject or make light of it.

PITFALLS

"There is a well known joke in France about Madame de Brinvilliers, the famous poisoner, to whom some gastronome compared a bad chef, saying, the only difference between La Brinvilliers and him is that he had good intentions."
ROBERT COURTINE.

- **Wine cork breaks or gets stuck in the bottle neck:**
  Push the cork into the bottle with a skewer and leave it skewered. Clear and clean the neck of the bottle in order to decant the wine. If the wine is corked, filter through muslin or a coffee filter.
- **Burnt food:**
  Obviously, food burnt beyond recognition has to be thrown away.
  Slightly singed food can be disguised with garnishing or trimmed discreetly. Failing all this, inform your guests that charcoal is good for you!
- **Whilst cooking the oven smokes, you burn the toast, there is a large build up of steam in the kitchen:**
  Keep the kitchen door leading into the house closed, and open kitchen windows or outside door.

APERITIFS

The origin of the word 'Alcohol' is the subject of an ongoing debate, some say that it could derive from the Arabic words 'Al kohl' meaning 'like kohl' (a fine powder substance used as a cosmetic). Others believe it evolved from the Arabic word 'Alguhl' meaning ghost or evil spirit. Most vegetable matter can produce alcohol under favourable circumstances. Distillation is a complicated process and the first accurate instructions for distilling alcohol were compiled by the Arabian Alchemist Geber in the eighth century AD. It was subsequently introduced to the Western World by Moorish chemists.

An apéritif is served before a meal, to stimulate the appetite, not to drown it. Take this into consideration when preparing the drinks. Serve with canapés or little savouries i.e. olives, nuts etc.

WHISKIES

The major producers of whiskies are: Ireland, Scotland, America and Canada. It is interesting to note the different spelling of the word 'whisky'. Irish and American are spelt with an 'e' before the 'y' (whiskey). Scottish and Canadian are spelt without the 'e' (whisky).

IRISH WHISKEY

During the fifth and sixth century missionary monks from the Continent brought the art of distilling to Ireland. Whiskey was referred to as 'uisce beatha' 'water of life'. In 1170 the troops of King Henry II of England invaded Ireland and called their new discovery whiskey because they were unable to pronounce 'uisce'. In 1608 Sir Thomas Phillips, who was the Deputy of King James I in Ulster, granted licence to distill legally. Irish whiskey is distinctive by its smooth and light taste. Its aromatic flavour differs from the smoky taste of Scotch whisky. It is made using a combination of Irish-grown malted and unmalted barley, with the addition of oats, wheat and rye. Once upon a time there were hundreds of distilleries; now only six remain, concentrated in Middleton, County Cork, and at the old Bushmills distillery, County Antrim.

SCOTCH WHISKIES

It would seem that history repeated itself - Irish monks brought whiskey to Scotland in the twelfth century. They found the climate ideal for this new industry, which began to prosper. Malt was first mentioned in an official document in 1494 and in 1505 a decree placed its distillation in Edinburgh under the good offices of the Royal College of Surgeons! In the seventeenth century the taxing authorities put a levy on the manufacturing of Scotch whisky as it was so popular and profitable. As always this encouraged smuggling and illegal distilling. There are over one hundred and twenty Malt distilleries throughout Scotland. The end product, which is endowed with a highly characteristic flavour, is either sold individually, or to other companies for blending. Blended Scotch whiskies are grain whiskies combined with a malt. These whiskies have a malt content of between 25% and 50%. There are hundreds of brands of blended Scotch whiskies.

AMERICAN WHISKIES

American whiskeys were created by Irish and Scottish immigrants. They are divided into seven different categories: bourbon, rye, corn, sour mash, Tennessee, bottled-in-bond and blended.

CANADIAN WHISKIES

In 1800 Canada produced too much grain, the farmers happily solved the problem by distilling the surplus and making whisky in their own holdings. Canadian whisky is often referred to as 'Rye', and is aged in oak for at least 3 years.

G I N

Gin was invented in Holland in 1650 by Doctor Selves, who added oil of juniper to alcohol and called the mixture 'Geneva'. This was originally used as a medicine for those suffering from kidney disorders. The base for the alcohol is grain spirit, redistilled with juniper berries and other flavouring such as orange peel and coriander seeds. Gin was quickly adopted by the British and caused wide-spread drunkenness and misery. By 1727, six million English were consuming 5 million gallons each year. The slogan "Drunk for a penny, dead drunk for tuppence, clean straw for nothing" was actually found over the door of one tavern, in the poorer urban parts of London. By the start of the nineteenth century workers no longer used the squalid gin shops as drinking houses; gin palaces were built which were the forerunners of pubs and restaurants. The advent of dry gin was in the 1870s; it was quite pungent and heavily sweetened. Gradually the distilling process became more sophisticated and the quality of spirit improved greatly. Gins produced today are almost all dry, although a few sweet gins are still made. Holland, England and Germany produce gin, each one uniquely different from the other.

DUTCH GIN

Dutch Gin called 'Genever' falls into two categories jonge (young), and oude (old), the adjectives specifying the technique not the age. Dutch gin does not mix well, and should be drunk well chilled and neat.

GERMAN GIN

Is known as Wacholder, the German word for Juniper. Made with a neutral spirit, and traditionally drunk chilled and neat in small glasses followed by a beer chaser.

ENGLISH GIN

The most popular gin today is made using the 'London Dry' method which is smooth, crystal-clear and very dry. The process originated in London towards the end of the 19th century. Virtually all English and American gins are made in the 'London Dry' style.

OLD TOM GIN

The only gin made today which is very similar to the gin produced up until the 1850s. This gin is the correct gin to use in a Tom Collins cocktail.

PLYMOUTH GIN

Is produced only in Plymouth (England), with water from the Devon moors. Members of the Royal Navy claim that it is the only gin suitable to make the cocktail Pink Gin because of its aromatic flavour.

FLAVOURED GINS

All gin-producing countries make flavoured gins such as: Pimms No 1.

RUM

The earliest record of rum being distilled dates back to 1526 in the West Indies: it was made from crushed sugar cane.

Because rum contains vitamin C, sailors were given a pint of rum with lime juice, each day, to prevent scurvy. As you can imagine the effects, it was quickly reduced to half a pint twice daily, watered down and nicknamed 'grog'.

The traditional tot of rum continued in the Navy until 1969, when it was abolished. In London by 1969, there were over three hundred 'grog shops'. Rum became so popular in France that strict tariffs were imposed to protect the brandy industry.

VODKA

There have been many arguments between the Polish and the Russians as to who can claim credit for the invention of Vodka. Vodka, meaning "little water", was first recorded in the 14th century and became extremely popular and widespread all over Eastern Europe in the centuries to follow. Records show that vodka was first made in a laboratory in 1810 in St Petersburg, and in 1818 Peter Smirnoff founded his vodka distillery in Moscow. Vodka is a white grain spirit, filtered through charcoal to produce a nearly pure spirit, but it can be made from any agricultural product i.e. potatoes, rye, corn and even molasses. Vodka is served as an accompaniment to smoked fish, spicy appetisers, oysters and caviar.

COCKTAILS

A cocktail is a drink made by mixing spirits or wine with fruit juices, bitters, liqueurs, or other ingredients, and subsequently by stirring, blending or shaking. Numerous charming stories surround the origin of cocktails, here are two such tales.

The Aztec legend tells of a beautiful slave called Xochtil, (pronounced cocktail), who belonged to the Emperor Axoloth. Xocktil presented an illustrious guest with a jewelled cup filled with a delicious concoction she had made. She drank from the cup first and handed it to the handsome stranger. Their eyes met, they fell in love, they married and made many little cocktails !

Betty Flanaghan, the keeper of a tavern in the state of New York during the War of Independence (1775-1782), was said to have mixed drinks cleverly for both French and American officers. One day she was given several chickens stolen from the British troops. She cooked a feast and decorated the glasses with cock feathers. One of the French gentlemen dipped a feather in his drink and cried "Vive le cocktail".

In America cocktails came into their own during the Prohibition, it was an effective way of disguising the poor-quality liquor which was made during the bootlegging era. It is estimated that approximately seven thousand cocktail recipes were invented between 1920 and 1937.

E Q U I P M E N T   L I S T

Cocktail shaker
Coil-rimmed strainer
Citrus squeezer
Long handle-bar spoon for
stirring
Corkscrew

Bottle opener
Can opener
Ice bucket with lid
Tongs
Small hammer & clean tea
towel for crushing ice

Chopping board and sharp
serrated knife
Cocktail sticks
Swizzle sticks
Ladle for serving punches
Champagne bucket

GLASSES

- **The Highball:** is a tall thin straight-sided glass.
- **The Snifter:** is a balloon-shaped glass.
- **The stemmed wine glass:** the size is up to you.
- **The fluted or open- bowled Champagne glass**.
- **The old-fashioned or on-the-rocks glass:** is a short tumbler.

You may wish to utilise any glasses of your choice or even hollowed-out coconut or pineapple shells.

GLASS PREPARATION:

- To create a sugar frosting around the rim of a glass, rub a piece of citrus fruit around the top edge and then dip into sugar, dyed sugar can be used to give different coloured frosting.
- To frost a glass, put the glass in the freezer for a couple of hours (do not put crystal glasses in the freezer).
- To chill a glass, pack it with ice and leave for 10 to 15 minutes.

DECORATION:

- To decorate a cocktail use umbrellas, bright straws, plastic animals, shaped and coloured ice cubes.
- To make coloured ice cubes, put a drop of grenadine, or any coloured syrup of your choice, in the water. Ice cubes can also be made with mixers i.e. tonic water, ginger ale, or Russian.

Fresh fruits (slices of orange, lemon, lime, pineapples, whole cherries, strawberries etc.) and vegetables (cucumber slices, cherry tomatoes, mint leaves, radishes, olives etc.) are colourful garnishes and can be eaten afterwards!

A SELECTION OF COCKTAILS

In the following recipes we are using a basic terminology such as 'part' 'squeeze' and 'dash', thus leaving to your discretion the quantity of spirits and juices you use to make each cocktail. A cocktail combines two or more ingredients which mix well together. No one ingredient should overwhelm the other.

Do not mix grapes and grain!

BLOODY MARY: *Created at Harry's New York Bar in Paris by Pete Petiot.*
1 part Vodka
5 parts tomato juice
Squeeze of lemon
Dash of Tabasco & Worcestershire sauce
Pepper & salt
Shake of celery salt
Ice cubes
Served as a long chilled drink with a stick of celery and slice of lemon.

HARVEY WALLBANGER: *Harvey, a surfing champion, was drowning his sorrows after having lost a championship by drinking Screwdrivers into which he was adding galliano. When he left the bar he was literally bouncing from one wall to the other (wall bang bang). A long drink stirred or shaken.*
Ice
1 part vodka
3 parts orange juice
1 tbs of galliano
The ice is served in the drink. The galliano can be served floating on top of the drink, or stirred in. Garnish with a slice of orange.

SCREWDRIVER: Screwdrivers made vodka popular. It is basically a shaken mixture of vodka and freshly squeezed orange juice served as a long drink. A dash of grenadine and some egg white can be added before shaking.

MANHATTAN: *Created at the Manhattan Club in New York by Winston Churchill's mother to celebrate the nomination of Samuel Tilden as Governor of the State of New York.*
Ice
1 part vermouth (sweet or dry)
2 parts whisky (rye bourbon or blended)

They are many recipes for the Manhattan cocktail which is generally mixed or shaken and served in a stemmed glass. Shake the ingredients together and strain into a glass. Garnish with a maraschino cherry and a twist of lemon.

WHISKEY SOUR:
8 parts rye or bourbon   *½ tsp caster sugar*
2 parts lemon juice
Shake with ice, strain into a short glass, garnish with a slice of lemon and a maraschino cherry. Two or three dashes of Angostura added to the Whiskey sour adds a little "je ne sais quoi".

TOM COLLINS: *They are many variations of the Tom Collins cocktail believed to have been named after several members of the Collins family. Tom Collins is a long drink served in a highball glass (there has been a special glass created for this cocktail).*
1 part lemon juice   *1 tsp of caster sugar*
3 parts gin
Pour over the ice and top up with soda water to taste.

MARGARITA: *In Virginia City in the days of the Wild West a bar keeper watched his lady love being shot by a hail of bullets. To drown his sorrows he mixed this tequila-based cocktail. The lady's name was Margarita.*
1 part Triple Sec   *Juice of half a lemon or lime*
3 parts tequila
The rim of a short glass should be rubbed with citrus rind or dipped in Cointreau and then in coarse salt. Shake the liquid ingredient with the ice and strain into a glass, decorate with a sliver of lemon or lime rind.

DAIQUIRI:
Ice   *4 parts white rum*
1 part lemon juice   *1 tsp of caster sugar*
Place all the ingredients in a shaker and shake vigorously, serve in a cocktail glass or an open style Champagne glass.

TEQUILA SUNRISE: Serve in a highball glass.
½ orange juice to tequila   *1 tsp of caster sugar*
Ice   *Soda water*
3 parts gin   *Grenadine syrup*
1 part lemon juice
Shake the orange juice and tequila with ice. Strain into the glass. Very slowly pour the grenadine syrup into the drink, which will settle at the bottom giving the appearance of a sunrise.

PIÑA COLADA:
1 part coconut milk   *1 part pineapple juice*
2 parts white rum
Shake all the ingredients together with plenty of ice, strain into a highball glass.

WHITE LADY: *First created in 1919 in the Siro's Club in London by Harry MacElhone. His second version, created in 1925, is now the classic recipe.*
1 part Cointreau   *2 parts dry gin*
1 part lemon juice
Prepare in a shaker with crushed ice, strain, serve in a stemmed glass.

SIDE CAR: *Created by Harry MacElhone at Harry's New York Bar in Paris in 1933.*
1 part Cointreau   2 parts brandy
1 part lemon juice
Shake well with ice, strain, serve in the stemmed glass.

ALEXANDER: *Created for Queen Alexandra, the wife of Edward VII.*
1 part Cognac   1 part fresh cream
1 part crème de cacao
Prepare in a shaker with crushed ice, mix well, serve in a cocktail glass or open style Champagne glass. Sprinkle with grated nutmeg.

NEGRONI: *Created by the Italian Count Negroni in the Hotel Baglioni in Florence.*
1 part red vermouth   1 part dry gin
1 part Campari
Prepare directly in a medium-size tumbler, stir all the ingredients together with ice, decorate with a slice of orange.

MARNIER: *Created by Michel Bigot in the Concorde La Fayette in Paris.*
Crushed ice   Tonic water
1 part Grand Marnier
Made directly in a tumbler and stirred with a swizzle stick.

RITZ COBBLER:
1 part Cointreau   Juice of half a lemon
1 part cognac
Mix in a shaker with crushed ice, pour into a highball, top up with brut Champagne. Garnish with fresh mint leaves and a cherry.

ANGEL FACE:
Ice   1 part apricot brandy
1 part dry gin   1 part Calvados
Place all the ingredients in a shaker, mix, and serve in a stemmed glass.

DRY MARTINI: *Dry Martini is the most internationally famous of all cocktails; three books have been written about it. The outstanding American essayist Bernard de Voto called the 'Dry Martini' the supreme American gift to World culture. Franklin Delano Roosevelt and Sir Winston Churchill thought highly of them, and the list of Martini drinkers reads like a roll-call from 'Who's Who'.*
1 part dry vermouth   7 parts dry gin
The highest-quality gin must be used, and the most pleasing proportion to the average palate is a ratio of seven to one. Shake with ice or stir in a Martini glass, garnish with an olive.

SINGAPORE GIN SLING: *A classic cocktail said to have first been made in the Raffles Hotel, Singapore in 1915; no two recipes are ever the same.*
2 parts gin   Heaped tsp of caster sugar
2 parts lime or lemon juice
Pour over crushed ice in a highball glass, top up with soda water, add a generous dash of Cointreau and cherry brandy, stir. Decorate with lemon and cherry.

EXOTIC WILLIAM: *Created for 'L'Art de Recevoir' by William French.*
1 sugar lump   1 dash lime cordial
4 drops bitters   2 parts white rum

Top up with tonic water, ice cubes, twist fresh lime. Pour the bitters over the sugar lump. Add the lime, and leave to dissolve. Add the rum and top up with the tonic water and ice. Serve.

CHAMPAGNE COCKTAILS

TRADITIONAL CHAMPAGNE COCKTAIL:
1 sugar cube   *Champagne*
1 tsp Angostura bitter
Place a cube of sugar saturated with Angostura bitters in a chilled Champagne glass, top up the glass with Champagne, add a twist of lemon or orange peel.

MAHARAJAH'S BURRA PEG:
1 part brandy   *5 parts Champagne*
Mix and serve.

BUCKS FIZZ:
Mix equal parts of fresh orange juice with Champagne.

KIR ROYAL: *Kir was a monk in Nolay in France and he had the idea of adding cassis cream (blackcurrant syrup) to white wine. 'Kir Royal' is the use of champagne instead of wine.*
l tsp. of creme de cassis added to a glass of chilled Champagne.
Other syrups can be added to white wine or Champagne, for example raspberry, strawberry, peach etc. Champagne with raspberry syrup is called 'Champagne à la framboise.'

BLACK VELVET: *A traditional English cocktail. There is in Cambridge a very exclusive students' club called 'The Natives' with twelve members, all from Jesus College. They meet once a year to drink Black Velvet and eat oysters, wearing morning suits with blue carnations (specially prepared by a florist) to match their ties.*
½ part Guiness to ½ part Champagne.

CAREVE: *Created for 'L'Art de Recevoir' by Evelyn and Caroline.*
Chilled vintage Champagne   *Dash of brandy*
Pureed fresh strawberries
Mix 1 part strawberry with 2 parts Champagne and a dash of brandy. This cocktail is very adequate on a summer afternoon tea party.

TOUR D'ARGENT: *Named in honour of this famous Parisian restaurant.*
1 tsp of cognac   *Sugar cube*
1 tsp of Cointreau   *Slice of orange*
Chilled Champagne
Pour the Cointreau and cognac in the glass and top up with Champagne. Place the slice of orange on the surface, soak the sugar cube with Cointreau and place on top of the slice of orange.

LOVING CUP: *This eighteenth century recipe was created to celebrate a betrothal. The voilets are a symbol of everlasting love. Makes ten to twelve cups.*
Bottle of light red wine   *Zest of one orange, cut in the same fashion*
Bottle of non-vintage dry Champagne   *Ice cubes*
5 fl oz (150 ml) of curacao   *8 oz (215 g) of sweet black grapes, skinned,*
4 oz (75 g) icing sugar   *halved & seeded*
Zest of one lemon cut thinly in a long twist *A handful of crystallised violets*
Mix all the liquid ingredients in a large bowl and chill for one hour in the refrigerator. Before serving add plenty of ice and garnish with grapes and violets.

TIPS ON SERVING CHAMPAGNE

A Champagne cork should be eased out of the bottle. Pour only half a glass at first, and then top up when the froth has subsided

PUNCH

MULLED RED WINE (GLUHWEIN):
For each bottle of red wine:

4 to 6 oz (110 g to 175 g) of lump sugar   *2 cloves*
Pared rind of one lemon   *Blade of mace*
2" (5 cm) stick of cinnamon   *Slice of lemon for serving*

Mix all the ingredients into a large jug which you then stand in a large saucepan filled with water, heat slowly over a gentle heat until the wine is piping hot, but not boiling. Serve in warmed glasses.

SANGRIA:
An authentic Spanish recipe. Makes 8 to 10 glasses

1 bottle of red wine   *5 fl oz (150 ml) of brandy*
2 oranges, sliced   *Block of ice*
2 lemons, sliced   *One litre of chilled soda water*

Marinate the orange and lemon slices in the brandy for one hour in the refrigerator. Put a block of ice in a large jug, add the marinated brandy and fruits, and then stir in the wine. Top up with soda water and serve in wine glasses.

TODDIES

Toddies are drunk piping hot.

GROG:

1 part lemon juice   *1 tsp honey*
2 parts rum
Top up with boiling water.

TODDY:

1 measure of whisky   *1 tsp honey or sugar*
Cognac or rum   *A small piece of cinnamon stick*
Top up with boiling water

NON-ALCOHOLIC COCKTAILS

"'Have some wine,' the March Hare said in an encouraging tone. Alice looked all around the table, but there was nothing on it but tea. 'I don't see any wine,' she remarked. 'There isn't any,' said the March Hare."
CARROLL

PUSSY FOOT:
1 part orange juice	Dash of grenadine
1 part lemon juice	1 egg yolk
1 part lime juice	Sparkling water

Shake well with crushed ice and strain into a large cocktail glass. Decorate with various fresh fruits.

PRESTON'S POTION: *A well known soft drink in the County of Meath - one of the few Irish soft drinks !*
Juice of two lemons	Sparkling water
4 sprigs of parsley	2 tsp sugar

Put the parsley, sugar and lemon juice into a blender with two or three ice cubes and blend for thirty seconds. Pour into a large cocktail glass and top up with sparkling water, stir. Mix finely chopped parsley to sugar, and frost to decorate the rim of the glass.

LUSSI: *An Indian drink that can be drunk in two ways, either sweet (Meeta) or salted (Numkeen).*
½ pt (275 ml) yoghurt	½ tsp of kewra essence
½ pt (275 ml) milk	Salt or sugar to taste
Juice of one lemon	Ice cubes

Blend the yoghurt, milk, lemon juice and kewra essence in a liquidiser (rose water can replace the kewra), with ice. Pour into a highball glass and add sugar or salt to taste. Serve with a slice of lemon and a straw.

The following non-alcoholic cocktails have been created for 'L'Art de Recevoir' by Evelyn and Caroline.

POMME D'AMOUR:
Ice	Dash of Tabasco & Worcestershire sauce
1 part Tomato juice	Squeeze of lime or lemon
1 part vegetable juice	Celery salt, black pepper

Mix together and serve with a stick of celery and cucumber shavings.

FRENCH TEASE: *Delightful served in a pineapple shell.*
Pineapple juice	Juice of a lemon
Fresh kiwi fruit	Dash of lime juice

Blend all the ingredients with plenty of ice for 30 seconds, strain into a large cocktail glass, decorate with a slice of pineapple and kiwi fruit.

CITRON VERT:
Ice	Zest of 2 lemons
Mint leaves	Juice of eight lemons
Sugar	½ pt (275 ml) of water

Lemonade.
Heat the water, mint leaves, sugar, lemon juice and lemon zest until the sugar is dissolved, leave to steep until cool, add the ice and lemonade. Serve in frosted tall glasses, decorated with lemon and fresh mint.

BOLD: Use as many fresh soft fruits as possible : banana, pineapple, raspberry, strawberries, black currants, red currants, cherries (stoned), lychees etc.
Liquidise with plenty of ice and strain into large cocktail glasses, top up with coconut milk, stir, and decorate with slices of fruits of your choice.

SWEET TOOTH: *Orange juice, pineapple juice, peach juice, grenadine.*
Shake all together with plenty of ice, serve in a large cocktail glass and decorate with fruits of your choice.

ICE CREAM SODAS AND MILK SHAKES: To make an ice cream soda, blend together a fruit juice of your choice, soda water, and a tablespoon of ice cream or a sorbet. Milk shakes are made by blending fruit syrups or flavoured powders with milk. Ice cream and whole fruits can be added to thicken the drink.

WINE

"A man cannot make him laugh, but that's no marvel, he drinks no wine."
SHAKESPEARE

Wine making probably dates back to the dawn of civilisation. The Bible mentions Noah who, after brewing his wine, grew to appreciate it so much that he became the oldest recorded alcoholic!

The Vine was brought to Europe by an explorer from Phocaea called Euxene, who landed on the Meridional coast of France, in an area governed by the King Nami. Euxene was an enterprising man and he began to plant the vine with great success. His luck did not stop there, he met, seduced and quickly married Gyptis, the King's daughter. History does not tell us whether he and Gyptis had any children, but we know that the union of the vine and the indigenous soil was very fruitful. Incidentally, Euxene's other claim to fame is to have founded 'Massilia', later to become Marseille. The Gaulois, who were not the barbarians we have been led to believe, developed the industry from Euxene and his people. Their method was not very sophisticated, the wine had to be drunk within a year.

The Greeks were the first to discover wine preservation by using earthenware jars (amphorae) sealed with wax to protect the wine from the air. The amphorae were buried in cool ground.

The Romans also used this method. Chronicles of the time claim that some of their vintage could be drunk as old as 125 years! When the Romans invaded Gaule they taught the natives their processes of refrigeration, concentration by heat, plastering, filtering etc. Very soon the pupils overtook their masters and began selling their wines to the whole of the Roman Empire. Transport was mainly by river; where the water ways were not navigable it became necessary to create new roads to join the regions of the Atlantic to the Mediterranean.

In the year AD92 the Emperor Domitian issued a decree throughout the Roman Empire: half the vines had to be pulled out and replaced by wheat. However, the Gaulois, not renowned for their obedience, found a way round it by removing the inferior vines and jealously rationing the best growing areas. Birth was thus given to those most famous wine growing areas of France.

A few centuries later Clovis, the King of the Francs, united Gaule and became a Christian. He was baptised in Reims with Champagne wine (it was not yet Champagne as we know it). The new religion favoured by the King spread rapidly throughout France. Monasteries and abbeys were built all over the country and the monks began the task of cultivating the vine with great enthusiasm!

After the collapse of the Roman Empire and throughout the Middle Ages, the use of the cork was lost and with it the ability to age wine, most wines produced then had to be drunk within a year. It was in Champagne around 1690 that Dom Pierre Perignon, cellar-master of Hautvillers Abbey, re-invented the cork and combined its use with newly developed strong glass bottles. This breakthrough would revolutionise the conservation of all wines.

Another rediscovery took place at about the same time: the properties of Botrytis. In Hungary a delayed harvest forced wine growers to make wine from shrivelled grapes. The result was astonishing, a beautiful wine with a new taste. The process was soon adopted and honoured with a place on the table of Louis XIV of France.

Wine-growing spread from Europe throughout the world - to Mexico, Peru, Chile, Argentina, South Africa, California, Australia, New Zealand etc.

By the middle of the nineteenth century, the viticultural fraternity had regained most of the lost arts and was enjoying steady evolution.

In 1863, calamity and disaster struck in the shape of 'PHYLLOXERA VASTATRIX' in the southern part of the Rhône Valley. It is a pest which lives and feeds in the root of the vine, eating the very life from the plant, which then withers and dies. It was brought over from America on vine cuttings to be used for experimental purposes.

The plague multiplied at a frightening pace. By 1860 the whole of the Rhône Valley and the Bordeaux area were contaminated. During the 1870's most of Portugal, Spain, Austria, Germany, and Hungary were affected. The nature of the disaster was not understood and cuttings from infected areas were transported from one side of the globe to the other by wine makers in despair.

However, from the pest's very birthplace came the remedy. The American vine was resistant to Phylloxera! By grafting European vines on to American ones, growers found that they had the answer. It was not a popular move at first; the very thought of grafting France's finest vines on to vulgar roots was a sacrilege. Nevertheless the process was adopted throughout France and the rest of Europe. The recovery was rapid but not without pain. The rootstocks used were not always suited to the soils which had produced the fine wines. It took several years to strike the right balance. Today the art of grafting has become very sophisticated. It is interesting to observe that although French vines are being planted all over the world with some success, it is never with the same results. The key to this mystery lies in the delicate interaction between the climate, the soil structure, the hours of sunshine and the lay of the land. French wine growers will tell you that the secret formula is, some 2000 years of trial and error, the knowledge carefully handed down through generations and to crown it all 'loving care'!

There are many fascinating anecdotes throughout French history, where wine plays a major rôle. We have selected two, the first in 1513, when an army of 30,000 Swiss and German soldiers laid siege to Dijon which was then only defended by a small garrison. When asked to surrender, the governors of the town sent out several envoys and many barrels of the best Burgundy wines. The opponents started negotiating and drinking; very soon a spirit of friendship prevailed and the assailants decided to go home in the best of moods, taking with them as many barrels of wine as they could carry.

The second is at Morlaix in 1522, when the English fleet was going up the estuary of Dossen. A spy informed the admiral that a great part of the French population had left the city to participate in some county festival. The English took the town easily. It was a hot day and the troops decided to have a drink. They went into the cellars and found the best wines. When the people of Morlaix came back they discovered the entire fleet blissfully merry and incapable of fighting. The English put to sea having lost the majority of their men and without taking anything.

WINE REGIONS OF FRANCE

The synergy between soil, climate, vine and the expertise of the 'vigneron' (vine grower) is of paramount importance.

Each wine draws unique characteristics from the composition of the soil, the grapes, and the microclimate.

The exact position of a vineyard is a crutial factor in the microclimate equation (for example it may be in a valley or on a slope, exposed to the wind or protected from it, it can enjoy a lot of sunshine and adequate rain fall, etc.)

THE GRAPES
Main Red Grapes

Cabernet Sauvignon	Is found mainly in the Bordeaux area, it produces a very fruity wine with a strong tannic content, high in alcohol.
Cabernet Franc	Is found in Chinon, Bourgueil, Touraine, it produces an aromatic light fruity wine.
Merlot	Is found in St Emilion, Pommerol, Médoc and Graves Bordeaux). It produces a powerful wine with colour and suppleness.
Pinot noir	Is the Burgundy grape par excellence, also found in Champagne and in Alsace. It produces fine wines with great aroma.
Pinot Meunier	Is found in Champagne, it produces a very supple wine.
Malbec	Is also called Cot in Touraine and in Auxerre, it produces a firm and fleshy wine.
Gamay	Is the Beaujolais grape found also in Touraine. A very precocious grape which produce vins primeurs, Beaujolais nouveau. Light, fruity, aromatic, vigorous, Gamay is drunk young.
Syrah	Is found in the South of France, Côtes du Rhône. It produces a robust, colourful, full-bodied wine with a high tannic content.
Grenache noir	Is found in the South of France, it produces a wine with a high alcohol content and a strong very distinctive bouquet. It is often blended with other grapes.
Carignan	Is found in the South of France. It is used blended with other grapes and produces a strong wine high in colour.
Cinsault	Is found in the South of France, it is used to produce rosé wine or for blending. It produces a supple wine with an elegant aroma.
Mourvèdre	Is found in the South of France in particular to produce Bandol wine. High in alcohol, very colourful, fleshy, with a wild bouquet.
Poulsard	Is found in the Jura, it produces a very elegant, colourful wine with a rich aroma.

25

Trousseau	Is found in the Jura it produces a wine with a strong tannic and alcoholic content.

Main White Grapes

Chardonnay	Is found in Burgundy, Chablis and Champagne. It produces the finest white wines. The wines are very well balanced, elegant, with a fine aroma and great breeding.
Chenin	Is found in the Loire, it produces a dry, mellow wine.
Gewürztraminer	Of Saxon origin, the grape produces an aromatic medium dry smooth wine.
Riesling	Of Saxon origin, it is now found close to the Rhine frontier of France and produces a dry or slightly liquorous very fine wine.
Sauvignon	Is found in Bordeaux and Loire, it produces a dry, light and aromatic wine. It is also used to produce a sweet wine of great distinction (Sauternes).
Ugni-Blanc	Of Italian origin, it is now cultivated in the South of France, Corsica, Armagnac and Cognac.
Pinot Blanc	Produces a very fine aromatic wine.
Muscat	Is widely used to produce dry wines (Alsace), liquorous wines (Rousillon and Languedoc) and mousseux wines (Clairette de Die).
Sylvaner	Used mainly in the East of France, producing average wines.
Sémillon	Is found in Bordeaux, it used to produce dry white Graves and Sauternes. This grape is never used alone, it is blended with Sauvignon.
Muscadelle	Is found in the Bordeaux area.
Aligoté	Is found in Burgundy and the wine produced bears its name (Bourgogne Aligoté). Can be excellent, although not of the Chardonnay quality.
Muscadet	Is found in Nantes, produces a fresh, light wine with a delicate aroma.
Clairette	Is found in the South of France and produces a heady aromatic excellent wine.
Mauzac	Also called 'blanquette', it produces a mousseux wine.
Folle Blanche	Is found in Nantes, Armagnac and Cognac.
Macableu	Is found in the South of France, it produces powerful wines.
Courbu	Is found in Bearn and Jurançon.
Manseng	Is found in Jurançon
Grenache	There are three grenache - white, grey and black, which produce a highly aromatic wine with a high alcoholic content.
Viognier	Is found on the Côtes du Rhône.
Roussanne	Is found on the Côtes du Rhône, it produces a fine wine.
Marsanne	Is found on the Côtes du Rhône.
Chasselas	Produces wines to be drunk young.
Roussette	Is found in Savoie, it produces fresh wines.
Savagnin	Is found in Jura, it produces the famous yellow wine.

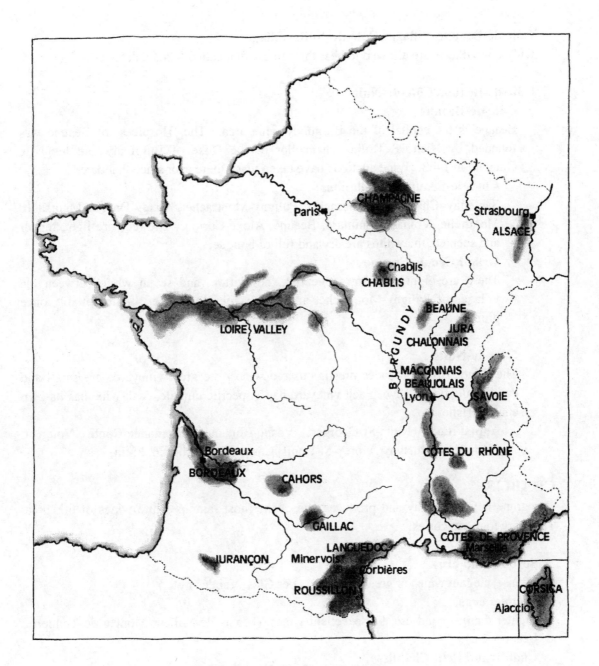

THE REGIONS

BOURGOGNE (BURGUNDY)

CÔTE D'OR

The Côte D'Or comprises the Côte de Beaune and the Côte De Nuits.

Classification in this area is very elaborate, it was finalised in 1984.

Cru means growth, however the term refers to a vineyard which meets strict criteria.

Grand Cru is a title given to a cru of great quality.

Grand cru

There are thirty of them. The wines bear the names of the vineyard i.e. Musigny, Corton, Montrachet, Chambertin.

Premier cru

The wines bear the name of their village followed by the name of the vineyard.

Côte-de-Beaune-Villages/Côte-de-Nuits-Villages
Only few villages are allowed to bear the name, often called 'Clos de'.

Côte-de-Beaune/Côte-de-Nuit
Côte-de-Beaune
Beaune is the capital of the Burgundy wine area. The 'Hospices' of Beaune was founded by Nicholas Rolin, Chancellor of the Duke of Burgundy and his wife Guigone in 1443. Wine auctions have taken place there ever since that date.
Côte-de-Beaune Appellations
Santenay, Chassagne-Montrachet, Puligny-Montrachet, Auxey-Duress, Meursault, Monthélie, Volnay, Pommard, Beaune, Aloxe-Corton. The reds are light, tender and scented, the whites are dry and full of bouquet.
Grand Cru de Beaune
There are eight of them - one red, the Corton, and seven white between the villages of Puligny-Montrachet and Chassagne-Montrachet - unforgettable once drunk!

Côte-de-Nuits
The 'Pinot Noir' produces prestigious red wines, the great vineyards are small and their production is low. Each vineyard has a specific climate, each wine has its own characteristics.
Appellations Nuits-St-Georges, Vosne-Romanée, Romanée-Conti, Vougeot, Chambolle-Musigny, Morey-St-Denis, Chevrey-Chambertin, Fixin.

CHABLIS
The grape is Chardonnay and produces one of the most famous white wines of this area. There are four categories:

Seven grand crus
Intense, elegant wines of great breeding. (Les Clos, Vaudésir etc.)
Premier crus
Lighter than a grand cru, but excellent wines. (Monts de Milieu, Montée de Tonnerre, Beauroy etc)
Chablis and Petit Chablis
Pleasant wines drunk young.

BEAUJOLAIS
The grape is the Gamay for red or rosé and the Chardonnay for the white. There are about sixty villages and seven thousand people producing Beaujolais. Only thirty out of these sixty are allowed to use appellation Beaujolais-Village and nine only produce the grand cru of Beaujolais.

Beaujolais Primeur
Known in England as 'Beaujolais Nouveau', it is a primeur wine, drunk in November.
Beaujolais-Villages
They come from the North of Beaujolais and are stronger than the Beaujolais Supérieur.
Grand Cru de Beaujolais
They are fine wines, capable of growing old.

Chiroubles	Fruity, scented, quite brilliant.
Brouilly	Full of flavour, particularly the Côte-de-Brouilly.
Fleurie	Light wine, exquisite and seductive.
Morgon	Fleshy and generous and can be keep for several years.
Saint-Amour	Deserves its name, adorable, very easy to drink.
Chénas	Full-bodied and generous, keeps for five years.
Juliénas	Vigorous and with body, matures with laying.
Moulin-à-Vent	Can be kept for ten years. Powerful and a joy to drink.
Régnié	Fine and elegant with intense ruby colour

MACONNAIS

The white wines of this area are superior to the red and rosé. The grape is the Chardonnay which produces wines of quality, the best being the Pouilly-Fuissé, dry, pale, refreshing, must be drunk when young (five years).

CHALONNAIS

Mercury	Red wine, deep and delicious.
Montagny	White wines, fresh and pleasant.
Rully	Very fine red or white wine. The latter is often made into Champagne.

BORDEAUX

Classification of the Crus - There are two thousand Châteaux in the area of Bordeaux.

Outstanding red Bordeaux wines have been 'classified' since 1855
Premier Cru (First Growths)
Deuxième Cru (Second Growths)
Troisième Cru (Third Growths)
Quatrième Cru (Fourth Growths)
Cinquième Cru (Fifth Growths)

Outstanding white Bordeaux wines have been 'classified' since 1855
Premier Grand Cru
Premier Cru
Deuxième Cru

Médoc
Produces red wines of great quality.

Haut-Médoc
Produces red wines such as:
St-Julien, St-Estèphe, Pauillac, Château-Margaux, Château-Lafite, Château-Latour, Château-Mouton-Rothschild and Château-Haut-Brion.
There are sixty other crus, delicate, fine, subtle and distinguished.

Saint-Emilion
The wine is very vigorous and full of body.

Eight villages are allowed to use the name **Saint-Emilion.**

Five others are allowed to add it to their names.

Les Châteaux: **twelve premiers grands crus**, Château-Cheval-Blanc and Château-Ausone head these, splendid and magnificent, full of body.

Followed by **grand crus**, about seventy of these are velvety and unctuous, lesser known. It is best to drink them when they are at least five years old.

Graves

The area produces white dry wines and strong reds.

The white are more numerous as we are close to the Sauternes area.

Famous grand crus:

Château-Haut-Brion (first classified as a Haut-Medoc in 1855).

Château-de-la-Brède (owned by Montesquieu), St. Morillon.

The reds, however, are very fruity and very distinguished:

Château-Haut-Brion, Château-Haut-Bailly, fine and crisp with a deep aroma.

Pomerol

The wines are close to Saint-Emilion and from the same grapes as Médoc but they have their own particular character and flavour.

Château-Pétrus heads a **dozen grands crus**, Château-La-Fleur, Château-la-Conseillante, Château-L'Evangile. Very smooth and fleshy wines with a slight flavour of truffle and a beautiful ruby colour. Can be drunk from five years old.

Entre-Deux-Mers

The red wine of the area is sold as a Bordeaux. The white wine is allowed the appellation 'Entre-Deux-Mers', it is dry, supple and fruity. There is, however, no grand cru.

Sauternes

Almost picked grain by grain and stored in barrels for two to three years prior to bottling, Sauternes is a naturally sweet wine. Once bottled the Sauternes keeps for many years.

There are **five villages**: Sauternes, Barsac, Bommes, Preignac and Fargues.

One **premier grand cru**, the Château-d'Yquem, a **dozen premier crus**, and a **dozen deuxièmes crus**. They are unique in the world and very smooth.

Fronsac

The wine is rustic; Côtes-de-Fronsac and Côtes-Canon-Fronsac produce a good cru which ages pleasantly.

Côtes de Bourg et de Blaye

The wines bear the appellation 'Premières-Côtes-de-Blaye', five very pleasant wines.

WINES FROM THE LOIRE VALLEY

Pouilly	Pouilly-sur-Loire is light and sharp and Pouilly-Fumé is fruity and harmonious.
Sancerre	Dry white wine from Sauvignon grapes.
Reuilly	Dry, lively white wine to be drunk young.
Jasnières	Medium sweet, can be kept for a long time.

Anjou	This area produces a lot of wines, red, rosé and white. The different appellations contrôlées for this area are: **Coteaux du Layon, Bonnezeaux, Quarts de Chaume**. Light rosés and white wines, they are well balanced and keep well.
Coteaux de la Loire	White wines, light, dry and fine.
Saumur	White wine, fruity and sturdy, some are made into 'mousseux Champagne'.
Vouvray	Two different whites, dry white and smooth white, part of it is made into Champagne. The rosé is produced from Cabernet grapes.
Chinon	Mainly red, supple and fruity
Muscadet	They are two Muscadet, Muscadet de Sèvre et Maine, Muscadet Côteaux-de-la-Loire, fresh and exuberant, should be drunk young.

WINES FROM THE RHÔNE VALLEY

A O C: The appellation 'Côtes-du-Rhône' groups one hundred and fifty villages including red, rosé and white wines. The appellation 'Côtes-du-Rhône-Villages' is allowed for fifteen villages. The grape is the Syrah.

Côte-Rotie	Very hot summers produce a very generous heady wine. Will age nicely.
Chateau Grillet	Produces heady white wine, in small quantities.
St-Joseph	Is an elegant and delicate red wine, a supple and light white wine.
Condrieu	Is a subtle or medium dry white wine and very scented.
St-Peray	Is a white wine, part of which is made into 'Mousseux'.
Cornas	Is a vigorous red wine full of colour.
Hermitage	Is a rich wine, intense, smooth, full of bouquet.
Clairette de Die	Is an exuberant white mousseux.
Crozes-Hermitage	Is not as good as the Hermitage, but full of vigour.
Châteauneuf-Du-Pape	Is a rich, muscular red wine. It matures quickly.
Gigondas	Is a robust and well-balanced wine and produces red, rosé and white.
Rasteau	Is a sweet wine low in alcohol content, a delicious dessert wine.
Tavel	A very good dry rosé, exuberant and refreshing.
Lirac	Produces rosé, red and white wines, less known that Tavel. Exuberant and pleasing.

VINS DE JURA & ARBOIS

Vins Jaunes (Yellow Wines)
The method used to produce this wine is unique. It needs six to ten years to mature in barrels, which renders it expensive. Rare, strange and marvellous, it must be tried. Château-Chablis is considered the best.

Vins De Paille (Straw Wine)
Named 'straw wine' because the grapes are dried on straw, it has a very high alcohol content. It can be kept for a long time and is remarkably smooth.
Very rare wines, without comparison.
Three famous names are: Côtes-du-Jura, Vins D'Arblois, Vins de L'Etoile.

VINS DE SAVOIE & DAUPHINE

These wines are not well known.
Seyssel
A white and dry wine which can be made into mousseux
Crepy, Vins de Savoie des Abymes, d'Apremont de Chignin d'Ayze.

WINES FROM THE SOUTH

Languedoc Roussillon	Blanquette de Limoux is a mousseux of some renown, sweet, to be drunk young.
Gaillac	Wine to be drunk young.
Corbières	Good body wine.
Fitou	Red wine with body and scent.
Minervois	Mainly red wine.
Côtes-du-Roussillon	Produces a good solid red and a pleasant white.
Vins du Juraçon	The wine which was used to baptise Henry IV of France, sweet and golden, rich with a lot of bouquet.
Madiran	Is a fleshy and generous wine.
Bergerac	Is a generous and velvety wine.
Montravel	Haut-Montravel, Côtes-de-Montravel, are medium, sweet white wines.
Monbazillac	Is a sweet smooth white, can be kept for twenty years or more.
Cahors	Is a dark wine, dense and scented.

PROVENCE

The soil is good for the vine and produces excellent rosé.

Côtes-de-Provence	Are wines full of flavour, round and pleasant. There are four appellations controlée, and the bottles have a specific shape.
Vins de Cassis	The whites are heady and robust, and the rosé dry and smooth.
Vins de Palette et de Bellet	Are produced from small vineyards, the wines are supple and full of bouquet.
Bandol	The red and white are of exuberant quality, the rosé is light.

ALSACE

A good Alsace carries the name of its grapes and its place of origin.

Riesling	Is the best, a fine wine of excellent quality, well balanced with great breeding.

Gewürztraminer	A spicy, peppery wine with body.
Tokay	A heady and robust wine.
Muscat d'Alsace	A very dry wine with a fine bouquet.
Sylvaner	A light and fresh wine to be drunk young.

C H A M P A G N E

The late Madame Lily Bollinger, when asked by a journalist when she chose to drink her own wine, eloquently expressed:

"I drink it when I'm happy and when I'm sad. Sometimes I drink it alone. When I have company I consider it obligatory. I trifle with it if I'm not hungry and drink it when I am. Otherwise I never touch it - unless I'm thirsty."
MADAME LILY BOLLINGER

Champagne enjoys a world-wide reputation and is forever the symbol of celebration, tradition and savoir-faire. It is a superlative wine. A monk named Dom Perignon started the process and he has been immortalised by one of the great Champagne houses.

The Pinot Noir, the Pinot Meunier and the Chardonnay are the grapes used to produce it, they are collected and pressed as soon as they are cut to prevent discoloration of the juice. It undergoes three pressings: 1st **'Cuvée'**, 2nd **'Première taille'**, 3rd **'Seconde taille'**.
The third press is not used to make the best Champagne. The juice spends the winter in cuves (barrels). It is then put in bottles where it will carry on fermenting. After two or three years the bottles are placed upside down, and are turned each day, drawing deposit to the cork. The cork is then removed and the deposit taken away. The space is filled with identical Champagne. A new cork is then put in place. After several months of rest the wine is ready.
The name of the vineyard does not matter, as Champagne is a blend. It is the name of the Champagne House which is important. Those great houses produce a Champagne of constant quality year after year, the Champagne being sufficiently characteristic to be different from the other houses. The appellation 'Champagne' is for the champagne wine only. The name **brut, sec** must appear on the label.

Some of the great houses are:
Bollinger, Clicquot, Krug, Laurent Perrier, Moët-Chandon, Mumm, Perrier-Jouet, Piper-Heidsieck, Pol Roger, Pommery, Roederer, Ruinard, Taittinger.

WINE LABELS

From the beginning of the 19th century, wine-growers and merchants have tried to protect their unique products. In the 1930 massive overproduction prompted vine-growers to set up a body which would, implement strict guidelines, limit wine production and monitor standards. This difficult task progressed slowly and demanded great determination to succeed. However this was the forerunner of the Intitute National des Appelations d'Origine (INAO). The INAO France is a watchdog, with twelve regional committees. Its mission is to control ouput, maintain excellence, and protect the appelations both in France and abroad.

A.O.C (APPELLATION D'ORIGINE CONTROLÉE)
The Appellations d'Origine certifies that the wine does come from the area stated on the label and that the quality expected has been preserved.
See the previous chapter 'Wine Regions of France' for further classification.

NON A.O.C WINES
V.D.Q.S.
(Vin Délimité de Qualité Supérieure). This is the second category for wines which have not passed the A.O.C test. They are however better than ordinary wines and their prices reflect it.
Vin de Pays
Recent qualification due to the progress of technology. The wines are drunk young; their alcohol content is lower than that of A.O.C and V.D.G.S.

WINE STORAGE

The best way to store wine is in a cellar which should be kept at a temperature of 10° to 11° centigrade. Stack the wine in a rack by putting white at the lower level, which is the coldest section, rosé in the middle and red at the top. Bottles should be laid on their side so that the cork does not dry up. If you can no longer read the labels, tie a tag on the bottlenecks or place notices on the shelves.
Once put down, wine should be disturbed as little as possible.

Wine stored in quantity should be entered into a cellar book, which not only helps you keep a record of the bottles in store, but ensures that the relevant wines are drunk on time, and at their best.

If you do not own a cellar, any suitable storage place will do, but remember that wine should be stored in a cool place and in the dark. Apply the same rules as you would in a cellar.

Prior to consuming your wine, place white wine in the refrigerator, not in the freezer compartment, for a few hours allowing it to chill thoroughly to 8°C-10°C. Red wine should be allowed to settle at room temperature. Always bare in mind that wine is alive and dislikes violent changes in temperature. Under no circumstances should it be shaken while in the bottle.

After uncorking, wine will breathe and take in oxygen. For white and rosé wines, take the cork out a few minutes before drinking. Red wine should be uncorked at least one hour before drinking.

Decanting will benefit all red wines, young and mature, it is essential for older and full bodied wines which might have a deposit.

WINE TASTING

"On est savant quand on boit bien
qui ne sait boire ne sait rien."
(One is learned when one drinks well, he who does not drink does not know anything).
BOILEAU

Tasting wine involves three of your senses: sight, smell and taste. The mood of the moment will add an extra dimension.

Fill your glass to about a quarter full, raise it by the stem and examine your wine. Notice that the light enhances its delicate shades. A good wine should be beautiful to look at, clear, bright and transparent. This rule applies to all wines, clarity and limpidity should be seen even in a heavier red wine.

A light colour suggests a light wine, a more robust shade denotes a stronger wine. Brightness is paramount, a wine with a dull look has passed its best.

Shades of colour are an indication of the age of a wine. Take for example two red wines, one younger than the other; at first they will both appear to have a beautiful ruby colour but if you tilt them, either against the light or a white background, you will see that the younger wine is a shade more purple and the older wine has a softer garnet colour.
White wine will have three shades, with practice you will learn to recognise them:
- pale yellow-green for young wines.
- medium yellow for mature wines.
- honey-gold for older wines.

Swirl the glass **gently** to release the bouquet, take your time, breathe in all the aromas, you will find it fascinating as each wine has a particular fragrance, delicate and complex. These aromas can range from flowers to fresh or dry fruits, to herbs, spices, truffle, honey, etc.

Slowly sip the wine and let your tongue and palate relish it. Do not swallow it too quickly as your taste buds will need a little time to get accustomed to the flavour.

WINE GLASSES
- The glass must be clear so one can admire the wine's colour and clarity.
- The glass must have a stem which permits a firm hold for swirling the wine and
  developing the bouquet without affecting its temperature.

The ideal wine glass has a rim which is narrower than the bowl at its largest part, to hold and concentrate the bouquet. A red wine glass is slightly bigger than a white wine glass. A wine glass should never be more than half filled.
A Champagne glass should be long stemmed and tulip shaped, it will retain the bubbles and with them its subtle aroma. A Champagne glass can be filled almost to the top.

WINE QUANTITY
½ bottle holds   3 glasses of 125 ml (4-5 fl oz) each

75 cl bottle holds	6 glasses of 125 ml (4-5 fl oz) each
A litre bottle holds	8 glasses of 125 ml (4-5 fl oz) each
Magnum	2 bottles
Double Magnum - Bordeaux	4 bottles
Jeroboam - Champagne	4 bottles
Rehoboam	6 bottles
Methuselah or Imperial	8 bottles
Salmanazar	12 bottles
Balthazar	16 bottles
Nebuchadnezzar	20 bottles

On average you should allow $1/3$ of a bottle per person per wine. Having said that it is almost impossible to foresee how much any one of your guests will drink, so we shall say:

2 persons	1 bottle
4 persons	2 bottles and so on

SERVING TEMPERATURE

Each wine has its own serving temperature, it is also a matter of personal choice. However this subject can lead to interesting debates with sommeliers !

Champage	5°C to 7°C
Sweet White & Rosé	5°C to 7°C
Dry White & Rosé	7°C to 10°C
Red Burgundy	15°C to 16°C
Red Bordeaux	17°C to 18°C
Red Beaujolais	9°C to 12°C
Red Côtes-du-Rhone	13°C to 14°C

VOCABULAIRE DU VIN (WINE TASTING TERMS)

ENGLISH...FRENCH TRANSLATION

Acidity	Basic savour, provides crispness	Acidité
Aroma	Scent of the wine	Arôme
Body	Consistency of the wine made of acid tannin and alcohol	Corps
Bouquet	Scent that develops in the wine during its evolution, aroma	Bouquet
Brilliant	Great, brilliant	Brillant
Coarse	Rough, poor quality	Grossier
Corked	A rare fault, very unpleasant smell	Bouchonné
Crisp	Refreshing and relatively acidic	Nerveux
Deep	Very full, many nuances of flavour	Profond
Dry	Low sugar content	Sec
Delicate	Light wine of quality	Délicat
Elegant	Of exceptional high quality and distinction	Elégant

Exuberant	Lively, easy to drink	Pétillant, Vif
Fine	Great distinction and grace	Fin
Finesse	Great distinction and grace	Fin
Firm	Strong and well balanced	Ferme
Fleshy	Full-bodied	Charnu, Etoffé Corsé
Fruity	Fruity	Fruité
Full-bodied	Full of flavour, powerful	Corsé
Generous	Rich, open	Généreux
Great	Noble	Grand
Green	Sharp, made from under-ripened grapes	Vert
Harmonious	Balanced to perfection	Harmonieux
Heady	High in alcohol	Capiteux
Intense	Deep and complicated	Dense
Mellow	Mature and soft	Moelleux
Muscular	Robust, full-bodied, assertive	Ample, Corsé
Nouveau	New wine drank within the year	Primeur
Perlant	Wine with a light sparkle	Perlant
Round	No sharp edge, mellow	Rond, ample Charpenté
Scented	Pleasant reminder of flowers or herbs	Parfumé
Sharp	With a bite, acid	Acide, Vert Acerbe
Smooth	Smooth	Moelleux
Solid	Firm and well structured	Solide
Spicy	Spice-like taste and smell	Epicé
Sturdy	Strong	Robuste
Supple	Easy to drink, soft and seductive with no sharpness	Souple
Sweet	High sugar content	Doux
Syrupy	Very sweet	Liquoreux
Tannin	Tannic acid which mellows with time	Tannin
Unctuous	Of great smoothness	Onctueux, Suave
Velvety	Smooth, like velvet	Velouté
Vigorous	Lively and strong with gentle taste	Vigoureux

SERVING WINE

Choosing and drinking wine is an infinitely personal matter. One does not need to be an expert to enjoy it, however there are a few easy and logical rules to observe.

T H E   F I R S T   O N E is what the French call 'monter la Gamme', roughly translated, it means 'go up the scale' (music). Very simply it is the young wine before the old, the light before the full-bodied and so on and so forth. A sip of water between each wine to clear the palate is a must. Do not serve too many wines at any one time.
When Champagne is served with the first course it must always be served throughout.

T H E   S E C O N D is the rule of marriage between wine and courses.

Dry white	Shellfish, oysters, crustacés, grilled or fried fish, snails, white poultry, veal.
Medium Dry white	Fish with sauces, vol-au-vent, poultry with sauces, rice, macaroni.
Rosé and light red	Grilled red meat, white meat, poultry, lamb, cheeses.
Full-bodied red	Red meat with sauces, duck, game, strong flavoured dishes, strong cheeses.
Champagne	Any food.

T H E   T H I R D rule is logical, wine should not be served with:
- spicy foods i.e. curry
- vinaigrette
- or with desserts containing oranges or chocolate.

The following quick reference table will help you further

STARTERS
HORS D'OEUVRE	**WINE**
Any dish with strong dressing	No wine
Soup	No wine
Eggs	Light wine
Ham	White
Foie Gras	Sweet white: Sauternes
Pâté	Rosé or red
Oysters	Dry white: Entre-Deux-Mers, Chablis Pouilly-Fuissé
Shellfish	Dry & smooth white: Clos des Mouches Puligny-Montrachet, Chassagne-Montrachet
Snails	Dry white: Chablis, Alsace
Frogs' legs	Light dry white: Graves
Quiches	Medium Dry White
Vol-au-vents	White: Côte-de-Beaune
Any pasta with cheese base	Smooth white

FISH

Smoked salmon	White: Sauternes, Burgundy, Alsace
Fish served cold with sauce	Dry white
Fish served hot with sauce	Dry or smooth white Muscadet, Chablis, Sancerre

POULTRY

Chicken roasted or in a white sauce	White
Chicken in red wine sauce Coq au vin	Red: Beaujolais, Volnay
Rabbit	White, rosé or red (the sauce will dictate)
Duck	Red: Châteauneuf-du-Pape, Côtes-du-Rhone, Gigondas
Duck à l'orange	White: Alsace or Champagne
Goose and turkey	Medium dry white
Pigeon and Guinea fowl	Red: Côte-de-Beaune, Chambertin, Côte-de-Nuits, St-Emilion

MEAT

Beef	Red: Bordeaux, Burgundy, Côtes-du-Rhône
Veal	Dry white: Muscadet, Pouilly-Fumé
Veal, roast, stuffed or braised	Red or rosé
Lamb boiled, grilled	Light red: Côte-de-Beaune, St-Amour
Lamb	Red: Bordeaux, Côtes-du-Rhône
Pork in white sauce	White
Pork	White or rosé
Offal	Young, untannic red wines, Beaujolais, Chinon
Sweetbread	Light young fruity white wine. Sancerre

GAME

Pheasant	Red: Pommard, Volnay
Partridge	Fully bodied red
Grouse	Light red: Beaujolais, Burgundy
Small birds	Red: Côte-de-Beaune
Hare	Fully bodied red

CHEESE

Non-fermented, fresh and creamy	Light rosé
Fermented, soft: Brie, Camembert, blue	Red wine: Bordeaux, St-Emilion, Burgundy, Nuits-St-Georges, Côte-de-Nuits, Côtes-du-Rhône
Fermented, firm: Tomme de Savoie Cantal, Saint Paulin	Light wines: white, rosé or red
Emmenthal, gruyère, Edam etc	Strong red
Goat's cheese	White, dry and fruity

DESSERTS

Any creams, (except chocolate and coffee) flans, puddings, crêpes,	White, smooth and Champagne

40

beignets, ice cream (except chocolate
and coffee)

PASTRIES

Choux, brioches, gateaux, pastries,   Sweet wines: Sauternes, Straw wine,
rum-babas, tarts.   Champagne

FRUITS

Citrus fruits   No wine
Pears   Light red wine
Peaches, apricots, red fruits   Light red wine
Melon   Port
Dried fruits   Any wine

LIQUEURS

"I am convinced digestion is the great secret of life."
REV, SYDNEY SMITH

The Latin word '**liqueur**' means liquid. Another name for liqueur is 'cordial' meaning 'heart cordis'. The French call liqueurs 'digestives' because they are served after a meal to aid digestion. Other terms for liqueur are 'elixir' and 'balm'.

The science of distilling, which concentrates the strength and flavour of any alcohol by removing most of the water, had been known in the East for thousands of years. It surfaced in Europe in the thirteenth century, at which time the Church was the guardian of learning, knowledge and wealth. Enterprising monks began experimenting with this new process of distilling. Their creation was undoubtedly strong-flavoured and crude by our standards, sugar and herbs had to be added to make the concoction palatable.

By the sixteenth century liqueurs were praised and valued as medicines. Needless to say, not just as medicine by those who could afford them! In the same period, sugars and spices from the New World became more easily accessible and liqueur-making expanded rapidly.

Many of today's proprietary brands originated in the nineteenth century. Liqueurs got another boost at the time of Prohibition, as they were used to disguise the poorer spirits.

A liqueur is defined as a spirit mixed with a flavour, and contains 2.5% to 40% sugar. Liqueurs with large amounts of sugar are called crèmes.

TYPES OF LIQUEURS

Liqueurs such as Benedictine or Chartreuse have a unique formula which is a closely guarded secret. No other manufacturers have been able to successfully copy them.

Advocaat
A thick mixture of eggs and brandy produced in Holland.
Amaretto
Made from apricot stones, it has a bitter almond flavour.
Absinthe
First created to treat malaria in 1792. Made from the root of the wormwood plant. It has a bitter liquorice flavour. Aniseed replaced wormwood because of its narcotic effect, and many liqueurs have been made carrying the name of anis, anisette, anesone, Pernod, pastis, ouzo.
Bailey's Irish Cream
Creamy chocolate and Irish whiskey liqueur.
Benedictine
Sweet liqueur produced by the Benedictine monks in France.

Chartreuse
Made by monks in France, high in the mountains of the Haute Savoie. There are two kind: one is yellow, the other green.

Cherry Brandy
Sweet cherry-flavoured liqueur.

Cointreau
Triple sec orange curaçao.

Crème de Cassis
The flavour for this liqueur comes mainly from blackcurrants.

Crème de Menthe
Several mints, but mainly peppermint, are used to flavour this liqueur. When this drink is produced it is a clear liqueur and harmless colourings are added.

Crème de Noyaux
Made from fruit stones which give it an almond flavour.

Curacao
The name has come into general use for any orange-flavoured liqueurs.

Drambuie
A Scottish whisky liqueur.

Grand Marnier
A cognac-based orange-flavoured liqueur.

Kummel
The chief flavour for this comes from cumin and caraway, with a touch of anis. There are dozens of varieties of this liqueur and it is believed to aid digestion. Served alight, with a coffee bean floating on the top.

Sloe Gin
The black, plum-like, fruit of the blackthorn provides the flavour for this liqueur. The fruit is steeped in gin.

Tia Maria
Jamaican coffee liqueur.

Triple Sec
A white curaçao produced by many manufacturers.

Pousse Cafe
Pour several liqueurs of different densities into a straight-sided glass. The liqueurs form layers, and to achieve the best dramatic effect use liqueurs of different colours. Gently pour each liqueur into the glass, chill in the refrigerator for one hour before serving.

Serving Liqueurs

Liqueurs are served after a meal, as a digestive in a small-stemmed liqueur glass. A 'frappé' is a liqueur poured over crushed ice in a Champagne saucer.

C O G N A C

The appellation controlée Cognac covers two 'departments' in Charente in France - 37,500 farmers grow the white 'UGNI BLANC' grape. They pick the grape before it is ripe which ensures a wine perfect for distillation. In the heart of Charente lies the town of Cognac. The soil there is as chalky as in Champagne, this is why the area is named 'Grande champagne', and the finest Cognac is produced there. Regions of progressively less chalky soils surround it, there are five in total. In decreasing circles we move from 'Grande

Champagne' to 'Petite Champagne' to borderies and 'Fins Bois' to 'Bons Bois' and 'Bois Ordinaires'. The quality of the Cognac varies from exquisite fineness in the inner circle to a more full-bodied and light-flavoured spirit in the outer circles.

Cognac is distilled in the winter months, two distillations are needed to get the right equation. The liquid running out of the still is white and clear and contains seventy percent alcohol; it takes ten barrels of wine to make one barrel of brandy. Once distilled, the ageing process must take place. Limousin oak is the perfect medium, it is porous and has a low tannin content. Three years in a barrel is the minimum, and most quality brandies have had three years or more. VSOPs (Very Special Old Pale) have five years or more. Evaporation during those years is astronomical. More cognac is lost in the air each year than is drunk in the whole of France!

The classification is:
- ☆☆☆: three years
- **VSOP:** five to nine years
- **XO NAPOLEON:** twelve to twenty years
- **VIEILLE RESERVE & GRAND ROYAL:** thirty years or more.

ARMAGNAC

Armagnac is produced eighty miles south of Cognac, in the Gascony region, and is divided into three areas:
- Haut-Armagnac
- Tenazère
- Bas-Armagnac.

Bas-Armagnac produces the best quality brandy. Soil and climate are one of the differences between Cognac and Armagnac. Armagnac is distilled once at a much lower strength than Cognac, this way, the spirit retains more flavouring elements within it. Armagnac is aged in black oak barrels which gives it its distinctive flavour and speeds the ageing process. Armagnac is drier than Cognac and does not need sugar; it possesses great smoothness, lingering flavour and an enormously captivating scent. There are no great houses like Martell or Hennessy in Armagnac, but a large number of small producers, which bear on their labels infinitely romantic and picturesque names.

BRANDIES

"Claret is the liquor for boys, port for men, but he who aspires to be a hero must drink brandy."
JOHNSON

A brandy should be served in a tulip-shaped glass, tall enough to allow a reasonable amount of aroma to build, but small enough to let the hand warm the glass. Brandy is brilliant in colour, the bouquet pleasant and subtle or intense and fruity. A superior brandy will have a lingering mellow after-taste. Unlike wine, brandy is stored in its bottle, upright and securely sealed, it will last indefinitely.
To flambé brandy: The brandy must be at room temperature. Pour the brandy over the food and ignite. Beware of setting both yourself and the kitchen alight!

EAU DE VIE (water of life)

This term refers to all white spirits or brandies made from fruits other than grapes. The French also call these 'alcools blancs' (white alcohols). For example:

Apple brandy
French 'Calvados', American 'Applejack'

Cherry brandy
Called 'Kirsch' in Alsace and 'Kirschwasser' in Germany and Switzerland. It takes 60lbs (25 kg) of cherries to make five bottles.

Raspberry brandy
French 'framboise', Germany 'himbeergeist'. It takes 60lbs (25 kg) to make one bottle. It is therefore extremely expensive.

Pear brandy
'Eau de vie de poire'. A pear is grown in the bottle on the tree. It is produced in France and Switzerland.

Plum brandy
French 'mirabelle' from yellow plums, 'reine' from greengage plums and 'quetsch' from Alsatian blue plums.

Strawberry brandy
Made with cultivated strawberries known as 'fraise' in France and 'Himbeergeist' in Germany.

Wild strawberries
'Fraises des bois', an authentic product hard to find and fabulously expensive.

Genévrier
A brandy that is almost a gin and made from juniper berries.

Many fruit brandies are local specialities.

FORTIFIED WINES

SHERRY

In the British Isles sherry still remains the most favoured apéritif. It is a fortified wine made from the Palomino white grape. Sherry made in the area of Jerez de Al Frontera is the only one entitled to use the name 'Sherry'. All other sherries, must always be labelled with the country of origin. Sherry should be consumed within one week of opening as it will deteriorate. Colour is a good guide to the sweetness of the sherry, and the following definitions are broadly accurate.

Fino: Very dry and pale.

Amontillado or Oloroso: Medium dry, a little darker and stronger than Fino.

Manzanilla: Very dry Fino from Bodegas of Sanlucar de Barremeda on the coast; delicate salty taste.

Amoroso: Extra sweet.

Cream: Sweet dessert sherry, either dark or pale.

Vino De Pasto: Fairly dry Fino.

PORT

In the early eighteenth century the French stopped exporting wine to Britain. Wine had to be imported from Portugal, as its quality was inferior a shipper had the bright idea of adding brandy to the wine whilst it was fermenting. The result was port, which had an immediate, spectacular success with the British, and has remained popular ever since. The chief distinction between ports is in the vintage, which is only declared if it has been an outstanding year. The wine is aged in wood for two years and bottled. Maturing takes place in the bottle, and so vintage ports need decanting as deposits form. Brandy and wine take a long time to blend satisfactorily, so a vintage port is not ready to be drunk for a least fifteen years. Non-vintage port is left in the barrel, and not bottled until it is considered drinkable.

Ruby port: The least sophisticated of the group. Blended from several wines and aged in casks for 3 years before bottling.
Tawny port: Made like ruby, but the wine used is of better quality. Tawny port is paler and drier.
White Port: A popular apéritif made with white grapes and fortified. Disconcertingly close to sherry.

MADEIRA

Madeira originates from the island of Madeira. The flavour is rather like caramel because the wine is baked at a high temperature before the end of fermentation. The amount of grape sugar still present at this stage will determine whether the finished product is dry or sweet. The sweet varieties are called Malmsey and Bual, and the dry, Verdelho and Sercial.

MARSALA

Based on the strong white wine of West Sicily. A popular drink in the Royal Navy of Nelson's time, but today it is used mainly in cooking. The superior variety, named Virgin, has a pleasant nutty flavour.

VERMOUTHS

Covers a multitude of red and white wines based drinks, to which sugar, flavourings, and alcohol have been added. Most vermouths come from Italy and France.

BITTERS

Bitters were developed in the nineteenth century as a tonic to fight malaria. A bitter is a digestive and a pick-me-up for the 'morning after'. It is also used to flavour drinks such as pink gin and Campari.

CIGARS

"One breathes with ones lungs, but one smokes a cigar with ones organs of smell and taste."
UNKNOWN CIGAR-SMOKER.

After dinner, with coffee and brandy, offer your guests a good selection of cigars, a cigar cutter is an essential implement.

The word 'cigar' is derived from the Mayan name 'Sik'ar', meaning smoking. Christopher Columbus recorded in his log book on 6th November 1492, that a few of his crew had sighted natives smoking in Watling Island near Cuba. The indigenous were seen rolling a leaf in their hands, put it in their mouths, light it at one end and inhale the smoke.

Manufacture

A cigar is made with the dried and fermented leaves of the 'Nicotiana Tabacum'. Climate, soil and man's expertise contribute to the quality and suitability of these leaves. Brazil, Cuba and Indonesia, have a particularly favourable soil for growing tobacco.

The leaves of the plant are gathered by hand. After the harvest the leaves are then dried in purposely constructed sheds. The leaves then undergo a process unique to cigar-tobacco. They are gathered in piles to generate a high temperature. This fermentation reduces sugar content and harmful bacteria is destroyed, it also improves flavour and colouring. After an average period of approximately ten weeks the leaves are selected and sorted.

Cigars are made of: **filler, binder and wrapper**.

The **filler** is a blend of tobaccos; often as many as twenty are used. Each brand of cigars has its own formula and a unique taste and aroma. It is a great art to maintain a constant taste as every crop of tobacco varies.

The **binder** has two very important functions. It holds the filler together, and regulates the burning rate. It maintains an even taste and full aroma. A good cigar should have a pure natural binder as well as a pure filler.

The **wrapper** is the outer leaf of the cigar, and again this should be 100% pure tobacco.

How to light a cigar

Cut a small slice off the tip of the cigar, with a cigar cutter, after moistening the end. You may light your cigar with either a gas-lighter or a match, but always wait until the sulphur has burned off. Heat the cigar by holding the flame a couple of inches below the tip until the tobacco begins to smoulder. Then draw on the cigar gently until it burns properly. Never draw rapidly as it will create a high temperature that will ruin the cigar's flavour.

Do not inhale the smoke but taste the cigars flavour by 'rolling' the smoke around the tongue before puffing it out. Cigars should be enjoyed like a good glass of wine. Ash tempers the heat of the cigar. Therefore hold the ash as long as possible. Never press out your cigar, but lay it in an ashtray and it will go out by itself without leaving any unpleasant smells.

Cigars will keep for a long time if they are bought in prime condition, and then stored correctly.

A cigar should feel soft when pressed gently, if it crackles and appears dry it is not in good condition. Cigars should be stored away from strong smelling items such as perfume, as this will destroy their aroma. Ideally one should have a humidor box. Good tobacconists will supply these. The box is usually wooden and lined with cedar-wood. A strip of metal or plastic with a cloth that one keeps damp is inside the box and provides the necessary moisture. In the winter when the moisture rate is high, keep your cigars in a warm, dry place. Trial and error will serve you well. Cigars do not like central heating, or the extreme of wet places.

THE CHEESE BOARD

On the Continent cheese is served before the dessert, but in England it is still served at the end of the meal, or to replace the dessert.

A cheese board should be large enough to accommodate four to five cheeses, a knife, and a small bunch of grapes. Leave a comfortable space between each cheese for ease of cutting. Serve with a selection of appetising accompaniments, such as celery, cherry tomatoes, radishes, dates, grapes or, as an alternative apple purée. Remember to offer salt with the cheese.

Cheeses of different textures and tastes should be offered, for example: Stilton, Brie or Camembert, a farmhouse Cheddar, a goat's cheese and Emmenthal or Yarlesberg.

Tips on purchasing:
1. Cheese should not have numerous cracks running through it.
2. Avoid cheeses which are sweaty looking and wrapped in cling film.
3. Avoid cheeses with dried edges.

Tips on storing cheese:
1. Cheese should be kept in a plastic container in a cool larder, but if this is not possible, a refrigerator is the next best place.
2. When stored in the refrigerator cheese should be removed two hours before serving so it is at room temperature when eaten.
3. Cheese should be wrapped in greaseproof or wax paper, as cling film and polythene make cheese sweat.

Note: Some cheeses have a strong aroma, and will taint other foods in the refrigerator.

BRITISH CHEESES

Ayrshire soft cheese: A Scottish cheese with a nutty, slightly salty flavour. The texture is soft and creamy.
Caboc: A soft, full, creamy rich cheese, almost white and rolled in toasted oatmeal, rarely available south of Scotland.
Caerphilly: A moist white cheese, with a mild slightly salty flavour.
Caithness: A soft yellow-coloured cheese with a medium to strong flavour. This cheese is often wrapped in a tartan package.
Cheddar: The most popular of the English cheeses. A strong yellow colour with a close creamy texture, its full nutty flavour varies in strength.
Cheshire: The oldest of the British cheeses, with a savoury, mellow, slightly salty flavour. There are two kinds of Cheshire, white and red.
Blue Cheshire: A very rare cheese as it has to be stored under special conditions to develop the blue veins. It has a stronger flavour than ordinary Cheshire, and is comparable to Stilton.
Cottage cheese: This pure white cheese is made from skimmed milk curds, has a low fat content and a mild bland flavour.

Crowdie: The Scottish equivalent to cottage cheese.

Derby: A close textured honey-coloured cheese with a mild flavour.

Sage Derby: Chopped fresh sage is incorporated in layers as the cheese is being made.

Dunlop: A moist Scottish cheese similar to English Cheddar, but with a softer texture and milder flavour. This cheese is the colour of pale butter.

Gloucester: This firm smooth texture cheese may be mellow and creamy or have a distinct bite to it, but should never be pungent. Traditionally this cheese has the colour of Guernsey milk.

Hramsa: A Scottish soft cheese made with double cream and flavoured with wild garlic gathered in the highlands.

Lancashire: An off-white crumbly cheese, when at its best it spreads like butter. Used to make Welsh Rarebit.

Leicester: A flaky-textured mild cheese, which can be red or golden in colour.

Lymeswold: A soft creamy mild-flavoured cheese with a blue vein.

Morven: A mild Scottish cheese sometimes flavoured with caraway seeds. Its texture is similar to Dutch Gouda.

Red Windsor: A crumbly texture, similar in flavour to mild cheddar.

Stilton: Stilton is the king of English cheeses. It is rich and creamy with distinctive patches of blue and at its best between November and April.

Wensleydale: A creamy yellow crumbly cheese with a mild flavour. In the North of England it is traditionally served with apple pie.

FRENCH CHEESES

"On ne peut rassembler les Français que sous le coup de la peur. On ne peut peut pas rassembler à froid un pays qui compte 365 spécialités de fromages."
The French will only be united under the threat of danger. Nobody can simply bring together a county that has 365 kinds of cheese.
CHARLES DE GAULLE

Many varieties of cheeses are produced in the regions of France, but unfortunately only a small proportion are imported into Britain.

Banon: Banon is dipped in 'Eau-de-vie', and traditionally left to mature for a couple of months in stone jars. A cream-coloured medium-soft cheese made from either goat's or cow's milk.

Bleu d'Auvergne: A close-textured blue cheese made from ewe's, goat's and cow's milk.

Bleu de Bresse: A soft creamy rich dark-veined blue cheese, made from skimmed cow's milk.

Bleu des Causses: A soft blue cheese, less piquant than roquefort, and made from cow's milk.

Boulette de Cambrai: A spicy cheese flavoured with herbs and made with buttermilk.

Boursin: A soft cream cheese flavoured with herbs, garlic or pepper.

Brie: Brie is one of France's greatest cheeses. It is a soft creamy white cheese with a delicate flavour made from cow's milk. The crust is edible.

Camembert: Camembert is world famous and comes from Normandy. A soft creamy pale yellow cheese, with a distinct flavour. It is made from cow's milk and has an edible crust. A ripe camembert should be soft; when it is over-ripe it turns pale brown and tastes of ammonia.

Cantal: A hard, strong cheese made from cow's milk. It is one of the largest French cheeses and comes from the Cantal and Auvergne regions of France. It has a flavour similar to cheddar.

Carre de l'Est: A square soft cheese with a high fat content, similar to camembert but with a milder flavour.

Comté: A firm yellow cheese with small holes running through it.

Demi-sel: A soft cream cheese, with a little salt content which tastes almost like cream.

Eppoisses: This soft round cheese has an orange crust. It is made from curdled milk and sometimes flavoured with black pepper, cloves or fennel, then soaked in wine or eau-de-vie. This cheese comes from Provence.

Fromage de Monsieur: A double cream cheese with a high fat content. It is oval in shape and can be eaten when slightly under ripe. This cheese is produced in Normandy, and has a slight salty taste.

Gruyere: The true gruyère is only ever made in the French-speaking area of Switzerland. It is a firm pale cheese with small holes throughout and a crinkly, slightly greasy golden brown rind. Gruyère is used in 'fondue' cooking.

Crème de Gruyère: This is processed gruyère cheese which is softer and has a mild taste.

Livarot: A soft yellow cheese with a dark reddish-brown rind. It is made from skimmed milk and has a strong flavour.

Maroilles: Produced more than 1,000 years ago by the monks of the Abbey of Maroilles, it is the oldest and most popular cheese of Northern France. It is a semi-hard, slightly salted yellow cheese with a reddish-brown rind. It has a strong flavour and is pungent.

Mimolette: This is a round orange cheese with a grey rind, and is similar to a hard dry cheddar.

Munster: A pungent semi-soft cheese, with a creamy texture and a reddish rind. It originates from the Alsace region, and is sometimes flavoured with cumin or aniseed.

Petit Suisse: A creamy unsalted cheese, made from whole milk and extra cream. It tastes faintly sour and is often eaten with sugar. It is always sold in little rolls individually wrapped.

Pont l'Evêque: A semi-soft pale yellow cheese with a crinkled yellow crust. Pont l'Evêque is square, and has a camembert flavour.

Port Salut: A bland semi-hard cheese both in flavour and colour with an orange rind.

Reblochon: A soft cheese which is pale in colour and has an orange-to-chestnut rind.

Roquefort: Roquefort takes its name from Roquefort-sur-Soulzon, a village surrounded by limestone caves where the cheese is ripened. Sheep's milk from Perigord, the Pays Basque and even Corsica is used.

It is a crumbly blue cheese with a salty and piquant flavour. Charlemagne and Charles VI were said to be exceedingly partial to Roquefort, and a nineteenth century Papal envoy, Monseigneur Bounet, was never allowed to leave France for the Vatican without carrying with him a case of Roquefort.

Saint Gorlon: A sharp blue cheese, comparable to gorgonzola.

Saint Marcellin: A small round crumbly cream cheese made from goat's milk which has a mild slightly salty taste. When louis XI was the dauphin, the legend is that two woodcutters found him after he had been attacked by a bear in the forest of Lenta. They fed him coarse bread and local cheese (St. Marcellin), which restored his health.

Saint Nectaire: A semi-hard, bland, pale yellow cheese with a yellow rind. Produced in the Auvergne region of France, it dates back to roman times.

Saint Paulin: A semi-hard yellow cheese, with a bland flavour similar to port salut.

Tomme de savoie: A semi-hard yellow cheese with a reddish rind and a distinct flavour.

Tomme de Raisin: A slightly chewy white cheese similar to tome de savoie, but covered with a mixture of dried black grape-skins and pips.

Trappiste de Belval: The name comes from the area of Artois close to Saint-Polsur-Temoise, where the Abbey from which it originates is situated.

Valençay or Levroux: A soft and creamy full-flavoured goat's cheese dusted with grey ashes.

CHEESES
FROM AROUND THE WORLD

"as I was crawling through the holes in a Swiss cheese the other day it occurred to me to wonder what a Swiss cheese would think if a Swiss cheese could think and after cogitating for sometime I said to myself if a Swiss cheese could think it would think that a Swiss cheese was the most important thing in the world just as everything that can think at all."
DON MARQUIS

Bel Paese: An Italian soft cheese which has an ivory colour, a thin dark yellow rind and a delicate slightly salty flavour. It is usually served as a dessert cheese and only occasionally used for cooking.

Bergkäse: An Australian hard dull yellow cheese with a dark brown rind. It has a high fat content and a nutty flavour.

Caciocavallo: A mild, semi-sweet-flavoured, white-to-straw coloured Italian curd cheese. The rind is smooth and thin, with thread like surface marks.

Danbo: A Danish mild, firm-textured cheese, sometimes flavoured with caraway seeds. This cheese has many regular even sized holes throughout.

Danish Blue: A blue-veined, soft-crumbly-textured cheese which was first produced in 1914. It has a strong salty flavour with a high cream content.

Dolcellate: An Italian blue-veined cheese, off-white in colour, with a robust full flavour and creamy moist texture.

Edam: A Dutch mild flavoured cheese with a rubbery consistency, encased in a red wax rind. Edam is similar to Gouda in flavour.

Edelpilz: A German cheese with a strong flavour and crumbly texture. The cheese is white around the edges and mottled blue in the centre.

Emmenthal: A Swiss cheese originally, but also produced in Germany and Denmark. The cheese is a dull yellow colour and has many holes the size of cherries throughout. Its flavour is nutty and it is suitable as a dessert and cooking cheese.

Fetta: A Greek semi-soft curd cheese, made from ewe's milk. It is white with a salty taste.

Fontina: Produced in the mountains in Northern Italy. It is a soft full-fat cheese, slightly straw-coloured with a few small holes. The rind is orange and thicker than most other rinds of cheeses. Imitations of this cheese are Fontal and Fontinella.

Gorgonzola: An Italian cheese named after the village of Gorgonzola, near Milan. This straw-coloured cheese is mottled with green and has a coarse brown rind. The flavour is strong and sometimes slightly spiced. Gorgonzola should be firm and dry.

Gouda: A Dutch cheese with a high butter-fat content. It is produced in squat moulds, and has a golden yellow colour. Gouda is not recommended for cooking.

Halumi: A Greek cheese similar to Fetta cheese.

Limburger: A very strong-smelling spicy cheese with holes throughout. It is bright yellow with a dark brown shiny rind.

Molbo: A Danish mild cheese with a slightly acid after-taste. It is close-textured with a few holes, yellow coloured with a red rind.

Mozzarella: A soft compact Italian curd cheese with a slightly sour flavour, used in pizza-making.

Parmesan: A very hard strong Italian cheese. It is off-white with a black rind.

Quargel: A hard Austrian cheese with a piquant flavour.

Riccotta: A soft bland Italian cheese with a low fat content made from sheep's milk. The rind of the cheese is ridged.

Samsoe: A Danish, sweet mild nutty flavoured cheese. This yellow firmly textured cheese has shiny round holes.

Vacherin: A Swiss cream cheese which is off-white and has a rough mottled rind.

Roulade: A full-fat cream cheese. Roulade can have various flavours.

SAVOURIES

A savoury follows the dessert or sometimes replaces it. It should be freshly made served very hot and highly seasoned. Savouries resemble hors d'oeuvres and can be served at cocktail parties. A savoury is more substantial in size than an hors d'oeuvre.

DEVILLED SOFT ROES

❀ ☆☆☆
PREPARATION TIME: 5 MINUTES
COOKING TIME: 10 MINUTES

Ingredients:

2 oz (50 g) of butter	*Salt, pepper & cayenne*
½ lb (225 g) of soft roes	*Lemon juice*
Seasoned flour	*Hot buttered toast*

Method:
Clean the roes by removing any membranes, toss the roes in seasoned flour. Heat a pan and add the butter, when foaming add the roes, brown on both sides, sprinkle with the seasoning. Squeeze lemon juice over the roes and serve immediately on hot buttered toast. Garnish with parsley and a lemon wedge.

SARDINES ON TOAST

❀ ☆☆☆
PREPARATION TIME: 10 MINUTES
COOKING TIME: 5 MINUTES

Ingredients:

8 sardines	*1 tsp of vinegar*
1 tsp grated onion	*1 pinch of salt*
1 tsp of French mustard	*4 slices of toast*
3 tsp of butter	

Method:
Make the toast. Combine the above ingredients to a smooth paste. Spread the mixture on the toast and put under a hot grill for approximately 5 minutes until piping hot. Garnish with a sprinkle of either finely chopped fennel and freshly ground black pepper, or lemon wedges and cayenne.

FINNAN HADDOCK

❀ ☆☆☆
PREPARATION TIME: 10 MINUTES
COOKING TIME: 10 MINUTES

Ingredients:
1 finnan haddock or 1 Arbroath smokie   *Seasoning*
Buttered toast

Method:
Flake the finnan haddock or smokie with a little butter or cream, season well and put on to the buttered toast. Grill until piping hot. Garnish with tomato, parsley, and lemon wedges.

ANGELS ON HORSEBACK

✽ ☆☆☆☆☆
PREPARATION TIME: 5 MINUTES
COOKING TIME: 10 MINUTES

Ingredients:
1 dozen oysters   *1 dozen slices of smoked streaky bacon*

Method:
Roll one oyster in one rasher of bacon and secure with a skewer and either grill or bake in a hot oven for 5-6 minutes. Serve two rolls per person on hot buttered toast. The recipe can be adapted, using kidneys instead of oysters and cooking for about 12 minutes.

DEVILS ON HORSEBACK

Use the same method as for 'Angels on Horseback' substituting the oyster with stoned prunes. Secure the prunes and bacon with a small wooden cocktail stick and cook in a hot oven for 15 minutes.

COCKTAIL SAUSAGES

✽ ☆☆☆
COOKING TIME: 20 MINUTES

Ingredients:
Chipolata or cocktail sausages   *Smoked streaky bacon*

Method:
To make cocktail sausages, twist a chipolata sausage in the centre and cut. Wrap a piece of bacon around the sausage and secure with a cocktail stick. Cook in a hot oven for 15 to 20 minutes.

PRUNE & DATE KEBAB

✽ ☆☆☆
PREPARATION TIME: 10 MINUTES
COOKING TIME: 10 MINUTES

Ingredients:
Whole stoned prunes   *Stoned dates*

Walnuts chopped coarsely	*Bay leaves*
Chutney	*Butter*
Rashers of streaky bacon	*Watercress*
Dessert apple	

Method:

Mix the nuts and chutney. Slit the prunes and dates and fill with a little of the mixture. Wrap a piece of streaky bacon around the fruit. Arrange on skewers alternating with a slice of apple and a bay leaf. Brush with melted butter, and grill. Garnish with watercress.

CAMEMBERT CROQUETTES

❀❀ ☆☆☆
PREPARATION TIME: 15 MINUTES
RESTING TIME: 1 HOUR
COOKING TIME: 7 MINUTES

Ingredients:

1 medium ripe camembert	*Dash of Tabasco sauce*
1½ oz (40 g) of butter	*1 egg yoke*
1½ oz (40 g) of flour	*Dry white crumbs*
½ pt (275 ml) of milk	*Deep fat for frying*
Salt, pepper, cayenne	*Grated Parmesan cheese*

Method:

Remove the rind from the cheese and press through a wire sieve. Make a roux with the butter and flour, gradually add the milk and stir until boiling. Season well and leave until cool, then add the Camembert and egg yolk. Spread on a plate and chill. Shape into pieces the size of a walnut on a floured board. Dip into beaten egg and then roll in dried white crumbs. Deep fry until golden brown. Serve immediately with grated parmesan cheese.

HOT CHICKEN CROUTES

This recipe is ideal for using left-over chicken.

❀❀ ☆☆☆
PREPARATION TIME: 15 MINUTES
COOKING TIME: 5 MINUTES

Ingredients:

½ pint (275 ml) of béchamel sauce	*Fried round bread*
1 tsp of curry paste	*1 tbs grated parmesan & gruyere cheese*
3 tbs cold diced chicken	*1 tbs of butter*
3 tbs cold diced ham or tongue	*Fried parsley to garnish*
Salt, pepper, cayenne, lemon juice	

Method:

Make béchamel sauce (see page 304), add the curry paste, diced chicken, ham or tongue. Season and add a squeeze of lemon juice. Heap the mixture onto the fried bread. Put another round of fried bread on top. Work the cheese and butter together to a paste, and spread over the top of the fried bread. Brown quickly under a hot grill and serve hot, garnished with the fried parsley.

HAM CORNUCOPIAS

❀❀ ☆☆☆
PREPARATION TIME: 15 MINUTES
COOKING TIME: 15 MINUTES
OVEN TEMP: 190C 375F M5
Special Equipment: Cornet Moulds

Ingredients:

Short crust pastry
Beaten egg
½ pt (275 ml) of béchamel sauce

6 oz (175 g) of minced ham
Seasoning

Method:

Roll the short crust pastry on a floured board and cut into approximately 12" (30cm) long and ½" (1cm) wide strips, brush these with water. Take one strip of pastry, starting at the pointed end of the mould, gradually wind the strip around, slightly overlapping the pastry until the mould is covered. Brush with beaten egg and place on a damp baking sheet. Bake until golden brown. Meanwhile make the béchamel sauce, adding the ham and seasoning. When the pastry is golden brown remove from the oven. Hold carefully with a clean tea towel and very gently twist the metal mould from the pastry. The mould should come away very easily to leave you with a conical pastry case. Fill and serve hot or cold.

WELSH RAREBIT

❀ ☆☆☆
PREPARATION TIME: 10 MINUTES
COOKING TIME: 10 MINUTES
OVEN TEMP: 400F 200C M6 OR HOT GRILL

Ingredients:

Slice of bread toasted on one side only
Grated cheddar cheese
Butter
Dried mustard

Worcestershire sauce
Cayenne, salt & pepper
Tobasco (optional)

Method:

Blend the cheese, butter, mustard and seasoning to your required taste, spread over the untoasted side of the bread and garnish with thinly sliced tomatoes and chopped parsley. Put in a hot oven or grill until the cheese has melted. Serve hot.

PETITS FOURS

Petits fours are 'sweet meats', of mouthful size, very delicate and elegant. Petits fours should be presented on a sweet plate. If they contain chocolate, leave them in the refrigerator until the last moment.

CHOCOLATE ICE-CREAM BALLS

❀ ❀ ☆☆☆ **These can be made well in advance and stored in the freezer.**
PREPARATION TIME: 30 MINUTES
FREEZING: SEVERAL HOURS

Ingredients:

10 fl oz (275 ml) of vanilla ice cream
Grated zest of 1 orange

Few drops of orange liqueur essence
5 oz (150 g) of plain chocolate covering

Method:
Soften the ice cream slightly and then beat in the orange zest and the flavouring essence. Put in a plastic container and re-freeze. Place a baking sheet in the freezer so it gets very cold. Using a melon baller, scoop the hard ice cream into small balls and put onto the cold baking sheet and put a cocktail stick into each ball. Return the ice-cream balls to the freezer and allow to become very hard. Melt the chocolate in a double saucepan and working very quickly dip the ice-cream balls into the melted chocolate and put back onto the tray in the freezer. Keep frozen until ready to serve.

FRESH FRUITS DIPPED IN CHOCOLATE

❀ ☆☆☆
PREPARATION TIME: 30 MINUTES

Ingredients:

Strawberries
Cherries
Orange segments

Pineapple
White & Black grapes

Method:
Melt the chocolate in a double saucepan, or in a bowl that sits on the rim of a pan of boiling water. Prepare the fruits, keeping the stalks on the strawberries, cherries and so on. Dip the fruits in the chocolate, place in petits fours cases and put in the refrigerator to set. Serve.

TOFFEE GLAZED FRESH FRUITS

❀ ❀ ☆☆☆ **Make a few hours before they are to be eaten, because the juice from the fruit turns the caramel sticky if left too long.**
PREPARATION TIME: 20 MINUTES
COOLING TIME: 30 MINUTES

Ingredients:

4 oz (110 g) of strawberries

4 oz (110 g) of white grapes

1 small orange or tangerine   *7 oz (200 g) of sugar*

Method:
Wash the strawberries but do not hull them, and leave the grapes in sprigs of two. Remove all the pith from the orange and divide into segments. Lightly oil two baking sheets. Put 4 fl oz (100 ml) of water and the sugar into a saucepan and stir over a gentle heat until the sugar has dissolved. Increase the heat and bring to the boil until the syrup is a pale golden-brown colour. Remove from the heat. Holding the strawberries by the hull quickly dip into the caramel and put onto the baking sheet, then do the same with the grapes; using tongs to dip the orange segments. Serve in paper petits fours cases within two hours.

ORANGE-ALMOND PETIT FOURS

❀ ☆☆☆ **These can be made well in advance and stored in an airtight tin for some weeks before use.**
PREPARATION TIME: 25 MINUTES
COOKING TIME: 15 MINUTES
OVEN TEMPERATURE: 180C 350F M4

Ingredients:
2 large egg whites
4 oz (110 g) of caster sugar
5 oz (150 g) ground almonds
Grated zest 1 orange

Few drops orange oil or essence
Candied orange peel for decoration
Butter for greasing

Method:
Heat the oven and grease the baking sheets. Whisk the egg whites until stiff. Combine the sugar, almonds and orange zest, add the orange oil. Fold into the egg whites. Fit a piping bag with a ½" (1 cm) star nozzle and spoon in the mixture. Pipe little rosettes onto the baking tray pushing the nozzle down to flatten the biscuit. Place a piece of candied peel into the centre of each biscuit and bake for 15 minutes until the biscuits are even in colour and firm. Cool on a wire tray.
Note: Lemon flavouring may be used instead of orange, and flaked almonds or cherry to decorate.

CIGARETTES RUSSE

❀❀ ☆☆☆
PREPARATION TIME: 1 HOUR
COOKING TIME: 6 MINUTES
OVEN TEMPERATURE: 200C 400F M6
MAKES: 15-20

Ingredients:
Few drops of vanilla essence
2 large egg whites
4 oz (110 g) of sifted icing sugar
1½ oz (40 g) of flour

2½ oz (60 g) of melted butter
1 oz (25 g) of dark chocolate
Butter & flour for greasing

Method:

Heat the oven, grease and lightly flour the baking sheets (tap off the excess flour so it is covered with a fine layer). Whisk the egg whites until stiff, sift the icing sugar into the egg whites and gently beat them together with a wooden spoon. Sift the flour onto the mixture and combine, beat in the melted butter. Drop one tablespoon of the mixture onto the baking sheet. Smooth out thinly and evenly with a knife to an even circle. Bake in the oven for 5-6 minutes until the biscuit is set and golden brown. Run a palette knife or fish slice under the cooked biscuit and turn it upside down, then quickly roll it around a pencil. Cool the biscuit on a wire tray. Cook the remaining biscuits in the same way in pairs. Melt the chocolate in a double pan and dip one end of the biscuit into the chocolate. Put back onto a wire tray until the chocolate has set. Store in an airtight container in a cool place until ready to serve.

CHOCOLATE MARZIPAN DATES

❀❀ ☆☆☆
PREPARATION TIME: 30 MINUTES
1-2 HOURS DRYING
MAKES: ABOUT 15

Ingredients:
8 oz (225 g) of marzipan   *1 lb (450 g) of dates (stoned)*
2 tbs of brandy   *8 oz (225 g) of milk or plain chocolate*

Method:
Combine the marzipan and brandy, shape into small sausages enough to insert into the dates. Push the sides of the dates together to conceal the marzipan. Melt the chocolate in a bowl over a pan of boiling water. Use a cocktail stick to dip the date into the chocolate in order to coat it evenly. Set the dates on a wire tray which has been covered in foil. Prepare all the dates in the same way, and decorate with tiny marzipan balls. Chill for at least one hour. Serve in petits fours cases.

FONDANT ICED FRUITS

❀❀ ☆☆☆
PREPARATION TIME: 30 MINUTES

Ingredients:
Cape gooseberries   *8 oz (225 g) of icing sugar*
Fresh cherries   *Pink food colouring*
Fresh strawberries   *Water*

Method:
Peel the lantern casing from around the Cape gooseberries but do not remove. Leave the hull on the strawberries and the stalks on the cherries, preferably in pairs. Sieve the icing sugar into a bowl, and gradually add a tiny amount of water until you have a mixture that leaves a gentle trail in the bowl, but will gradually even out. Dip the fruits in the fondant icing until evenly coated and place on a baking tray covered in foil until set. Serve.

COFFEE

"Coffee, (which makes a politician wise,
And see through all things with his half-shut eyes)
Sent up in vapours to the Baron's brains
New stratagems, the radiant lock to gain."
ALEXANDER POPE

The coffee plant is an evergreen; the fruit looks like a wild cherry, each berry containing two green beans. Coffee beans are the seed kernel of the coffee tree. The plant was first discovered in its wild state in the region of Ethiopia called Kaffa. The natives observed that woodland animals were clearly stimulated by feeding freely from the berries, and they investigated its effects.

The word coffee originates from the Turkish 'kahveh', which first of all meant wine. There are many legends about coffee's early beginnings, but in fact it is not until the thirteenth century that the process of cleaning and roasting the beans was discovered. The Moslems adopted it with great relish, and by the middle of the fifteenth century coffee was being drunk in Mecca, Cairo, Damascus and Constantinople.

Coffee made its first appearance in Europe in the seventeenth century when Turks fleeing from Vienna left behind a wagon-load of raw coffee. The Viennese people found this new drink to their liking and the Viennese coffee house became 'the mother of cafés'. Needless to say it was only the upper classes who could afford to drink it.

From Vienna its fame spread to Zurich to the Café Odeon, where famous people such as James Joyce, Sigmund Freud, and Trotsky met their friends and entourage. There, over endless cups of steaming coffee, they passionately discussed ideas which were to change the world.

In England, the first coffee house was opened in Oxford by a Turk. It was immensely successful. People were curious to try this mysterious beverage which had been advertised as stimulating, and possessing many health giving properties.

In France, it was in Marseilles that the first 'café' house made its debut, quickly followed by Paris. French cafés were exclusive establishments.

Coffee became very fashionable for the middle classes and had a faint aura of Eastern exoticism; it had to be as hot as fire and as black as coal. Bach gave coffee its 'lettre de Noblesse' by composing his famous Coffee Cantata. However, it was not altogether welcomed everywhere. The Church considered it a hellish brew and coffee was prohibited several times in many countries.

Coffee in its original state has no smell, and it is only through roasting that the coffee exhales its delicious aroma. The kernel contains 1-2 per cent caffeine (which is removed in decaffeinated coffee), tannic acid and volatile oils. Coffee is now grown in 40 countries, and there are numerous varieties covering a wide range of prices, quality and tastes. The staff in specialised shops will be glad to advise you by pointing out the strength and flavour of the various beans. Ground coffee does not keep as long as the beans.

SERVING COFFEE

Coffee should be served either very hot or iced. Each country has its own method of making coffee.

Café au lait: The French serve hot milky coffee for breakfast in a large cup or bowl.

Espresso: The Italian method of making coffee using a dark roasted bean in an espresso machine which forces hot water through the ground coffee. It is then served in small cups.

Cappuccino: The milk added to the coffee has been heated by steam which causes it to froth. Chocolate powder is sometimes sprinkled on the froth.

Pharisee: Coffee with rum. An excellent cold remedy. One thing is certain, it does send you to sleep.

Turkish coffee: Is made with a mild roasted bean. The ground coffee is boiled with water in an individual metal jug and then poured into a small cup. Sugar is optional.

Gaelic coffee: Is made with strong hot coffee and two to three tots of Irish whiskey and then sweetened. Cream is then very carefully poured on top of the coffee. To do this successfully, use the back of a teaspoon and pour the cream over it slowly.

Iced coffee: Make the coffee and chill in the refrigerator. Serve in a tall glass with piped cream or vanilla ice cream on top.

Emperor coffee: Beat together one egg yolk and two tablespoons of cream into a cup of hot coffee, sweeten with a little sugar and flavour with brandy.

Café Noisette: Make the coffee and flavour with a little sugar and cherry brandy.

Viennese coffee: Add chocolate powder and thick cream to the coffee.

Prince Charles: Coffee with a tot of Drambuie.

Monk's coffee: Is coffee with a tot of Bénédictine.

Calypso: Coffee with a tot of Tia Maria.

Coffee essence: Is a syrup made from coffee, chicory and caramel.

TEAS & TISANES

"A hardened and shameless tea-drinker, who has for twenty years diluted his meals with only the infusion of this fascinating plant, whose kettle has scarcely time to cool, who with tea amuses the evening, with tea solaces the midnight, and with tea welcomes the morning."
JOHNSON

We take tea very much for granted, yet it has a fascinating history and was, once upon a time, a rare commodity.
It is believed that the Chinese were the first to discover tea; it has been drunk in China for thousands of years. Around the time of Christ it was introduced to Japan. The first to bring the leaf tea to Europe were the Dutch, around the end of the sixth century. It cost £15 per pound (roughly a man's yearly salary) and was an exotic, rare luxury.

It was not until the seventeenth and eighteenth centuries that tea drinking became fashionable amongst the gentlemen frequenting the London coffee shops. The ladies soon became aware of the new craze and exploited it to the full. They bought fine imported porcelain tea sets which they would show off to their guests. The lady of the house would personally blend and make tea. She would wear, for the occasion, a stylish and fashionable tea gown. The tea leaves were kept in beautiful and elaborate tea caddies, which were always locked so that the servants could not steal any of their precious contents. The lady of the house was the only person who had a key and this was secured around her waist. The caddies contained blending bowls, sugar tongs, tea canisters and a caddy spoon or mole spoon.

One of the most famous names to be linked with tea is Twinings. In 1706 Thomas Twining set up as a tea merchant in the London Strand. A few years later Richard Twining was to play a major rôle in the history of tea. In 1784 the tea trade was undergoing a severe crisis - heavy taxes, wholesale smuggling of teas from Holland and very high retail prices forced many of the small companies to close down. Richard Twining was the Chairman of the Tea Dealers. A determined and energetic man, he requested and obtained several interviews with William Pitt. As a result of those discussions the Commutation Act of 1784 was passed. The Act considerably reduced the heavy duty on tea, prices fell and consumption rose greatly. The industry was saved. Merchants began advertising extensively, claiming that tea was a cure for many ailments.

In the first half of the eighteenth century tea gardens opened where one could stroll in good company. When the ladies were tired of walking, they could sit around small tables to sip tea and eat dainty morsels.
Afternoon tea really took off in the nineteenth century. Anna, the seventh Duchess of Bedford, found that she was feeling hungry in the middle of the afternoon. There was a long gap between lunch and dinner and so every afternoon at about 4 O'clock she would have a pot of tea and some light refreshment. Eating alone was no fun and so she started inviting friends to join her. Little did she realise that she was starting not only a fashion but a custom.

Afternoon tea became 'à la mode', the rage spread rapidly, and tea shops began to thrive.

Tea is divided into three main categories:
- **Black tea**
- **Oolong or red tea**
- **Green tea**

First sifting and broken leaves are used for tea bags, and because of this the tea brews darker and stronger in a shorter time but has a less distinctive flavour than loose tea.

BLACK TEA

The leaves of black tea are dried after plucking. They are then machine-rolled and oxidised which turns them a bright coppery colour because they have absorbed oxygen. This process is called fermenting in the tea trade. After oxidisation the leaves are dried in hot-air chambers, and during this stage the leaves turn black, and the sugar in the leaves caramelises giving the tea a slightly burnt aroma which distinguishes the black teas from the red oolong and green teas. Black tea is high in caffeine, but the level is lower than in coffee. In Britain black teas are usually drunk with the addition of milk, but some delicate china teas such as Lapsang Souchong are pleasant without.

Assam: A north East Indian tea which gives a reddish brew with a strong flavour.

Ceylon: Has a delicate fragrance and full taste.

Darjeeling: Grown in the foothills of the Himalayas. This tea is often referred to as the champagne of teas. Its bouquet is similar to that of Muscatel, with a rich flavour.

Earl Grey: Earl Grey is named after a nineteenth Century British statesman. The Second Earl Grey was given the recipe after a diplomatic mission to China. This tea is a blend of China teas mixed with oil of bergamot.

English Breakfast: Is a blend of Ceylon and Indian teas, with a full-bodied strong flavour.

Keemun: A China tea from the Auhui Province, producing a light-coloured fragrant clear liquid, with a slightly nutty sweet taste.

Kenya: A fine-flavoured tea, which produced a reddish-gold liquid.

Lapsang Souchong: The best-quality leaves come from the Fujian Province in China; its flavour and aroma are smoky.

Orange Pekoe: The term Pekoe denotes the leaf size. It can be used for any tea, for example: Assam, Orange Pekoe or Darjeeling Orange Pekoe. It is also sold as a highly scented Souchong, or blended with Jasmine tea to add flavour.

OOLONG RED TEA

Oolong red teas are produced in several provinces in China. The leaf tea is processed in the same way as black tea, but the oxidation period is much shorter. Its colour and flavour are mid-way between black and green tea. These teas are low in caffeine.

Formosa/China Olong: This tea produces a straw-coloured liquid that has a slightly peachy flavour.

Formosa/China Pouchong: The leaves are scented with gardenia, jasmine or yulan blossom. The tea is a pale pinky-brown with a mild flavour.

GREEN TEA

Green tea comes from the Zhejiang Province in China. The leaves are first steamed to prevent fermentation, then machine-rolled and fired under a current of hot air to give green-grey pellets. All of the green teas are low in caffeine.

Gunpowder: There is a legend that this tea got its name when the British first arrived in China. They were shown the green pellets, and they nicknamed it gunpowder because it so resembled the grey lead ball shot. This tea is the most popular green tea in the West, and it produces a delicate straw coloured liquid, with a penetrating taste.
Jasmine: It is either a green, or a blend of green and black teas mixed with jasmine flowers.

SCENTED OR FLAVOURED TEAS

Scented or flavoured teas are a blend of teas mixed with dried fruits or flowers for added flavour. They are drunk without the addition of milk.

INFUSIONS & TISANES

Infusions and tisanes are brewed from roots, seeds, leaves, flowers, fruits and herbs. These infusions are caffeine free, and refreshing. Infusions are served without milk. Infusions are taken for their particular properties.

Burdock:
To purify the blood and cure skin diseases.
Camomile:
To induce sleep and ease aches and pains.
Elderflower:
Remedy for gout and to soothe nerves.
Ginseng:
Remedy for impotence.
Lime Blossom:
Alleviates headaches and colds.
Rosehip:
Supplements intake of vitamin C.
Rosemary:
Stimulates the memory.
Sage:
Eases sore throats and loss of voice.

TO MAKE THE PERFECT CUP OF TEA

1. The kettle must always be filled with fresh water from the cold tap.
2. The tea pot should be warmed with hot water, which should then be poured out.
3. You should allow one teaspoon of tea per person, and then add one extra for the pot.
4. Boil the water and fill the pot.
5. Brew for 3-5 minutes.
6. Stir the tea before pouring it.

EQUIPMENT USED FOR TEA MAKING

The tea caddy: The word caddy originates from the word 'cathy', the oriental measure for weighing tea. Loose tea will keep up to two years if unopened in an airtight container, but tea bags only about six months.

Teapots: The teapot was first brought from China to Europe in the early seventeenth century. It was made of china, and was broad and squat with wide spouts that would not clog with leaves. The pots were small as each person had their own. In the eighteenth century pots of all shapes and sizes were made. A teapot should not be washed in detergent or soap as the lingering taste leaves a tang which spoils the tea. To remove the tannin, soak the teapot for several hours in a mixture of 4 teaspoons of bicarbonate of soda dissolved in hot water. When choosing a teapot make sure that the handle can easily be grasped without your knuckles burning on the side of the teapot. Choose a pot with a hole in the lid as this allows the air to escape from the pot when the tea is being poured, and therefore prevents dribbling from the spout.

Infusers: An infuser is used so that the leaves can be removed from the pot to prevent the tea from stewing once the desired strength has been reached.

Tea strainers: These are bowl-shaped and placed over the cup whilst the tea is being poured.

Tea cosies: These should only be used if tea bags or infusers are being used. The tea bag or infuser should be removed from the pot when the tea has brewed, and the cosy placed over the pot to keep the tea hot. When leaves are being used, a cosy will keep the liquid too hot and cause an overdraw giving a stewed taste.

Tea cups: The Chinese still use the original tea cup which was a tiny bowl about two inches (5 cm) high holding no more than a few thimblefuls of tea. The handle came from the English 'posset' cup which was used for hot drinks. When the English potteries began to expand, tea cups with a handle were produced, and their shapes and sizes varied greatly.

Milk jugs and creamers: The original milk jugs were in the shape of a cow, but small jugs and creamers have replaced these.

THE NIGHT
&
THE MORNING AFTER

"To be a good housewife does not necessarily imply an abandonment of proper pleasures or amusing recreation."
MRS BEETON'S BOOK OF HOUSEHOLD MANAGEMENT, 1861.

Preparation and organisation are the key words!

DURING A PARTY

1. Empty ashtrays throughout the evening.
2. Throw away empty bottles.
3. Put cutlery to soak (any acid will stain silver.) Scrape food debris off the plates.
4. The main objective is to clear as you go along.

Before the party, clear the kitchen. You will need the work surfaces later on in the evening, so start clean and tidy.
Treat spillage immediately, it is not churlish to do this in front of guests, as disasters can be avoided if action is taken quickly.   Spilt liquids will mark wood badly.

AFTER THE PARTY

For safety, check the ashtrays to ensure there are no burning cigarette ends. If possible, open a window to allow fresh air into your rooms to rid them of smoke, food and alcohol odours.

Cover food you wish to keep with cling film and put into the refrigerator. Wash any silver as it will tarnish.

Empty liquids from glasses, to prevent the smell of alcohol lingering.

Lock doors.

HANGOVER REMEDY

At least once in a lifetime, you wish that the night before had never happened! To be wise after the event is easy, however a little forward planning goes a long way.

- Drink a pint of milk to line the stomach before going out.
- Always avoid drinking on a empty stomach.
All of the following remedies are not medically proven, the only certain fact is that the body needs time to recover. You need Vitamin C, and B, which the excess alcohol has destroyed, and plenty of liquid because of dehydration, **NOT MORE ALCOHOL.**

On returning from a heavy session:
- Drink a pint of water before going to sleep.
- Take a proprietary brand of hangover cure before sleep.
- Vitamin B and C.

In the morning depending on how you feel take the following (but not all at once!):
- Fresh air.
- Water.
- A teaspoon of honey to replace glucose.
- A proprietary brand of hangover cure.
- ½ pint milk with a raw egg whisked in and a little salt (if you have the stomach for it).
- Dried toast.

Avoid the following:
- Fatty food.
- Do not drink milk followed by orange juice as they do not mix well in the stomach.
- More alcohol.
- Noisy children or noisy animals!

CHRISTMAS

The Christmas period officially stretches from the 25th of December to the 6th of January, or Twelfth Night.

In the ancient world, the 25th December was the height of the festivities for the Sun-worshippers. The Roman Saturnalia was a time of great revelry and sacrifice. The same rituals and celebrations took place over Northern Europe. The early Christians chose the date of the rebirth of the sun as the time for the birth of their God, the symbolic gesture of a new beginning for mankind. This duality of religion and merry-making has been part of Christmas ever since.

In 1644 Parliament banned the 'heathen' celebrations on this day to make the occasion a more religious one. With the restoration of the Monarchy and the return of Charles II, England began to celebrate Christmas Day again.

In Victorian England, Prince Albert brought over the German Christmas tradition of decorating the house and the Christmas tree on Christmas Eve. Children hung their stockings by the chimney. Boar's head, goose, roast beef or chicken were served.

Father Christmas is a more recent figure; he is the descendant of the fourth century Dutch Saint Nicholas and much influenced by America's Santa Claus, who first appeared in England in 1870. It is customary for children to leave Father Christmas a glass of sherry, mince pies and a carrot for the reindeer.

The custom of kissing under the mistletoe is an ancient pagan ritual. Mistletoe represents male virility and the male can assert his supremacy by demanding a kiss, or several kisses, one for each berry. Once upon a time the main decoration in the house was the kissing booth, a bell of evergreens adorned with ribbon and fruits from which hung mistletoe and presents.

In France, Christmas Eve parties were originally held on the return from midnight mass, when gentlefolk's came home to a blazing fire and a warming supper. The family would gather round the tree and open their presents. Today it is celebrated with a formal light supper when Champagne is served and presents are exchanged.

CHRISTMAS EVE BUFFET

Hot Cheese Rolls
Cocktail Sausages
Devils on Horseback
Chestnuts Catherine Wheels
Cocktail Vol-au-Vent
Hot Mincemeat Tarts with Brandy Butter

White wine:

⬚ Petit Chablis

⬚⬚ Meursault (Beaune, Burgundy)

⬚⬚⬚ Bâtard-Montrachet (Beaune, Burgundy)

Champagne throughout is ideal for this intimate buffet.

HOT CHEESE ROLLS

✳ ☆☆☆ **These can be made well in advance and frozen**
PREPARATION TIME: 30 MINUTES
COOKING TIME: 15 MINUTES
OVEN TEMP: 375F 190C M5

Ingredients:

1 large loaf of cut white or brown bread (medium or thin-sliced)
8 oz (225 g) of Cheddar cheese, finely grated

3 oz (75 g) of melted butter
Cayenne pepper

Method:
Take the crusts off the bread slices, and with a rolling pin flatten the bread until thin. Brush each slice of bread with melted butter. Sprinkle some of the grated cheese over the bread and add cayenne pepper. Roll the slice of bread tightly to form a cigar shape. Do this with all the slices of bread. Arrange them side by side tightly so they do not unroll during cooking, and brush them with the remaining butter. (At this stage you may freeze the rolls or store in a cool place for 24 hours. Defrost before cooking). Cook until golden brown, which will be after approximately 15 minutes. Serve.

CHESTNUT CATHERINE WHEELS

❀ ☆☆☆ **These can be made 24 hours in advance or frozen**
PREPARATION TIME: 30 MINUTES
COOKING TIME: 15 MINUTES
OVEN TEMP: 375F 190C M5

Ingredients:

1 lb (450 g) of puff pastry
8 oz (225 g) of sausage meat
8 oz (225 g) of chestnut purée

1 tsp of parsley, finely chopped
Salt & black pepper
1 egg

Method:
Roll the pastry on a floured surface to form a large square approximately 15x15" (39x39cm). Mix the sausage meat with the chestnut purée, parsley and seasoning. Spread the sausage meat mixture over the pastry leaving a 1" (2.5cm) border. Dampen the edges with beaten egg and roll the pastry up like a Catherine wheel, sealing the edges. Glaze the pastry with the remaining egg. Leave to rest in a cool place until firm. With a sharp knife slice the roll into ¼" (5 mm) thick wheels, place on a damp baking sheet and cook in a hot oven for 15 minutes until golden brown.
Note: If you want to freeze the wheels, lay them on a sheet of greaseproof paper. Defrost before cooking.

COCKTAIL VOL-AU-VENT

❀ ☆☆☆
PREPARATION TIME: 30 MINUTES
COOKING TIME: 12 MINUTES
OVEN TEMP: 200C 400F M6

Vol-au-vent cases, Ingredients:

40 small cocktail vol-au-vent cases

1 beaten egg

Method:
Glaze the cases with a beaten egg, place on a damp baking sheet and cook until risen and golden brown. With the rounded end of a teaspoon handle carefully remove the lid whilst still hot, and put aside. Fill the vol-au-vent cases, put the lids back on the top, and garnish with a small sprig of parsley

Chicken & mushroom filing:

½ pt (275 ml) of béchamel sauce
4 oz (110 g) of chicken, finely minced

3 oz (75 g) of mushrooms, finely chopped
1 heaped tbs of chopped onion

Method:
Sauté the onion until clear, add the mushroom and chicken, cook for 5 minutes, stir in the béchamel sauce and season.

Ham & egg filing:

½ pt (275 ml) of béchamel sauce

4 oz (110 g) of ham, finely minced

1 hard-boiled egg, finely chopped

1 heaped tbs of chopped onion

Method:

Sauté the onion until clear, add the béchamel, ham and hard-boiled egg and gently heat.

HOT MINCEMEAT TARTS WITH BRANDY BUTTER

❀ ☆☆☆ **(24 Tarts)**
PREPARATION TIME: 20 MINUTES
COOKING TIME: 15 MINUTES
OVEN TEMP: 375F 190C M5
Special Equipment: Tartlet tray

Ingredients:

1 lb (450 g) short crust or puff pastry

1 lb (450 g) of mincemeat

4 tbs of brandy (optional)

1 large cooking apple, finely chopped
(optional)

Method:

Roll the pastry on a floured surface, cut circles to line the bun tins. Mix the mincemeat with the brandy and chopped apple, and fill the tartlets approximately half full (not more as it will overflow and burn). Leave the pastry to rest in a cool place for about an hour and then cook in the oven for approximately 15 minutes. Serve hot with a generous teaspoon of brandy butter. Make sure your guests have a napkin and small plate as the butter tends to drip.

BRANDY BUTTER

❀ ☆☆☆☆☆
PREPARATION TIME: 15 MINUTES

Ingredients:

4 oz (110 g) unsalted butter

4 oz (110 g) caster sugar

4 tbs of brandy

Method:

Beat the butter until you obtain a smooth white cream (to save time and effort use an electric beater). Gradually incorporate the sugar and then pour a few drops of brandy at a time, beating continuously, be careful that the mixture does not curdle towards the end. Put into a glass dish and leave to harden in the refrigerator. Serve.

✍ **To complete this buffet: Cocktail Sausages (See Page 55), Devils on Horseback (See Page 55).**

CHRISTMAS DAY MENU FOR EIGHT PERSONS

Smoked Salmon Parcels

Roast Turkey
Chestnuts & Forcemeat Stuffing
Chipolatas & Roast Chestnuts
Brussels with Chestnuts
Roast Parsnips, Roast Potatoes
Leeks in White Sauce
Cranberry Sauce & Bread Sauce

Christmas Pudding with Brandy Butter
Cheese Board
Marrons Glacés - Fruit Liqueurs - Chocolates

White wine for the first course:

Château-Bonnet (Entre-Deux-Mers, Bordeaux)

Château-Rahoul (Graves, Bordeaux)

Corton-Charlemagne (Beaune, Burgundy)

White or red for the main course:
Red wine:

Château-Cantemerle (Médoc, Bordeaux)

Château-Beychevelle (Saint-Julien, Bordeaux)

Château-Cheval-Blanc (Saint-Emilion, Bordeaux)

Champagne is suitable throughout the meal.

SMOKED SALMON PARCELS

❀ ☆☆☆☆☆
PREPARATION TIME: 40 MINUTES

Ingredients:

8 large slices of smoked salmon   2 tbs of fresh chives, finely chopped
8 oz (250 g) of cream cheese   Watercress to garnish

Method:

Mix the chives with the cream cheese and season to taste. Lay the smoked salmon slices out and arrange a portion of cream cheese in the centre, folding the salmon around it to form a neat parcel. With two long lengths of chive, decorate the salmon to look like string on a parcel. Garnish with lemon wedges, tomato and watercress, and serve with brown bread and butter

ROAST TURKEY

✿✿ ☆☆☆
PREPARATION TIME: 30 MINUTES (including stuffing)
COOKING TIME: (See Page 212).

Ingredients:
Turkey weighing approximately 16 lbs (7.2 kg)

Method:
Cover the turkey with foil, wrap extra pieces around the legs and wings to prevent them from burning. The most important thing to remember when you cook the bird is not to dry it out by prolonged cooking.
Use the fat and juices from the bird to make an excellent gravy (see page 306).
A turkey is always better stuffed, it adds flavour and keeps the bird moist during cooking.

Two suggested traditional stuffings for turkey:

FORCEMEAT STUFFING

✿ ☆☆☆
PREPARATION TIME: 15 MINUTES

Ingredients:

1 lb (450 g) of sausage meat	*Salt & black pepper*
8 oz (225 g) of fresh white breadcrumbs	*1 large onion, finely chopped*
Parsley, finely chopped	*1 egg*
Fresh thyme	*3 oz (75 g) of margarine*

Method:
Sauté the onion in the margarine until transparent. Bind together all the ingredients until well mixed, and stuff the bird.

CHESTNUT FORCEMEAT STUFFING

Ingredients:

Same as forcemeat stuffing	*Fresh chestnuts*
1 tin of chestnut purée	

Method:
Follow the recipe for forcemeat stuffing, adding a tin of chestnut purée and some fresh peeled chestnut pieces.

ROAST CHESTNUTS

Roast the chestnuts in a small ovenproof dish with some fat from the turkey.

CHIPOLATA

Wrap a small piece of bacon around each chipolata and roast in a similar way.

CHRISTMAS PUDDING

Note: It is better to make your Christmas puddings two or three months before Christmas. They will actually keep until the following year, providing that you have cleaned the outside of the bowl adequately, and put fresh paper over the top of the puddings.
Makes two Puddings

❀ ☆☆☆☆
COOKING TIME: 5 HOURS

Ingredients:

1 small orange
1 small banana
½ lb (225 g) of raisins
Pinch of salt
½ lb sultanas
2 oz (50 g) of dried apricots
3 oz (75 g) of mixed peel
5 tbs of brown ale
2 large eggs

1 oz (25 g) ground almonds
3 oz (75 g) plain flour
1 level teaspoon mixed spice ½ lb (225 g)
Stoned dried prunes
4 oz (110 g) of dark brown sugar
(Barbados)
1 oz (25 g) fresh breadcrumbs
5 oz (150 g) shredded suet

Method:

Liquidise the prunes, apricots, orange peel and juice, banana, mixed peel, brown ale, almonds and eggs. Add the mixture to the remaining ingredients and combine well.

Grease two 1½ pint (700 g) pudding basins with vegetable oil or margarine (but not butter). Divide the mixture between two bowls and cover with two layers of greased greaseproof paper then a layer of tin foil. Tie securely into position under the rim of the basin. Cook in a steamer for six hours.

To make your own steamer, lay a saucer upside down in the bottom of a saucepan large enough to fit the pudding basin, pour boiling water halfway up the bowl, cover with a lid and cook in a cool oven. When the pudding is cooked leave to cool. Clean the outside of the bowl thoroughly and re-cover with two fresh piece of grease proof and tin foil. This way the pudding will keep for a long time.
Remember to get all the family to stir the pudding and make a wish.
Serving Suggestions: brandy butter (see page 72), custard or cream.

✍ **To complete this menu: Brussels With Chestnuts (See Page 245), Roast Parsnips (See Page 257), Roast Potatoes (See Page 260), Leeks Béchamel (See Page 253), Cranberry Sauce (See Page 275), Bread Sauce (See Page 314).**

BOXING DAY

Boxing Day is also know as 'St. Stephen's Day'. It commemorates the first male Christian martyr who was stoned to death in Jerusalem in 33 A.D. - remembered the carol 'Good King Wenceslas'.

On this day, by tradition, employers gave their servants small gifts of money. Folk hunted wrens, squirrels and small animals; a wren would be impaled on the end of a stick and feathers would be sold for good luck.

Nowadays, on Boxing Day morning, people take part in a sport of their choice, hunts, beagling and shoots take place.

It has become a tradition in recent years, to serve cold meats and salads, so that the hostess does not have to cook again.

NEW YEAR

January is the opening month of the Christian year. The word January is named after the Roman God Janus, which translated from Latin means 'opening'. Janus has two faces on his statue, one looking forward and the other looking back.

There are no Christian roots to 'New Year'; it is linked to old pagan celebrations of the winter and changing of the year. Fires used to be lit to encourage the sun and to protect against witchcraft and evil. It was known as 'burying the old year out' and is still done in various parts of the country. Windows and doors are often left open so that the old year can depart easily.

Once upon a time it was common for children to go apple gifting on the first of January. A decorated apple would be carried by means of three small sticks and at each house a 'New Year's Blessing' would be offered in exchange for small gifts of food or money.

In Scotland there is an old tradition called 'first footing'. A tall dark gentleman enters the house from the front door at the stroke of midnight and brings along a piece of coal or bread. In return he is offered a drink and some food to ensure a happy forth coming year. Should he arrive empty-handed it would bring bad luck to the household. He must leave through the back door.

The children soot their faces and go around the houses singing New Year rhymes hoping for gifts, money or drinks; this is called 'guising'. The guisers donate a piece of coal in exchange for their presents.

The British welcome the New Year in at midnight by joining hands and singing 'Auld Lang Syne', listening to the chimes of Big Ben.

We suggest that a selection of two wines or a Champagne throughout the meal will be sufficient.

White wines with the hors d'oeuvre and fish course:

🝙 Château-Talbot-Caillou-Blanc (Saint Julien, Bordeaux)

🝙🝙 Saint-Aubin (Beaune, Burgundy)

🝙🝙🝙 Château-Laville-Haut-Brion (Bordeaux)

Red wines with the main course:

🍷 Château-Tour-de-Mirail (Haut-Médoc, Bordeaux)

🍷🍷 Château-Calon-Ségur (Saint-Estèphe, Bordeaux)

🍷🍷🍷 Château-La-Mission-Haut-Brion (Bordeaux)

CONSOMMÉ

❁ ☆☆☆
COOKING TIME: 10 MINUTES

Ingredients:

4 tins of beef consommé
8 fl oz (250 ml) dry sherry

Pasta shells or julienne strips of vegetable

Method:

Simmer the soup with the pasta shells or julienne strips of vegetable. Serve with a glass of sherry which your guests may add to their soup.

HORS D'OEUVRES

❀ ☆☆☆
Choose a selection of different salami and dried meats. Allow one slice per person and about seven to eight choices. Garnish with a fanned pickled gherkin.

SOLE IN TARRAGON

❀ ☆☆☆☆
PREPARATION TIME: 10 MINUTES
COOKING TIME: 20 MINUTES
OVEN TEMP: 180C 375F M5

Ingredients:

2 fillets of sole per person	*Fresh tarragon*
½ pt (275 ml) of white wine	*Lemon wedges*
½ pt (275 ml) of water	*Cornflour*

Method:
Ask the fishmonger to skin and fillet the soles. Grease an ovenproof dish large enough to hold all the fillets. Roll the fillets up and arrange in the dish. Pour the wine and water over the fillets and add fresh tarragon, reserving some to garnish. Cook in the oven for 20 minutes. Remove the fillets from the liquid and drain. Keep warm. Strain the liquid and thicken with cornflour adding finely chopped fresh tarragon. Season to taste. Pour the sauce over the fillets and serve with lemon and parsley.

LEMON SORBET

Serve a small portion of lemon sorbet to cleanse the palate.

CHÂTEAUBRIAND

❀ ☆☆☆☆☆
PREPARATION TIME: 10 MINUTES
COOKING TIME: 20 MINUTES
OVEN TEMP: 220C 425F M7

Note: This is not strictly a Châteaubriand because we are cooking for 8 persons and a Châteaubriand is for 2. We are also going to cook the fillet in the oven instead of under the grill.

Ingredients:

3-4 lb (1kg 350 g - 1kg 800 g) fillet steak	*Butter*

Method:
Remove any fat, gristle and membrane from the fillet and evenly spread a thin layer of butter over it. Place in a roasting dish in the oven and cook for 25 minutes for rare, 35 minutes for medium and 45 minutes for well done. Remove from the oven and keep warm. Garnish with watercress and baked tomatoes.

CUCUMBER, WATERCRESS AND ONION TOP SALAD

✹ ☆☆☆
Add all the ingredients together and toss in a walnut French dressing (see page 315).

FRESH FRUIT SALAD WITH CRUSHED CARAMEL

✹ ☆☆☆
PREPARATION TIME: 20 MINUTES
COOKING TIME: 10 MINUTES

Ingredients:
Fresh fruit of your choice in season   *6 oz (175 g) white sugar*

Method:
Make the fruit salad using any fresh fruits in season. In a heavy-based saucepan dissolve the white sugar over a gentle heat. Allow to turn a light golden-brown and then remove from the heat and pour into a lightly-oiled baking sheet. The caramel will immediately harden. Crush the caramel and sprinkle over the fresh fruit salad. Add a drop of liqueur to the fruit salad syrup.

✋ **To complete this menu: Bearnaise Sauce (See Page 312), Buttered New Potatoes (See Page 262).**

NEW YEAR MENU FOR EIGHT PERSONS

Prawns in Wine Aspic

Roast Goose
Potatoes, Creamed Potatoes
Red Cabbage with Apple
Brusselsl with Bacon

Pineapple & Kiwi

Cheese Board
Coffee & Petits Fours

White wine for the first course:
🍷 Chablis
🍷🍷 Puligny-Montrachet (Beaune, Burgundy)
🍷🍷🍷 Chevalier-Montrachet (Beaune, Burgundy)

Red wine for the main course:

♟ Nuits-St George (Côte-de-Nuits, Burgundy)

♟♟ Pommard (Burgundy)

♟♟♟ Château-Latour (Pauillac, Bordeaux)

Champagne is suitable throughout the meal.

PRAWNS IN WINE ASPIC

✿✿ ☆☆☆☆
PREPARATION TIME: 20 MINUTES
CHILLING TIME: AT LEAST 2 HOURS
Special Equipment: Dariole Moulds

Ingredients:

16 oz (450 g) of prawns, cooked & peeled   *1 packet of aspic*
1½ pt (850 ml) of white wine

Method:

Prepare the aspic according to the instructions on the packet, using ½ white wine to water. Season to taste. Fill each dariole mould with the prawns and the aspic. Put in the refrigerator to set. When you are ready to serve, fill a small bowl with boiling water and quickly dip the mould in to release it; then turn out onto individual serving plates. Serve with Melba toast, French or brown bread and butter.

ROAST GOOSE

✿✿ ☆☆☆☆☆
PREPARATION TIME: 20 MINUTES
COOKING TIME: 2 HOURS
OVEN TEMP: 400F 200C M6

Ingredients:

1 goose of approximately 8 to 10 lbs (3.6 - 4.5 kgs)
Stuffing:

8 oz (225 g) of fresh white breadcrumbs   *2 tbs of fresh sage, finely chopped*
2 oz (50 g) of melted butter   *Seasoning*
1 onion, finely chopped

Method:

Melt the butter and fry the onion until transparent, add all the ingredients and mix until well combined. Stuff the bird.

A goose has a large amount of fat distributed around its body and so before cooking prick the flesh all over with a skewer. Place in a roasting pan with no extra fat, but cover the bottom of the pan with a little water.

Cover the bird closely with foil and place in the oven. Remove the foil 30 minutes before the end of cooking so the skin becomes brown and crispy.

Note: If you wish, before cooking the goose, rub its skin lightly with salt.

To complete this menu: **Red Cabbage with Apple (See Page 246), Roast & Cream Potatoes (See Page 260 & 262), Brussels with Bacon (See Page 245), Gravy (See Page 306), Pineapple & Kiwi Fruit (See Page 289), Petits Fours (See Page 58, 60).**
Cheese Board: Select cheeses which are not too rich i.e. Emmantal, Port Salut.

TWELFTH NIGHT

The Twelfth Night signifies the end of Yule, it used to be a time for games, feasting and dancing. Christmas decorations should be taken down, it is thought that any holly kept in the house after this date brings bad luck. Each leaf and berry turns into a mischievous spirit.

A Twelfth Night cake is baked in honour of the Three Kings; a dried bean and a pea are hidden inside it. Whoever finds the bean is the King, and whoever finds the pea is the Queen, (if a gentleman finds the pea he will choose his Queen and vice versa). The cake is made with flour, sugar, honey, ginger, pepper, dried fruits and up to eighteen eggs. It is then iced and decorated.

In France the Twelfth Night cake is called 'La Galette des Rois' in the North, 'Le Gateau des Rois' in the South, ('la Galette' is similar to the British cake, while 'le Gateau' is a brioche cake decorated with 'fruits confits').
The ritual of finding the bean and the pea and being proclaimed King is the same as in the United Kingdom, but there is a slight variation, as the King has to invite all the guests present to eat another cake thus prolonging the parties throughout the month of January.

The Italians also celebrate the 6th January and call it 'La Befana'.

BURNS NIGHT

Robert Burns (1759 - 1796)

Robert Burns is Scotland's greatest poet. On January 25th each year Scotland celebrates his memory with a traditional dinner of Haggis, merrymaking and drinking of toasts.

Burns Night dinner starts with a Scotch broth followed by The Haggis. The Haggis is brought to the table on a silver plate to the sound of Scottish pipes. Prior to cutting The Haggis tradition demands that a member of the party declame the 'Address to a Haggis'. At the end of the recitation, the diners will toast Burns and The Haggis with a wee dram of single malt Scottish whisky. Malt whisky will continue to be served throughout the meal. Haggis is made from sheep's stomachs stuffed with the heart, lungs and liver of the animal, and oatmeal. It is served with 'Chappit, Neaps and Tatties' which are mashed swedes and potatoes.

Throughout the evening Burns' poems are recited, the most famous being 'Tam o 'Shanter'. A popular toast is "Lang may your lum reek" meaning "Long may your chimney smoke". The evening is rounded off with the singing of 'Auld Lang Syne'.

SHROVE TUESDAY

Shrove Tuesday is the last day before Lent. For centuries the faithful took confession, made penance and were 'shriven' (given absolution by the priest) in preparation for Lent and fasting. It was the last opportunity to eat foods such as butter and eggs which would be prohibited by the Church during the forthcoming time of austerity.

In England today it is a light-hearted day in which sport plays a large part. In some towns and villages people run in pancake races, the most famous one being held in Olney, Bucks. The prize-winner gets a kiss which is bestowed by the vicar.

Shrove Tuesday is called 'Mardi Gras', in France. The children wear fancy dress. In Rio de Janiero a large carnival takes place.

Emulate this theme and hold a party at home with a festive atmosphere and fancy-dress costume.

PANCAKE BATTER

❀ ☆☆☆
PREPARATION TIME: 10 MINUTES
STANDING TIME: 2 HOURS
COOKING TIME: 2 MINUTES PER PANCAKE
Special Equipment: Omelette Pan

Ingredients: To make ten thin pancakes

4 oz (110 g) of plain flour	*Pinch of salt*
1 egg	*½ pt (150 ml) of milk*

Method:

Sift the flour and the salt into a bowl. Gradually make a smooth batter by adding the milk and egg to the flour, either with a hand beater or electric whisk. Leave to stand for a couple of hours.

Heat some oil in the omelette pan and when it is very hot add enough batter to cover the bottom of the pan with a very thin layer. Gently tilt the omelette pan around until the batter evenly coats the bottom. The pancake should take literally under a minute to lightly brown. Gently slide a fish slice under the pancake and turn. Brown gently, and serve.

If you are preparing pancakes for several persons you need to make them in advance. To do this, cut strips of grease-proof paper and lay them in between each pancake. You can either keep them in the plate-warming oven for immediate use or store them in an air-tight container for a few days, or freeze them.

SELECTION OF SAVOURY FILLINGS

1. The basic filling is béchamel sauce (see page 304).
Allow a ¼ pt (150 ml) of béchamel sauce per pancake.

Make the béchamel sauce of a coating consistency and add the other cooked ingredients. Arrange the mixture along the centre of the pancake and roll. Serve the pancakes hot or cold.

Fillings:
- Cooked diced chicken and ham, with finely chopped sautéed onions with either mushrooms or sweetcorn.
- Cooked cauliflower with grated Cheddar cheese and a teaspoon of mustard.
- Prawns with chopped hard-boiled egg and anchovy essence (optional).
- Smoked haddock with hard-boiled egg and finely chopped parsley.
- Sautéed green and red peppers with onions and any other vegetable you choose.
- Cooked chopped chicken with broccoli and grated cheese.

SAVOURY MINCE

❀ ☆☆☆
PREPARATION TIME: 10 MINUTES
COOKING TIME: 30 MINUTES

85

Ingredients: To fill eight pancakes

1 lb (450 g) of minced beef
1 medium onion, finely chopped
1 green pepper, finely chopped
1 crushed clove of garlic (optional)

1 tbs of oil
1 medium can of tomatoes
1 tbs of tomato purée
Fresh herbs of your choice

Method:

Heat the oil in a heavy-based pan, add the garlic onion and pepper, sauté until soft. Add the minced beef, tomatoes, tomato purée and herbs. Cook over a moderate heat for about ½ an hour.

Fill the pancakes and serve hot with a crisp green salad.

SMOKED SALMON PANCAKES

✽ ☆☆☆☆☆
PREPARATION TIME: 20 MINUTES

Ingredients:

A slice of smoked salmon per pancake
2 oz (50 g) of cream or cottage cheese per pancake

Chopped fresh chives or spring onion tops

Method:

Mix the chives or onion tops with the cream or cottage cheese, season. Spread the cheese over the pancakes evenly and lay a slice of smoked salmon over the cheese. Roll the pancake up. Serve cold, whole or sliced to look like Catherine wheels.

✋ **To complete this selection: Chilli Con Carne (See Page 203), Serve hot with garlic bread.**

SELECTION OF SWEET FILLINGS

- Freshly squeezed lemon or orange juice with caster sugar.
- Hot jam.
- Golden or Maple syrup with fresh cream and chopped bananas.
- Orange butter: Mix softened butter with caster sugar and orange juice, spread on the pancake and roll up.
- Ice cream with chocolate sauce (see page 317) with chopped nuts.
- Fresh strawberries or raspberries with whipped cream.
- Thick Greek Yoghurt with fresh figs.

VALENTINE'S DAY

The symbol of Valentine are two bluebirds representing two lovers bound together in spirit. Saint Valentine was the Bishop of Rome, renowned for his piety and chastity, he was martyred on the 14th February and soon after adopted as the patron saint of lovers.

Flambé King Prawn

Steak with Roquefort
Jacket Potatoes, Side Salad

Peaches with Sour Cream

White wine with first course:

⬛ Montagny (Côte-Chalonnaise)

⬛⬛ Pouilly-Fuissé (Mâconnais)

⬛⬛⬛ Aloxe-Corton (Beaune, Burgundy)

Red wine for the main course:

🍷 Macon Rouge (Mâconnais)

🍷🍷 Côte-Rôtie (Côtes-du-Rhone)

🍷🍷🍷 Château-Montrose (Saint-Estèphe-Bordeaux)

FLAMBÉ KING PRAWN

✱ ☆☆☆☆☆
PREPARATION TIME: 20 MINUTES
COOKING TIME: 10 MINUTES

Ingredients:

4 cooked king prawns per person	*2 tbs of chopped parsley*
2 oz (50 g) of butter	*4 tbs of brandy*
2 cloves of crushed garlic	

Method:
Peel the prawns, leaving the head and the tip of the tail on. Heat the butter in a frying pan, add the crushed garlic and 1 tablespoon of parsley. Add the prawns and gently heat through. Add the brandy, heat and flambé. Serve with chopped parsley and a lemon wedge.

STEAK WITH ROQUEFORT

❀ ☆☆☆☆
PREPARATION TIME: 10 MINUTES
COOKING TIME: 10 MINUTES

Ingredients:

2 fillet or rump steaks   2 slices of Roquefort cheese

Method:

Heat the grill to its maximum, and grill the steaks on one side for half the cooking time. Turn the steak over and allow to brown, then place a slice of Roquefort over the steak and grill until the cheese has melted and is bubbling. Garnish the steak with watercress and a grilled tomato half.

Sauce: Add the juices from the grill pan to a little red wine, a stock cube and a tablespoon of red currant jelly, bring to the boil.

PEACHES IN SOUR CREAM

❀ ☆☆☆
PREPARATION TIME: 5 MINUTES
COOKING TIME: 5 MINUTES
CHILLING TIME: 2 HOURS MINIMUM

Ingredients:

1 tin of peach halves   5 fl oz (150 ml) of sour cream
4 tbs of demerara sugar

Method:

Divide the peach halves between two ramekins with a little of the juice. Pour the cream over the peaches leaving a quarter of an inch at the top. Sprinkle the brown sugar heavily over the cream. Place under a very hot grill until the sugar melts. Chill in the refrigerator and serve.

Salmon Crêpes

Poussin Véronique
Broccoli, Cauliflower Florettes
Baked Potatoes

Port Jelly

White wine throughout the meal:

⚜ Muscadet-de-Sèvre-et-Maine (Loire)

⚜⚜ Pouilly-Fumé (Loire)

⚜⚜⚜ Chablis Grenouilles Grand Cru

SALMON CRÊPES

❀ ☆☆☆☆ **The crêpes can be prepared well in advance, or frozen.**
PREPARATION TIME: 10 MINUTES
COOKING TIME: 30 MINUTES

Ingredients:

4 crêpes (see page 85)   *Finely chopped parsley*
4 slices of smoked salmon   *Lemon wedges*
10 fl oz (275 ml) of single cream

Method:
Arrange a slice of smoked salmon on each crêpe and roll up neatly. Heat the single cream in a frying pan, add the crêpes and slowly heat through. The smoked salmon will turn opaque. Garnish with parsley and a lemon wedge.

POUSSIN VÉRONIQUE

❀ ☆☆☆☆
PREPARATION TIME: 15 MINUTES
COOKING TIME: 45 MINUTES
OVEN TEMP: 200C 400F M6

Ingredients:

2 poussins   *Lemon juice*
8 oz (225 g) of cottage cheese   *Cayenne pepper*
1 bunch of watercress   *12 oz (350 g) of seedless white grapes*
Salt & black pepper   *10 fl oz (275 ml) of single cream*
Butter   *1 glass of white wine*

Method:
Take half the bunch of watercress and chop roughly, mix with the cottage cheese. Season with salt and pepper, cayenne and a squeeze of lemon juice. Stuff the poussins with the mixture, arrange in a baking tin spreading some butter over the breasts and legs of the birds. Season with salt, pepper, cayenne and lemon juice and pour the glass of white wine in the bottom of the tin. Loosely cover and cook in a pre-heated oven. Cook for 30 minutes and remove the cover to allow the birds to brown.
Sauce: Gently heat together the juices from the pan, the cream and the seedless grapes. Garnish the poussins with the remaining watercress and the sauce.

PORT JELLY

❀❀ ☆☆☆☆☆
PREPARATION TIME: 30 MINUTES
SETTING TIME: 4 HOURS MINIMUM

Ingredients:

½ pt (275 ml) of ruby port
Juice of one lemon
½ oz (10 g) of powder gelatine

1 red jelly
¼ pt (150 ml) of boiling water
Juice of one orange

Fruit Cream:

5 fl oz (150 ml) of double cream
2 oz (50 g) of fresh raspberries

2 oz (50 g) of fresh strawberries

Method:

Dissolve the jelly in the boiling water. Soak the gelatine in 2 tablespoons of cold water and add to the jelly. When dissolved pour the port and strained orange and lemon juice in the mixture.

Take a 1½ pint mould and fill half way with the jelly and set in the refrigerator; (to speed this process up either place it in the freezer for a short period or dip the mould in a large bowl full of ice cubes). When the moulded jelly has set, sit a beaker or glass (bottom side down) on the centre of the jelly leaving enough room around the outside to pour the remaining liquid jelly. Place in the refrigerator until set.

In order to remove the beaker, pour hot water into it to loosen it from the jelly; (if using a glass be careful not to pour very hot water into it as it will crack the glass.)

Whip the double cream until stiff and add the fresh fruits. Pile into the cavity of the jelly. To turn the jelly out, loosen the top edge of the jelly with a sharp knife and dip the mould quickly into very hot water. Place a damp plate or serving bowl over the top of the mould and turn upside down. Remove the mould and refrigerate until ready to serve.

Vichyssoise

Lobster Mayonnaise
Buttered New Potatoes, Mixed Salad

Fresh Raspberries

An excellent choice for a romantic meal as everything can be prepared in advance. Champagne with the main course.

VICHYSSOISE

❀ ☆☆☆
PREPARATION TIME: 15 MINUTES
COOKING TIME: 1 HOUR
CHILLING TIME: 12 HOURS (Preferably make the day before)

Ingredients:

1 oz (25 g) of butter
4 small leeks
4 small potatoes
1 stick of celery
Fresh parsley & chives

1 pt of strong chicken stock
Salt & black pepper
¼ pt (150 ml) of single cream or top of milk

Method:

Heat the butter and add the finely sliced leeks, cover the pan and gently heat for about 15 minutes shaking the pan regularly, until the leeks are softened. They must not brown. Add the finely sliced potatoes and celery, the chopped parsley, stock and seasoning. Bring to the boil and simmer for 30 minutes until all the vegetables are cooked. Allow to cool and liquidise at this point if you wish. Season and add the cream. Chill in the refrigerator. Serve chilled, garnished with finely chopped chives.

LOBSTER MAYONNAISE

❀ ☆☆☆☆☆
Buy small lobsters, allowing one per person. Lobsters should be fresh (see page 237). Ask the fishmonger to cut the lobster in half and remove the stomach sack for you.
PREPARATION TIME: 20 MINUTES

Ingredients:

1 small lobster per person cut in half
Mayonnaise (see page 312)

Lumpfish
Mixed salad

Method:

When serving a lobster in its shell you do need a few tools. Either use a lobster pick and crackers, or a skewer and nutcracker. The fishmonger will have removed any inedible parts so that the lobster is ready to eat. Serve with mayonnaise and a side salad. Mix some red lumpfish with the mayonnaise.

Lobster mayonnaise can also be served out of the shell. To do this, remove all the flesh from the claws and body and mix with the mayonnaise. Either put the mixture back into the shell halves, or pile in the centre of a plate and garnish with the salad.

✋ **To complete this menu: Buttered New Potatoes (See Page 262), Mixed Salad of Your Choice, Fresh Raspberries.**

Stuffed Mushrooms

Châteaubriand
New Potatoes with Snipped Chives
Green Salad
Béarnaise Sauce

Strawberries & Greek Yoghurt

White wine with the first course:

Vouvray (Loire)

Château-d'Arche (Sauternes Bordeaux)

Clos-des-Mouches (Beaune Burgundy)

Red wine for the main course:

Côte-de-Nuits Villages (Burgundy)

Vosne Romanée Les Suchots (Côte-de-Nuits, Burgundy)

Richebourg Domaine de la Romanée Conti (Côte-de-Nuits, Burgundy)

STUFFED MUSHROOMS

✿ ☆☆☆
PREPARATION TIME: 30 MINUTES
COOKING TIME: 15 MINUTES
OVEN TEMP: 200C 400F M6

Ingredients:

Butter	*3 tbs of finely chopped parsley*
24 medium sized flat mushrooms	*Salt & black pepper*
6 slices of ham, finely minced	*2oz (50 g) of butter*
6 tbs of fresh white breadcrumbs	*1 clove of garlic crushed*

Method:
Melt the butter and add the garlic. Mix the ham, breadcrumbs, parsley and seasoning in with the butter, bind together. Peel the mushrooms and remove the stalk. If you wish to cut the mushrooms to the same size use a round pastry cutter and trim the edge of the mushrooms. Divide the mixture between the mushrooms and pack tightly. Cook in the oven with butter for approximately 15 minutes until tender. Serve.

CHÂTEAUBRIAND

François René Vicomte Châteaubriand (1768-1848) was a famous French novelist, poet and politician. Notwithstanding these achievements, he is also famous because his chef, Monsieur Montmirial, grilled for him a very thick slice of fillet of beef and served it with potatoes (pommes de terre Château) and a sauce!

✽ ☆☆☆☆☆ **Châteaubriand is served rare, for two persons.**
PREPARATION TIME: 10 MINUTES
COOKING TIME: 15 MINUTES

Ingredients:

Fillet steak weighing approximately   *Watercress*
1¼ lbs (450 g)   *Grilled tomato halves*
3oz (75 g) butter   *Asparagus spears*
Salt & black pepper

Method:
Trim the meat and season. Heat the grill, melt the butter in a saucepan. Put the meat under the hot grill and keep brushing the melted butter over it to keep it moist. Serve with grilled tomato halves and asparagus spears. Garnish with watercress.

STRAWBERRIES WITH GREEK YOGHURT

✽ ☆☆☆
PREPARATION TIME: 10 MINUTES

Ingredients:

8 oz (200 g) of natural Greek yoghurt   *3 oz (75 g) demerara sugar*
8 oz (200 g) of strawberries

Method:
Wash and hull the strawberries, gently mash with a fork and add to the yoghurt. Arrange in layers with the demerara sugar, finishing off with a layer of sugar. Put into the refrigerator to chill. Serve.

✌ **To complete this menu: Béarnaise Sauce (See Page 312).**

MOTHERING SUNDAY

4th Sunday in Lent

In medieval times on Mothering Sunday people visited their 'Mother' church, the Cathedral of their diocese. In the mid-seventeenth century it became a day for honouring not only the Mother of God but all mothers. Services were held in churches throughout the country to worship and give thanks. People who worked in service were given the day off. Simnel cakes were baked and taken home along with bunches of flowers.

Schoolchildren, several weeks in advance, make, draw, paint, or sew little presents for their mothers. The whole exercise is done in great secrecy and with much anticipation.

SIMNEL CAKE

Simnel cake is decorated with twelve marzipan balls, representing the months of the year, or crystallised flowers, little chocolate eggs and sprigs of fresh spring flowers.

Simnel cake can also be baked for Easter Day tea-time. In that case it should be decorated with eleven marzipan balls to represent the Apostles (Judas is not included).

☆☆ ❀❀❀❀ **Make 24 hours in advance**
PREPARATION TIME: 30 MINUTES
COOKING TIME: 2½ TO 3 HOURS
OVEN TEMPERATURE: 180C 350F M4 for the first two hours and 150C 300F M2
for the rest of the time
Special Equipment: 9" round deep cake tin

Ingredients:

1½ lbs (700 g) sultanas	*4 large eggs*
6 oz (175 g) of currants	*6 oz (175 g) of crystallised peel*
1 pint (570 ml) of ruby port	*14 oz (400 g) of plain flour*
Grated rind of 2 large lemons	*1 tsp of salt*
8 oz (225 g) of unsalted butter, softened	*1 tsp of baking powder*
8 oz (225 g) of soft brown sugar	*1 tsp of ground all spice*

For the almond paste:

8 oz (225 g) of ground almonds	*8 oz (225 g) of caster sugar*
8 oz (225 g) of sifted icing sugar	*1 large egg, beaten*

To glaze:

3oz (75 g) of caster sugar	*4 tbs of milk*

Method:

Soak the sultanas and currants overnight in the port. Drain and reserve the port.
Beat together the butter, lemon rind and sugar until light and fluffy. Add the eggs one at a time, beating well. Add the grated peel, drained and chopped dried fruits. Sift the flour, salt, baking powder and spices into the bowl. Fold into the creamed mixture. If necessary add 1-2 tablespoons of port to the mixture to achieve a soft dropping consistency. Grease and line the cake tin with greaseproof paper. Spoon in half the mixture and level the top.
Make the almond paste: Mix the ground almonds with the sugars. Add the beaten egg and enough lemon juice to make a pliable but not sticky paste. Sprinkle the working surface with sifted icing sugar and knead the paste lightly until smooth. Roll out and cut a circle the size of the tin. Place the almond paste circle on the cake mixture in the tin. Spoon the remaining mixture into the tin and smooth until even and level. Bake in the centre of the oven for 2½-3 hours, turning down the temperature after 2 hours.

To test whether the cake is cooked, insert a skewer into the cake, if it comes out clean the cake is cooked.
Let the cake stand in its tin for 15 minutes to cool before turning out (to prevent the marzipan layer from splitting). When the cake is cool, boil together the sugar and milk until thick and syrupy and brush over the top of the cake to glaze.
Decorate accordingly.

EASTER TIME

Easter time celebrates the resurrection of Christ.
Most of the Easter customs predate Christianity. The name of 'Easter' is derived from 'Eostre' the Saxon Goddess of Spring. The egg was the sacred symbol of rebirth, the hare was regarded as the embodiment of life and fertility. Pagan revelries took place during the Spring equinox, Eostre's worshippers used to bake small cakes and eat them during the celebrations. When Christianity began the small cakes were replaced by soft buns and adorned with a cross. They were believed to have holy powers, to protect from Evil. One bun would be kept, hung from the ceiling, when a member of the family became ill a small piece would be dissolved in warm milk and given to the patient in the hope of curing the ailment.

The Pascal Lamb which was slaughtered during the Jewish Passover become the symbol of Christ as the sacrificial lamb. It has long been the custom to celebrate the end of lent with a feast of roast lamb flavoured with herb rosemary. The blue flower of rosemary is said to be the colour of the Virgin Mary's robes.

Traditionally on Easter Day, in England, an Easter Egg hunt takes place for the children. In France, there is a charming legend that from each belfry the church bells fly over to Rome for Lent. They return on Easter morning bringing back an Easter Egg for each child in the parish, and in so doing ring with great glee.

GOOD FRIDAY MENU FOR SIX PERSONS

Melon with Parma Ham

Poached Salmon
New Potatoes, Cucumber Salad
Chicory & Walnut Salad

Syllabub

White wine throughout the meal:
Château-Carbonnieux (Bordeaux)
Saint-Véran (Mâconnais)
Les Aigrots (Beaune, Burgundy)

MELON WITH PARMA HAM

❀ ☆☆☆☆
PREPARATION TIME: 20 MINUTES

Ingredients:

2 ripe olga or chenterelle melons   *Endive leaves*
4 large thin slices of Parma ham

Method:
Cut the melons in half, and scoop out balls and put aside. Cut the Parma ham into thin strips. Arrange the melon on individual plates and lay the Parma ham strips over the top. Garnish with endive. Serve.

POACHED SALMON

❀ ☆☆☆☆
PREPARATION TIME: 40 MINUTES
COOKING TIME: Approx 8 MINUTES per lb (450 g) (when the fish weighs over 6 lbs (2,7 kg). A 10 lb (4,5 kg) salmon takes about 1¼ hours.)
Special Equipment: A Fish Kettle

Make a court bouillon. There are two ways of making this:

COURT BOUILLON (A)

Ingredients:

2 quarts of water   *1½ oz (40 g) of salt*
1 lb (450 g) of carrots, sliced   *¼ pt (150 ml) of cider vinegar or wine*
3 shallots or 2 medium onions, sliced   *vinegar*
1 bay-leaf   *1 bunch of parsley*
1 sprig of thyme   *12 peppercorns*

Method:
Put all the ingredients into a pan except the peppercorns and simmer for 1 hour. Ten minutes before the end of cooking, add the peppercorns. Strain and cool.

COURT BOUILLON (B): suitable for salmon and trout.

Ingredients:

3 quarts of water   *A bouquet garni & a bay leaf*
½ bottle of white wine   *12 peppercorns*
1 teacup of tarragon vinegar   *A blade of mace*
2 onion & carrots, sliced

Method:
Tie the peppercorns and the mace in a piece of muslin, and simmer with all the ingredients for ½ hour.

Note: Ask the fishmonger to gut and clean the fish for you, so that no blood deposit remains on the backbone, and wash away as many scales as possible. A whole fish looks very attractive as a centre piece, and can be skinned once cooked.

POACHED SALMON ON THE HOB

Place the whole salmon in the kettle or in a roasting tin. Pour enough court bouillon to half cover the fish. Bring to the boil and then simmer **very gently**. When the fish is cooked the flesh should come away from the bone easily. The juices from the fish should be a milky colour, like curd.
Note: If you do not have a fish kettle large enough, you can still cook your salmon in cutlets or poach it in the oven in a roasting tin.

POACHED SALMON IN THE OVEN

Make the court bouillon. Do not strain. Butter a fireproof dish large enough to hold the whole salmon, or the cutlets you are cooking. Pour the bouillon over the salmon, and cook in the oven (slow to moderate) for 45-60 minutes for a 4 lbs (1.8 kgs) fish. Baste frequently. If the oven temperature is too high the skin will crack. Cook the cutlets for 15 minutes, lightly covered with foil.
If you are serving the fish cold, leave in the bouillon, as this keeps the fish moist whilst cooling . To serve the fish hot, remove from the bouillon and drain well. The skin will be easily removed by using a round-bladed or fish knife.
This menu can be prepared in advance, the salmon cooked the day before, and the mayonnaise made and kept covered in the refrigerator.

✋ **To complete this menu: Syllabub (See Page 280), Cucumber salad (See Page 251), Chicory & Walnut Salad (See Page 149).**

EASTER SUNDAY MENU FOR EIGHT PERSONS

Anchovy Stuffed Eggs

Roast Spring Lamb
New Potatoes, Spring Cabbage
Lemon Carrots, Pear Boats
Fresh Mint Sauce
Purée of Root Vegetables

Cream Filled Brandy Snaps

White wine with the first course:

⬚ Côtes-de-Toul (Mosselle)

⬚⬚ Rully (Challonnais)

⬚⬚⬚ Château-d'Yquem (Sauternes, Bordeaux)

Red Wine with the main course:

🍷 Saint-Amour (Beaujolais)

🍷🍷 Lirac (Côtes-du-Rhone)

🍷🍷🍷 Vosne-Romanée (Côte de Nuits, Burgundy)

ANCHOVY STUFFED EGGS

✽ ☆☆☆
PREPARATION TIME: 30 MINUTES

Ingredients:

8 hard-boiled eggs
Anchovy essence
Tin of anchovy fillets

Mayonnaise
Cream cheese

Method:
Hard boil the eggs and peel. Cut lengthways in half and remove the yolk. In a bowl, cream the yolk with the other ingredients, keeping a few anchovies for garnishing. Season to taste. Put into a piping bag with a star nozzle and pipe into the egg halves. Decorate with the anchovy fillets and place on a bed of lettuce leaves and some tomato flowers.

ROASTED SPRING LAMB

✽ ☆☆☆
PREPARATION TIME: 10 MINUTES
COOKING TIME: 2 HOURS
OVEN TEMPERATURE: 400F 200C M6

Ingredients:

1 leg of English spring lamb
2 cloves of peeled fresh garlic, cut into slithers

Salt
Rosemary sprigs

Method:
With a sharp knife pierce the flesh of the lamb and insert the garlic slithers and rosemary. Melt some lard in the roasting pan, and sear the lamb in the hot fat, salt the skin, cover and roast in the oven for approximately 2 hours. Serve.
Note: Always leave a roast joint 15 minutes after cooking before carving.

PEAR BOATS

❀ ☆☆☆
PREPARATION TIME: 5 MINUTES

Ingredients:

1 large tin of pear halves   *1 jar of mint jelly*
1 jar of redcurrant jelly

Method:

Drain the pear halves, fill each pear half cavity with a teaspoon of either mint or redcurrant jelly. Just before serving your lamb arrange the pear halves around the joint.

FRESH GARDEN MINT SAUCE

❀ ☆☆☆
PREPARATION TIME: 10 MINUTES

Ingredients:

1 bunch of fresh mint   *Vinegar*
1 level tbs caster sugar

Method:

Chop the mint leaves very finely and put into a china sauce boat. Sprinkle the mint with caster sugar and dissolve it by pouring a couple of spoonfull of boiling vegetable water over. Add the vinegar. Serve.

CREAM FILLED BRANDY SNAPS

❀ ☆☆☆ **3 brandy snaps per person**
PREPARATION TIME: 20 MINUTES

Ingredients:

24 brandy snaps   *1pt (570 ml) of double cream*

Method:

Whip the double cream until it stands in stiff peaks. Pipe the cream into the brandy snaps. Serve.

✍ **To complete this menu: New Potatoes (See Page 262), Spring Cabbage, Lemon Carrots (See Page 247), Purée of Root Vegetables (See Page 265).**

HALLOWE'EN

Hallowe'en means 'the eve of ', 'the evening before'. The 31st of October precedes All Saints' Day, a very sacred feast. Religion and superstition go hand-in-hand in the folklore of each nation. This co-existence of good and evil explains the tradition of Hallowe'en which is a direct pagan descendant of the Celtic feast of Samhain. The night before this very holy day, the creatures of the supernatural come forth to accomplish their mischievous deeds. Witches on their broomsticks, goblins and other dreaded things take part in a macabre and merry dance.

Many years ago, in the villages, the tradition was to stay inside, out of harm's way, huddled together by a glowing fire. Folks would listen to spine-chilling tales of the dead rising from their graves, fortunes would be told and rituals would take place. These would vary from one part of the country to the other.

101

Fires were lit on hillsides to ward off evil spirits, and stones were thrown into the flames. At dawn the next day the villagers would come back in the hope of finding their stones in the ashes. If they did, they would be assured of good luck for that year; if they were unsuccessful, it meant bad luck or even death.

One could ascertain the initials of a future lover by peeling an apple carefully, keeping the peel intact, and throwing it over one's shoulder. The shape the peel would take would be the lover's initials.

By walking slowly backwards round a large tree three times in the darkness, a faint glimpse of the visage of one's future lover would appear....

Delightful, don't you think!

What a perfect theme for a fancy dress party for children and adults alike. Decorate your house with anything which will create a spooky atmosphere. Pumpkins carved into eerie faces lit up with candles, hanging spiders, cobwebs, witches' hats and broomsticks.

BUFFET PARTY FOR TWENTY PERSONS

Devils on Horseback
Olives & Gherkins
Spicy Tortilla Chips
Barbecued Spare Ribs
Jacket Potatoes with Soured Cream & Chives
Savoury Rice
Okra Mediterranean
Eyeball Jelly with Blood Cream
Baked Apples

PREPARATION ADVICE

The following can be:

prepared in advance:

- Devils on Horseback: cook on the evening
- Sour cream and chives
- Baked apples (remember to add lemon juice to the water to prevent discoloration)
- Potatoes (scrubbed)

cooked in advance:

- Rice: reheat by pouring boiling water through the rice
- Okra Mediterranean: reheat on the evening
- Barbecue sauce: reheat on the evening

COUNTDOWN

Approximately two hours before:

- Prepare rice ingredients
- Arrange spare ribs
- Turn out the jellies
- Make the blood cream
- Prepare the Glühwein
- Prepare fruit punch

Approximately one hour before:

- Cook the devils on horseback
- Cook potatoes
- Cook spare ribs
- Heat okra
- Heat barbecue sauce
- Make custard
- Heat the rice and add the vegetables

During the party:

After you have served the spare ribs, put the apples in the oven to cook.

BARBECUED SPARE RIBS

✻ ☆☆☆

PREPARATION TIME: 20 MINUTES
COOKING TIME: 20 MINUTES
OVEN TEMPERATURE: 200C 400F MARK 7

Ingredients:
3 spare ribs per person
For The Barbecue Sauce:

4 onions, finely chopped	*2 tbs of hot chilli sauce*
4 crushed cloves of garlic	*1 tbs of Worcestershire sauce*
2 green peppers, finely chopped	*1 tsp of Tobasco*
2 red peppers, finely chopped	*Salt & black pepper*
4 lbs (2 kgs) of fresh tomatoes, skinned	*3 tbs of olive oil*

Method:
To make the barbecue sauce:

Heat the oil in a heavy-based pan and add the onion, garlic, and peppers. Cook for approximately 5 minutes. Skin the tomatoes and roughly chop, add to the onion. Add the rest of the ingredients and cook over a gentle heat for about 20 minutes.

Arrange the spare ribs in roasting tins. Lightly sprinkle with salt and pepper and a little oil. Roast in the hot oven until crisp, approximately 20 minutes. Serve hot with the barbecue sauce.

JACKET POTATOES WITH SOURED CREAM AND CHIVES

❀ ☆☆☆
PREPARATION TIME: 10 MINUTES
COOKING TIME: 1 HOUR
OVEN TEMPERATURE: 200C 400F MARK 7

Ingredients:

1 jacket potato per person
l pt (570 ml) of sour cream

8 oz (225 g) of fresh chives
Green food colouring

Method:

Bake the potato. Finely chop the chives and add to the sour cream with a few drops of green food colouring (add as much colour as you desire).

SAVOURY RICE

❀ ☆☆☆
PREPARATION TIME: 10 MINUTES
COOKING TIME: 20 MINUTES

Ingredients:

2 lbs (900 g) long grain rice
8 oz (225 g) green peas
Green food colouring

8 oz (225 g) sweetcorn kernels
1 large onion, finely chopped
1 large green pepper, finely chopped

Method:

Cook the rice in boiling water with a tablespoon of green food colouring (remember that the food colouring will stain metal saucepans) and keep warm. Meanwhile sauté the onion, pepper, peas and sweet corn. Mix all the ingredients together.

EYEBALL JELLY WITH BLOOD CREAM

❀ ☆☆☆
PREPARATION TIME: 20 MINUTES
SETTING TIME: OVERNIGHT

Ingredients:

4 large tins of lychees (the lychees will represent the wizard's eyeballs)

4 pts (2 ltrs) of lime jelly

Method:
Make four pints of lime jelly according to the instructions on the packet, using the syrup from the lychees as part of the liquid. Divide the fruit between your chosen moulds and pour in the jelly. Allow to set. Turn out the jellies when set. Serve with blood cream.

Blood Cream:
1 pint (575 ml) of double or single cream with a few drops of cochineal mixed in to create the appearance of blood.

BAKED APPLES

❋ ☆☆☆
PREPARATION TIME: ½ HOUR
COOKING TIME: 40 MINUTES
OVEN TEMPERATURE: 200C 400F MARK 7

Ingredients:

1 cooking apple per person *12 oz (350 g) of demerara sugar*
1 lb (450 g) of dried mixed fruits *8 oz (225 g) of butter*
1 lb (450 g) of honey *1 pt (570 ml) of water*

Method:
Core the apples. Arrange on roasting tins. Mix the dried fruits with the sugar and fill the apples. Pour the honey over the apples, and put a knob of butter on top of each one. Pour the water into the roasting tin. Cover with tin foil and bake in the oven until tender, approximately 40 minutes. Serve with blue custard.
To make blue custard: Add a few drops of blue food colouring to the custard.

BEVERAGES

FRUIT PUNCH

Sparkling white wine, chilled *1 pt (570 ml) of orange juice, chilled*
¼ pt (150 ml) of lime cordial, chilled *Green food colouring*

To each bottle of sparkling white wine add the lime cordial and orange juice.
To add a touch of the spooks, float in the punch tomato tops which look like spiders and whole okra which look like green fingers or carrot slivers, which look like goldfish.

✍ **To complete this buffet: Devils on Horseback (See Page 55), Okra Mediterranean (See Page 256), Glühwein (See Page 19).**

GUY FAWKES

(O)n the 5th of November 1605, Guy Fawkes and his accomplices attempted and failed to blow up King James I and his Parliament. The plotters were captured. Guy Fawkes, Robert Catesby, Thomas Winters and others were condemned to be *"hanged by the neck, drawn, quartered and cut down while still alive, until death."* Ever since that day, November the 5th is celebrated with bonfires and fireworks displays.

November is a cold month. A suitable menu for an outdoor bonfire fire party is:

Roast Chestnuts in Their Skins
Jacket Potatoes with Sour Cream or Butter
Sausages In Baguettes
Goulash Soup
Corn on the Cob
Prawn Chowder
Chicken Drumsticks with Chilli Sauce

ROAST CHESTNUTS

☆ ❀❀❀
PREPARATION TIME: 10 MINUTES

Method:
With a sharp knife, make a slit in the skin of the chestnut. They are excellent roast in the bonfire in a wire receptacle, but are equally good roast in a hot oven for about 20 minutes. Serve sprinkled with salt.

JACKET POTATOES

☆ ❀❀❀
COOKING TIME: 1 HOUR

Method:
Scrub the potatoes; prick and wrap each one in tin foil, cook nestled around the edge of the fire as with the chestnuts.

SAUSAGES IN BAGUETTES

☆ ❀❀❀
PREPARATION TIME: 10 MINUTES
COOKING TIME: 25 MINUTES

Method:
Slit and butter the baguettes. Cook the sausages and serve hot inside the baguettes with fried onions, mustard or tomato sauce. Wrap each baguette in a paper napkin.

GOULASH SOUP

☆ ❀❀❀ **Can be made in advance or deep frozen.**
PREPARATION TIME: 20 MINUTES
COOKING TIME: 2 HOURS

Ingredients: To Serve Twelve Persons

3 lbs (1.3 kg) of lean stewing beef	*3 x 14 fl oz (380 g) can chopped tomatoes*
4 lbs (1.8 kg) of finely sliced onions	*10 tbs of paprika*
Seasoned flour	*2 tbs of caraway seeds*
2 pts (1.4 ltr) of beef stock	*10 fl oz (300 ml) of soured cream*

Method:
Cut the beef into strips about 1" (2.5 cm) long and ½" (1.2 cm) wide, toss in the seasoned flour. Heat the fat in a heavy-based saucepan and fry the onion until clear. Take the onions out, and fry the meat until lightly brown. Add the onions, beef stock, tinned tomatoes, paprika and caraway seeds. Season. Cook very gently for a couple of hours. Check every so often that there is plenty of liquid and add more if necessary. When the meat is tender the soup is ready. Just before serving, stir in the soured cream.

CORN ON THE COB

✩❀❀❀
COOKING TIME: 15 MINUTES

Method:

Boil them for 15 minutes in salt water, finish off under the grill with hot butter. Serve.

PRAWN CHOWDER

✩ ❀❀❀❀❀
PREPARATION TIME: 10 MINUTES
COOKING TIME: ½ HOUR

Ingredients: To Serve Twelve Persons

2 lbs (900 g) of peeled prawns   *8 oz (225 g) of garden peas*
1 lb (450 g) of cooked diced chicken   *3 pts (1.7 ltr) of chicken stock*
1 lb (450 g) of cooked sweet corn   *2 glasses of white wine*
2 large onions, finely chopped   *Cornflour to thicken*
Black pepper & salt   *¾ pt (425 ml) of milk*

Method:

Sauté the onions. Add all the ingredients in a large saucepan except the cornflour. Cook for approximately 20 minutes then thicken with the cornflour and ¼ pint of milk. Serve.

CHICKEN DRUMSTICKS WITH CHILLI SAUCE

✩ ❀❀❀
PREPARATION TIME: 10 MINUTES
COOKING TIME: 40 MINUTES
OVEN TEMP: 200C 400F M6

Ingredients: *Chicken drumsticks*
Sauce:

1 pt (570 ml) of chilli sauce   *1 tbs of oil*
1 large green pepper, finely chopped   *1 x 14 fl oz (380 g) can of tomatoes, finely*
1 large red pepper, finely chopped   *chopped*
1 large onion, finely chopped   *1 tbs of tomato purée*
2 cloves of garlic, finely crushed   *1 tbs of tomato chilli sauce*
1 finely chopped fresh green chilli   *Black pepper & salt*

Method:

Heat the oil in a saucepan, sauté the pepper, onion, chilli and garlic. Add the rest of the ingredients and simmer gently for about 20 minutes. Serve hot or cold with the chicken drumsticks.

✋ **To complete this menu: Glühwein (See Page 19).**

THANKSGIVING

Thanksgiving Day is a national holiday in the United States of America, celebrated on the fourth Thursday in November. In Canada, Thanksgiving takes place on the second Monday in October.

In 1621 the Pilgrim Fathers celebrated their first harvest and gave thanks to God, but it was not until 1863 that 'Thanksgiving' day became a national holiday.

When the Pilgrim Fathers arrived in New England in 1620, not only did they discover a land with great potential, they also found that food was in abundance, in particular, Indian corn, squashes, cranberries, wild berries, fish and seafood and wild fat turkeys.

English cooking methods were applied, and slowly evolved. Traditional national favourites began to emerge such as Boston baked beans and the Thanksgiving dinner of roast turkey and pumpkin pie.

A typical New England Thanksgiving dinner consists of, turkey with oyster stuffing, cranberry sauce, corn bread, Indian pudding and pumpkin pie.

CRANBERRY MOULD

❀ ☆☆☆ **America's festive way of serving cranberries with hot or cold turkey.**
PREPARATION TIME: 1 HOUR
CHILLING TIME: 6 HOURS OR UNTIL FIRM
Serves 10 persons
Special Equipment: 1½ Pint Ring Mould

Ingredients:

8 fl oz (225 g) of pineapple juice
2 tsp of powdered gelatine
8 fl oz (220 ml) of boiling water
5 oz (10 g) packet of cherry jelly
6 oz (175 g) of sugar
2 tsp of lemon juice

8 oz (225 g) of raw cranberries, finely chopped
Zest & flesh of 1 medium orange
8 oz (225 g) of canned crushed pineapple
2½ oz (60 g) walnuts
Lettuce leaves

Method:

Pour the pineapple juice into a bowl and sprinkle the powdered gelatine over it. Stand the bowl in hot water and stir until the gelatine has dissolved. Pour the boiling water over the cherry jelly and mix until it has dissolved. Add the sugar, lemon juice and the pineapple juice mixture, and chill until partially set, approximately 1 hour. Stir in the cranberries, orange zest, chopped orange flesh, pineapple and nuts, pour into a 1½ pint ring mould and chill until completely set. Unmould the jelly onto a plate, and garnish with lettuce leaves.

INDIAN PUDDING

❀ ☆☆☆ **Serves 6 Persons**
PREPARATION TIME: 20 MINUTES
COOKING TIME: 1¼ HOURS

OVEN TEMPERATURE: 150C 300F M2

Ingredients:

21 fl oz (600 ml) of milk
2 oz (50 g) of finely ground cornmeal
Pinch of salt
1 oz (25 g) of butter
2 medium sized eggs, lightly beaten
Vanilla ice cream to serve (optional)

1 tsp of cinnamon
½ tsp of ginger, nutmeg or allspice
Pinch of mace
2 tbs of sugar
3 oz (75 g) of raisins

Method:

Heat the oven. Scald the milk, bringing it almost to boiling point. Whisk in the salt and cornmeal, and mix until it thickens slightly. Stir in the butter. Remove from the heat and set aside to cool, placing a piece of grease-proof paper over the top to prevent a skin forming. When the mixture is slightly warmer than room temperature, add the rest of the ingredients. Taste the custard at this stage and add extra sugar or seasoning if you desire. Pour the custard into the mould or six individual ramekins and place in the oven for 1¼ hours until the custard is set. Serve warm with ice cream.

PUMPKIN PIE

Few Americans would dream of celebrating Thanksgiving without pumpkin pie.

❁❁ ☆☆☆ **Serves 8 Persons**
PREPARATION TIME: 30 MINUTES
COOKING TIME: 45 MINUTES
OVEN TEMPERATURE: 200C 400F M6
Special Equipment: Flan Ring or Case (10")

Ingredients:

2 large eggs
4 oz (110 g) of sugar
1 tbs of molasses
¼ tsp of ground ginger
1 tsp of ground cinnamon
½ tsp of freshly grated nutmeg

Pinch of ground cloves
½ tsp of salt
1 lb (450 g) of canned or stewed pumpkin
13 fl oz (400 ml) of milk
1 x 10" (25 cm) unbaked pastry case
10 fl oz (275 ml) of whipped cream

Note: If you use fresh pumpkin, buy 2 lbs (1 kg) and stew it over a low heat until virtually all of the liquid has evaporated.

Method:

Heat the oven. Combine the eggs with the sugar, molasses, spices and salt, blend well. Add the pumpkin and the milk, mix and check the spices. Pour into the unbaked pastry case. Cook in the centre of the oven for 40 minutes until set. Serve warm or cold with the cream.

ENGAGEMENT & WEDDING

ENGAGEMENT

The Protocol: The groom-to-be asks the father of the bride-to-be, for permission to marry his daughter. The groom's parents should be the next to be told; close family and friends should follow. An announcement can then be made in the social column of a newspaper, the wording of which will be taken care of by the newspaper.

The bride-to-be's family may organise a party at the bride's home, in a restaurant or hotel. The bride-to-be's father toasts the health and happiness of the couple, while the fiancé proposes a toast to the health of both sets of parents.
The young man is congratulated, but never the young lady, as this could be interpreted as being her catch rather than his. The same rule applies at the wedding.

In America, a friend holds 'a shower' for the bride-to-be, at which she is given personal gifts for her trousseau.

WEDDING

Forward planning is of paramount importance for any wedding. You will have to organise and co-ordinate everything and everybody. However, it need not be a daunting task. If you have the room or a large garden, take advantage of these assets and arrange your own reception.
We have chosen a wedding reception held at the bride's house using either a marquee or large reception rooms, and have drawn up a check-list and a three-month countdown.
You can obviously adapt this guide to your own requirements and timetable - do bear in mind that during the most popular season, June to September, arranging bookings with little notice will not be easy.

PLAN OF ACTION

Month Three
- Decide when and where you want to get married and consult the Vicar or the Registrar to fix the exact date and time of the ceremony. Discuss calling of the bans and the service you will have, the order of service, music, flowers, bell-ringing, church fees. Ask whether confetti, photographers and video cameramen are allowed inside.
- Compile your guest list.
- Book your reception venue, caterers, band or discothèque.
- Choose your attendants and best man.
- Choose your dress, accessories and bridesmaid outfits.
- Organise hiring of any morning suits.
- Book your honeymoon.
- Book the cars.
- Book the photographers.
- Compile wedding gift list.

- Order wedding stationery.
- Arrange floral decoration.
- Buy wedding rings.
- Order your wedding cake.
- Book any hotel rooms needed for guests.
- Book a hotel for your wedding night if applicable.

Month Two

- It is traditional to send out your wedding invitations six weeks before the date.
- Any wedding gifts you receive require an immediate reply thanking the sender.
- Buy gifts for the groom, bride, attendants, best man, and ushers.
- Final honeymoon bookings - check passports etc.

Month One

- Chase up late invitation replies and finalise the guest list.
- Prepare place cards for guests - write out a place chart to be displayed.
- Finalise the menu and wine, give the final numbers to the caterers, in writing, two weeks before the wedding day.
- Double check 'thank you' letters have been sent for all gifts received.
- Ensure that your own and attendants' wedding clothes are ready, and that any hair appointments have been made.
- Check that transport is organised.
- Prepare a newspaper announcement if applicable.

Week Before

- If it is a church wedding, you will have a rehearsal.
- Check the service sheets have been delivered to the best man.
- Make final checks on clothes, catering, cake, transport, flowers and photography.
- If you are going to display your presents, set a room aside for this purpose and arrange them as they arrive.
- Check you have everything packed and ready for the honeymoon.

THE COST

Custom and etiquette give guidelines, but it is for you to decide what will be done, in accordance with your personal circumstances.

-**The bride's father** bears the cost of the reception and the cake, transport (except for the groom and best man), any press announcement, wedding stationery, photographers, flowers and decorations (for the church and reception).
-**The bride** usually buys her own wedding dress and bridesmaid dresses, and any trousseau she requires. She also buys her groom a wedding ring, if applicable, and a present.
-**The groom** pays for the bride's engagement and wedding rings, the church or registrars fees, flowers for the bride, bridesmaids, mother of the bride and groom, buttonholes for the best man, ushers, and any close male relatives and of course himself. Transport for himself and the best man to the ceremony and presents for the bride's attendant, best man and ushers. Lastly, the honeymoon.

THE BRIDAL PARTY
PREPARATIONS & PROTOCOL

THE BRIDE

- She chooses her attendants, her dress, and theirs.
- She writes the 'thank-you' letters.
  On the day
- She receives the guests at the reception with the groom and both sets of parents.
- She gives her attendants their gifts.
- She opens the ball or the dancing with her groom.
- She throws her bouquet amongst the guests before leaving for the honeymoon.

THE BRIDE AND HER MOTHER

- They compile the guest list, consulting with the groom's parents.
- They make arrangements for the wedding reception, floral decorations, order the cake and send the invitations.

THE BRIDE'S FATHER

- He escorts the bride to the church and gives her away.
- He stands next to the bride during the speeches at the wedding breakfast and proposes a toast to the bride and groom.

THE GROOM

- He chooses his best man and ushers.
- He arranges the honeymoon.
  On the day
- He replies to the bride's father's speech, thanking the bride's parents for their daughter's hand and the guests for attending, and proposes a toast to the bridesmaid.

THE BEST MAN

- He checks the arrangements made by the groom and ensures he has the wedding rings.
- He organises the stag night.
  On the day
- He escorts the groom to the church.
- He organises the ushers.
- He escorts the chief bridesmaid to the signing of the register during the recessional and at the reception.
- He takes the role of calling for silence for the speeches, announces the cake cutting, replies to the groom's toast to the bridesmaids and makes a speech on behalf of the bride and groom, reading out any telemessages and cards.
- He ensures that transport has been organised for the couple's honeymoon.
- He sees that the couple leave the reception in good time with all their luggage.
- He looks after the groom's wedding suit.

THE USHERS

- They greet the guests in the church, providing them with the service sheet and guiding them to their pews.
- They escort the groom's parents and bride's mother to their seats.

THE CHIEF BRIDESMAID

- She helps the bride dress for the wedding and does the same for the younger bridesmaids.
- At the ceremony she makes sure that the other attendants are in the right order to follow the bride, and arranges her veil and train.
- She holds the bride's bouquet during the service and returns it to her after the signing of the register.
- After the reception she helps the bride to change and looks after her wedding dress.

CATERERS

The caterers should be competent and guide you adequately. Ask to compare several menus and each respective price. Ascertain whether they supply cutlery, china, linen, glassware and waitresses for serving and clearing. Find out whether they provide drinks and Champagne (which is traditional and should accompany the toasts and the cutting of the cake).

The wedding cake: If your caterers do not make it, they might recommend an alternative supplier. Remember to order well in advance.

The marquee: Some caterers will undertake to organise the marquee and seating arrangements. However, if they do not provide this service, there are many companies hiring marquees and all the necessary trappings.

THE FLOWERS

You should liaise with the florist of your choice, the church, and the caterers.

You will need:
- The bouquet for the bride, corsages for the ladies, button-holes for the gentlemen.
- Flowers in the church: remember flower arrangements put in the Church will have to stay there, and if the wedding takes place during Lent ask your vicar whether he will allow the church to be decorated with flowers for the occasion.
- Flowers for the reception.

BAND OR DISCOTHEQUE

It is important to have a meeting with the band (or the person running the discothèque) and discuss the programme they will play, to please all age groups and ensure variety.

THE DRESS

Wedding and bridesmaids' dresses can be bought off the peg or made to measure. Either way it will take time and planning. We recommend most strongly that you give yourself (or the dressmaker) plenty of time. Choose your dress, be totally happy with it and do not let other people over-influence your decision - you must feel it is 'you'. You can then co-ordinate the bridesmaids' or page-boys' outfits. Good communication should keep everyone involved, informed and happy.

Any bride's magazine will contain all the necessary up-to-date addresses and suggestions.

MORNING SUITS

Gentlemen from both sides of the family can get together to organise the hiring of their morning suits.

THE RINGS

The bride is always given a wedding ring during the ceremony. It is up to the couple to decide whether the groom should have one too.

THE WEDDING LIST

Large stores in your area will offer a bridal service. A wedding list not only avoids duplication, but ensures that you will get the things you need. Make it as comprehensive and large as you can, giving your guests the opportunity to choose according to their budget.

GIFTS

A room should be selected to show the presents. It is usual for the guests to have sent their gifts well in advance, to allow the bride and her family time to arrange a display.

INVITATION ETIQUETTE

Invitations should be sent out six weeks before the date. Guests should reply by return. Unless it is a very small wedding, engraved or printed invitations are suitable. In most circumstances the invitation will be sent from the bride's parents.

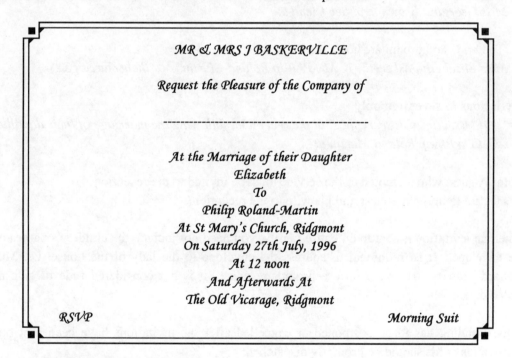

MR & MRS J BASKERVILLE

Request the Pleasure of the Company of

At the Marriage of their Daughter
Elizabeth
To
Philip Roland-Martin
At St Mary's Church, Ridgmont
On Saturday 27th July, 1996
At 12 noon
And Afterwards At
The Old Vicarage, Ridgmont

RSVP   *Morning Suit*

The wording of the invitation:

Let us list all the possible permutations:

1. Bride's parents are hosts:
   Mr. & Mrs. James Baskerville.... at the marriage of their daughter....

2. Bride's mother is widowed:
   Mrs. James Baskerville.... of her daughter....

3. Bride's mother has remarried and she and the bride's stepfather are hosts:
   Mr. & Mrs. David Culpepper .... her daughter....

4. Bride's father has remarried and he and the bride's stepmother are hosts:
   Mr. & Mrs. James Baskerville.... his daughter....

5. A step-parent is to be the sole host:
   Mr. George Gray (or Mrs. Julian Bromsfield).... his (her) stepdaughter....

6. Divorced parents jointly hosting their daughters' wedding:
   Mr. James Baskerville and Mrs. Helen Baskerville.... their daughter....

7. The bride's mother has subsequently remarried but is jointly hosting the occasion with the bride's father:
   Mr. James Baskerville and Mrs. Helen Bonnafoux.... their daughter....

8. The host is some other relation to the bride:
   Mr. & Mrs. Michael Knights.... their niece/ward or his (her) cousin/goddaughter....

9. No relationship, e.g. the host is a friend of the bride:
   Miss Georgina Brown.... of her friend....

10. The bride and groom are hosts themselves:
    Miss Elizabeth Baskerville & Mr. Phillip Roland-Martin.... at their marriage....

Invitations to reception only
Mr. and Mrs. James Baskerville.... at the reception, following the marriage of their daughter Elizabeth to Philip Roland-Martin at ....

Note: A guest who is invited to the service must be invited to the reception.
It is tactful to invite the vicar and his wife to the reception.

When an invitation is sent to an entire family, you need not include the children's names on the envelope. It is traditional to address the envelope to the lady of the house, i.e. Mrs. Edward Roberts. If you require a prompt response, it is not considered rude to give an RSVP date.

If the wedding has to be postponed or cancelled after the invitations have been sent out, notification cards should be promptly dispatched.

O N   T H E   D A Y

We have devised a hypothetical time-table for your guidance, with a twelve noon wedding service.
It is wise for the bride and her close family to have something to eat before going to the church. A few canapés which do not hang on the breath and a bottle of champagne will relax everyone.

AT THE CHURCH

The bride's family and friends sit on the left-hand side of the aisle, as you face the altar, and the groom's family on the right. On each side, the close family sits nearest the front.

The ushers should arrive approximately forty minutes before the ceremony to receive early guests.

The groom and best man should arrive at least twenty minutes before the ceremony and take their places in the front right-hand pew. The best man stands on the groom's right.
Guests should start arriving about fifteen minutes before the ceremony.
The bridesmaids should arrive about ten minutes before.
The bride's mother is the last person to take her seat before the ceremony starts. She ensures there is a seat beside her for her husband after he has given the bride away.

The bride proceeds slowly up the aisle on her father's right arm. She must remember to wear her engagement ring on her right hand. Her father leads her to the groom's left. Attendants are behind. The chief bridesmaid steps forward and takes the bride's bouquet which she holds until the bride has signed the register. If there is no chief bridesmaid or the attendants are very young the bride's father takes the bouquet and hands it to his wife who returns it to the bride in the vestry.

The service takes anything from 35 to 45 minutes and so you would arrive back at the house at about 13.30 allowing time for photographs to be taken. The instructions for getting to the reception should have been sent with the invitations, but one usher should remain behind and make sure the guests know where to go.

13.30. BACK FROM THE CHURCH

Guests can be announced by a master of ceremonies, this helps both side of the family, friends and guests to recognise everyone.

The receiving line: The bride and groom should be the first. Next are both sets of parents, mother of the bride with father of the groom and vice versa (or whoever may be standing in for them). Next the close family in order of seniority, for example grand parents or uncles and aunts before sisters, brothers or nieces and nephews.

At a buffet the guests choose where they would like to sit and the bride and groom circulate freely.
In the case of a formal meal a top table is reserved for the bridal party and the seating arrangement is as follows:

Best man
Groom's mother
Bride's father
Bride
Groom
Bride's mother
Groom's father
Chief bridesmaid

Speeches: The first speech is from the bride's father, who propose a toast to the bride and groom. This should be short.

The groom replies, thanking his parents-in-law for producing such a wonderful daughter and for organising the wedding, emphasising the role his mother-in-law has played in its planning and smooth running. He finishes his speech with a toast to the bridesmaids.

It is then the duty of the best man to reply on behalf of the bridesmaids. The best man's speech can be amusing but should not be too saucy.

After his speech the best man reads out any telemessages. (He must keep these to return to the bride after the honeymoon).

After the speeches the bride and groom cut the cake, his hand resting over hers to assist. A tier of the cake is often kept for christenings.

About half an hour after the cake-cutting the bride and groom will retire to change into their going-away outfits. As they are about to leave the bride tosses her bouquet towards the assembled guests, a single lady should catch it in the hope that she might be the next lucky bride. The best man is supposed to produce the honeymoon tickets and ensure transport for the couple to their destination. He is also responsible for the returning of any hired morning suits. In Scotland sweets and coins are thrown to children from the going-away car.

After the bridal couple depart, guests should thank the host and hostess and leave.

You might choose to have an evening function following the reception when guests who were not invited to the wedding reception come along to celebrate the occasion in a less formal manner.

REGISTRAR OFFICE WEDDING CEREMONY

The bridal party arrives about ten minutes before the service, and assembles in the waiting room. The couple are called in first to have the proceeding briefly explained to them and to pay the fees. After a short address by the superintendent registrar the service proceeds.

When you give notice to the registrar ask how many guests you may invite as registrars' offices vary in size.

After a civil wedding service you can if you wish have your marriage blessed in church. A service of blessing normally consist of a brief address, a reading, prayer and blessings. You should check with the minister whether he will accept traditional wedding clothes for this service and how many guests you may invite.

In some European countries the law requires that one should be first married by the Mayor in the registrars' office which is usually the town hall. For this civic ceremony the bride wears a formal dress or suit and a hat. She then goes home to change into her wedding dress. The religious ceremony follows with all the pomp and circumstance.

In France after the cutting of the cake, which is usually a 'Pièce Montée', as a keepsake and a good-luck token, the bride will tear her wedding veil and give a small piece of it to everyone. The guests will also receive a prettily wrapped packet of white 'dragées' (sweet sugared almonds). Halfway through the reception the bride and groom discreetly disappear, on their way to their honeymoon.

CHRISTENING

The birth of a child is cause for celebration. An announcement is usually made in the social column of the Times, the Telegraph or the local paper. The christening takes place when the mother feels fit again.

In England, it is traditional, that one of the tiers from the parents' wedding cake is kept for the child's christening. In this case, do examine the cake in advance, as the icing may have discoloured and may even have weebles. Do not be put off by this as it is usual and the cake will still be quite delicious once you have it re-iced.

Champagne is traditional for the toast. White wine, soft drinks and tea should also be offered during the reception.

On the continent the custom is to give the guests a small dainty box of sugared almonds (dragées) bearing the child's name on the lid; the almonds are blue for a boy and pink for a girl. These boxes are sent to members of the family and friends who were unable to attend.

FORMAL AFTERNOON TEA FOR TWENTY PERSONS

Selection of Sandwiches
Scones
Savoury Petits Croissants
Sardines Crescents
Pizzas
Fingers Eclairs, Rum Babas
Cherry Trifles, Danish Pastries
Paris-Brest, Cream Cakes
Fresh Fruit Tartlets
Dragées

A SELECTION OF SANDWICHES

✽ ☆☆☆
PREPARATION TIME: 2 HOURS

- Cream cheese mixed with chopped walnuts, or chopped celery, or any other ingredients you desire.
- Smoked salmon, lemon juice and cayenne.

- Finely grated Cheddar cheese mixed with mayonnaise, mustard and finely chopped tomatoes and seasoning, or instead of the mustard, some Marmite.
- Turkey slices with stuffing.
- Ham slices with Dijon or grain mustard.
- Egg mayonnaise: chop the hard-boiled eggs and mix with mayonnaise and a soft creamy cheese i.e. Primula, and season.
- Sardine butter: mash sardines in with butter, and season with lemon juice and cayenne. It is unnecessary to butter your bread when using this filling. Add sliced tomatoes.
- Watercress with cream cheese.

Method:

Sandwiches need to be fresh and so should be made at the last minute. To speed up the process, have all the fillings made in advance and work systematically. Ensure that the butter is soft before spreading on the bread. Butter all the bread you are using, and then fill the sandwiches. Alternate white bread with brown bread and even have three layers using the white and brown bread to create a Harlequin effect.

Be careful not to underfill or overfill the sandwiches. If you decide to remove the crusts, do so after filling the sandwiches. An electric knife is very useful for this task.

Cut the sandwiches into quarters crossways, or into smaller squares or into fingers. Garnish your plate with cress, tomato wedges, cucumber slices and lettuce leaves.

Bridge rolls: They should be approximately 2½" (5 cm) long and 1" (2.5cm) wide. They make a superb alternative to sandwiches; allow about 2-3 bridge rolls per person. Cut in half, butter, fill and garnish the rolls with cress, a tomato or cucumber slice.

SCONES

✹ ☆☆☆
PREPARATION TIME: 15 MINUTES
COOKING TIME: 12-15 MINUTES
OVEN TEMPERATURE: 220C 425F Mark 7
Special Equipment: 2" Diameter Plain Cutter

Ingredients: for approximately 8 scones

1 lb (450 g) of plain flour
1 tsp of salt
1 tsp of bicarbonate of soda

1½ oz (40 g) of butter
½ pt (275 ml) of buttermilk or fresh milk with 2 tsp of cream of tartar

Method:

Sift the flour, salt and soda into a bowl. Rub in the butter to a fine breadcrumb consistency. Add the milk and mix with a round-bladed knife to form a soft but firm dough. Turn onto a floured surface and knead lightly. Roll out to about ¾" (2 cm) thick. Stamp out 2" (5 cm) rounds, or make a large round with triangular incisions in it. Bake on a lightly floured baking sheet until risen and golden brown. Serve with whipped cream and strawberry jam.

SAVOURY CROISSANTS

✹ ☆☆☆ **Can be prepared in advance and frozen uncooked**
PREPARATION TIME: 30 MINUTES
COOKING TIME: 15 MINUTES

OVEN TEMPERATURE: 200C 400F MARK 6

Ingredients: for approximately 18 croissants

1 lb (450 g) puff pastry	*Cayenne pepper*
8 oz (225 g) grated strong cheddar or	*Beaten egg*
other cheese	

Method:
Roll the pastry and cut into 3" (7.5cm) squares. Sprinkle with the grated cheese and cayenne. Roll up tightly from a corner downwards. A crescent shape will form which you then gently curve round to form a croissant. (Freeze at this point if you wish to). Leave to rest for 2 hours. Glaze with beaten egg and cook for approximately 15 minutes in a pre-heated oven until golden brown. Serve hot.

SARDINE CRESCENTS

✻ ☆☆☆ **Can be prepared in advance and frozen uncooked**
PREPARATION TIME: 30 MINUTES
COOKING TIME: 15 MINUTES
OVEN TEMPERATURE: 200C 400F MARK 6

Ingredients: for approximately 10 crescents

1 lb (450 g) of ready-made puff pastry	*Salt*
2 tins of sardines	*Vinegar*
Lemon juice	*Beaten egg*
Cayenne pepper	

Method:
Roll out the pastry, and cut as many 3" (7.5cm) rounds as possible. Mash the sardines, lemon juice, cayenne and salt together. Add vinegar to taste. Brush the outer perimeter of the pastry circle with beaten egg, and pile a small amount of the sardine mixture in the centre. Fold the round in half and seal securely. (Freeze at this point if you wish to). Place the crescents onto a baking sheet and leave to rest for about 2 hours in a cool place. Brush with beaten egg before cooking and put in a pre-heated oven for 15 minutes until risen and golden brown. Serve hot.

PIZZA

✻ ☆☆☆ **Pizza keeps well in the freezer, and can be prepared well in advance.**
PREPARATION TIME: 1 HOUR
COOKING TIME: 15-20 MINUTES
OVEN TEMPERATURE: 220C 425F Mark 7
To Freeze: Bake for 15 minutes. Cool, wrap in foil and seal. When you need it, thaw at room temperature for about 2 hours, and reheat in a hot oven 220C, 425F Mark 7 for 10 minutes.

Ingredients: for 4 round pizzas, or 24 or more square pieces.

1 lb (450 g) plain flour	*½ oz (15 g) fresh yeast (2 tsp dried yeast)*
2 level tsp salt	*½ pt (275 ml) of warm water*

½ level tsp of caster sugar (optional)   *1 tbs oil*

Pizza Topping:

Strong grated cheddar cheese or mozzarella, fresh sliced tomatoes or a spicy tomato, onion, garlic, and herb sauce. With fresh or dried herbs of your choice, mushrooms, peppers, anchovies, salami, tuna fish, or any ingredients you desire.

Method:

For the pizza bases:

Mix the flour and salt in a bowl. Blend the fresh yeast with the warm water and allow to froth. Add to the dry ingredients along with the oil **(*)**. Mix to form a dough, then turn out onto a floured working surface and knead for about 5 minutes until the dough is firm and elastic. Place back in the basin and cover with a cloth and leave in a warm place until it has risen to double its size. Turn the dough out onto your working surface and press firmly with your knuckles to knock any air out. If you are making square pizzas, line a greased baking sheet with the dough. Brush with olive oil and cover with the toppings. Set the prepared pizzas in a warm place and leave to rise for about 15-20 minutes before baking. Cook in a pre-heated oven for approximately 20 minutes. Serve hot, cut into mouth-sized pieces.

(*) If using dried yeast, dissolve the sugar in warm water and sprinkle the yeast onto it. Leave to stand in a warm place for approximately 10 minutes until frothy, then add to the flour as above.

FINGER ECLAIRS

- CHOUX PASTRY

❀ ☆☆☆

PREPARATION TIME: 15 MINUTES

COOKING TIME: 20 MINUTES

OVEN TEMPERATURE: 200C 400F MARK 6

Ingredients: Make approximately 20 small éclairs

7½ fl oz (210 ml) of water   *3¾ oz (100 g) of flour*

3 oz (75 g) of butter or margarine   *3 eggs*

Method:

Put the water and fat into a saucepan and bring to a rapid boil. Draw aside and immediately add the sifted flour all at once. Beat vigorously until a smooth dough has formed. Leave the mixture to cool (so that you can lay your hand against the side of the pan without burning it). Beat the eggs, and add a little at a time to the dough, beating thoroughly all the time. You may not need to add all the egg, but ensure that your mixture is firm and keeps its shape at the end of beating. It should have a glossy appearance.

Grease a baking sheet, and pipe the mixture onto the sheet in small fingers about 1½" (3 cm) long. Cook in a pre-heated oven for about 15 minutes until risen and golden brown. Place the éclairs on a cooling rack and prick the sides with a skewer to allow the air to escape.

- GLACÉ ICING

❀ ☆☆☆

PREPARATION TIME: 10 MINUTES

Ingredients:

2-3 tbs of water
2-3 oz (50-60 g) of block chocolate, or
1-2 tbs of coffee essence

½-¾ lb (100-150 g) of icing sugar, sifted
1-2 tbs sugar syrup or water

Method:
Slowly melt the chocolate in the water until smooth. Add the sifted icing sugar and enough sugar syrup to make a thick cream. Heat the mixture very gently. Dip the tops of the éclairs into the icing. Fill with whipped double cream.

RUM BABAS

We suggest that you buy the rum babas sponge cases. Make a syrup of water and sugar, adding some rum. Pour the syrup over the babas cases so that they are moist. Mix fresh fruits with whipped cream and pile in the centre of the babas.
Note: Cream cakes can be bought from a good patissier, along with Danish pastries. If you feel that you are able to make your own fresh fruit tartlets do so, but do not attempt any job that will fluster you.

CHERRY TRIFLE

❀ ☆☆☆
PREPARATION TIME: 20 MINUTES
SETTING TIME: 2 HOURS MINIMUM

Ingredients:

1 packet of fruit jelly
1 packet of sponge fingers, or trifle
sponges
1 tin of fruit of your choice, or fresh soft
fruits

4 tbs of sweet sherry
1 pt (570 ml) custard
½ pt (275 ml) whipped cream
Cherries & angelica to decorate
2 oz (50 g) of grated chocolate

Method:
Dissolve the jelly. If you are using tinned fruit, add the liquid from the fruit. Lay the sponge on the bottom of your serving dish and pour the fruit, jelly and sherry over it. Leave to set in the refrigerator. When the jelly is set, make the custard and allow to cool. Pour the custard over the jelly and again leave to set. Decorate with whipped cream, cherries, angelica and grated chocolate.

PARIS-BREST

This sweet was created in the late nineteenth century in honour of the famous bicycle race. The route was circular from Paris to Brest and back again.

❀ ☆☆☆ **Serves 8 Persons**
PREPARATION TIME: 30 MINUTES
COOKING TIME: 30 MINUTES
OVEN TEMPERATURE: 200C 400F MARK 6

Ingredients:

1 oz (25 g) of unsalted butter
1 level tsp of caster sugar
¼ pt (150 ml) of milk
For the Chantilly Cream:
½ pt (275 ml) of double cream
3 level tbs of icing sugar

4 oz (110 g) of plain flour
3 eggs
1½ oz (40 g) of flaked almonds

1 egg white

Method:

- CHOUX PASTRY:

Put the butter, milk and sugar into a pan, and bring to a rapid boil. Remove from the heat and add the sifted flour. Beat vigorously until a smooth dough has formed. Stir the eggs one by one into the pastry, then add the yolk of a third egg if needed to make a smooth firm glossy dough. Spoon the paste into a piping bag fitted with a large plain nozzle. On a greased baking tray pipe a 8" (20 cm) circle approximately 1½" (4 cm) wide. Sprinkle the almonds over and bake for 30 minutes until golden brown and risen. Cool the choux ring on a wire cooling rack, then split in half horizontally with a sharp knife.

- CHANTILLY CREAM:

Whip together the double cream, sifted icing sugar and egg white until light and fluffy. Spoon into the hollow bottom half of the choux ring. Cover with the lid, and dust with icing sugar.

WEDDING ANNIVERSARIES

The most celebrated wedding anniversaries are Silver, Ruby and Diamond. On these occasions a large party is organised, usually by the immediate family.

For quick and easy reference we have included a table showing each year and its theme. Use the themes as a basis for your celebrations.

First	*Paper*	*Thirteenth*	*Lace*
Second	*Cotton*	*Fourteenth*	*Ivory*
Third	*Leather*	*Fifteenth*	*Crystal*
Fourth	*Fruit & flowers*	*Twentieth*	*China*
Fifth	*Wooden*	*Twenty-fifth*	*Silver*
Sixth	*Sugar & candy*	*Thirtieth*	*Pearl*
Seventh	*Woollen*	*Thirty-fifth*	*Coral*
Eighth	*Salt*	*Fortieth*	*Ruby*
Ninth	*Copper*	*Forty-fifth*	*Sapphire*
Tenth	*Tin*	*Fiftieth*	*Golden*
Eleventh	*Steel*	*Fifty-fifth*	*Emerald*
Twelfth	*Silk & fine linen*	*Sixtieth*	*Diamond*

FOURTH WEDDING ANNIVERSARY FOR FOUR PERSONS
Theme: Fruit & Flowers

Hot Baked Grapefruit

Roast Duckling
with Orange or Cherry Sauce
Cauliflower Polonaise, Roast Potatoes
Boiled Potatoes, Lemon Carrots
Mangetout Peas

Grapes Delight

Petits Fours

Wine is not recommended with the first course. For the main course red or white can be chosen.

White wine when serving orange sauce:

🏺 Bonnezeaux (Anjou)

🏺🏺 Condrieu (Côtes du Rhone)

🏺🏺🏺 Chablis Les Clos Grand Cru

Red wine when serving cherry sauce:

🍷 Minervois (Languedoc)

🍷🍷 Gigondas (Côtes du Rhone)

🍷🍷🍷 Château-Ausone (Saint-Emilion, Bordeaux)

Note: This menu is based on fruit, the Cauliflower Polonaise represents a flower. Do not be afraid to use flower heads to decorate your food, for example: a small flower in the middle on your baked grapefruit.

ROAST DUCKLING WITH CHERRY SAUCE

❀❀ ☆☆☆☆
PREPARATION TIME: 20 MINUTES
COOKING TIME: 2 HOURS
OVEN TEMP: 400F 200C Mark 6

Ingredients:
1 fresh duckling
Sage Stuffing:

Sieved fresh breadcrumbs	*Butter*
1 onion, finely chopped	*Seasoning*
Fresh sage leaves	*Orange zest*

For the cherry sauce:

1 lb (450 g) of fresh stoned cherries	*Juice of one orange*
(1 tin)	*Juice from the roast pan*
¼ pt (150 ml) of water (none if using	*Arrowroot to thicken*
tinned cherries)	*Cherry brandy or port (optional)*
1 tsp of sugar	

Orange Sauce (See Page 284)

Method:
Sauté the onion in butter. Add the sieved breadcrumbs, finely chopped sage leaves, orange zest and seasoning. If it is not moist enough, add a little orange juice. Mix together until blended and stuff into the cavity of the bird.

Prick the duck's skin and rub a little salt all over. Put into a roasting pan with about ½" (1 cm) of water, cover the bird with foil, put into the oven and roast for 2 hours. Thirty minutes before the end of the cooking remove the foil to allow the duck to brown and crisp.

Meanwhile make the cherry sauce. Stone the cherries and put into a pan. Add the water and sugar and bring to the boil, cook for 5 minutes. Pour in the orange juice and zest and put aside.

When the duck has cooked drain off most of the fat, leaving the juices in the bottom of the pan. Pour the juices into the cherry sauce and thicken with arrowroot to a pouring consistency. At the last minute add the cherry brandy or port. Serve hot.

ROAST POTATOES

Cook the par-boiled potatoes around the duck.

To complete this menu: **Hot Baked Grapefruit (See Page 277), Cauliflower Polonaise (See Page 248), Lemon Carrots (See Page 247), Grapes Delight (See Page 278), Petits fours: Toffee-Glazed Fresh Fruits (See Page 58).**

15TH WEDDING ANNIVERSARY FOR TEN PERSONS
Theme: Crystal

Chilled Consommé with Tio Pepe

Steak au Poivre
Jacket Potatoes with Sour Cream & Chives
Haricot Verts & Purée Carrots

Grapes in Sauternes

Coffee & Petits Fours

Red wine with the main course:

ᴵ Côte-de-Brouilly (Beaujolais)

ᴵᴵ Châteauneuf-du-Pape (Côtes du Rhône)

ᴵᴵᴵ Griottes-Chambertin, (Côte de Nuits, Burgundy)

The entrée and the dessert have the appearance of crystal. Try to use crystal glasses and dishes to keep in tune with the theme.

Note: Both the entrée and the dessert can be made the previous day, the carrot purée prepared in advance, the jacket potato scrubbed ready for the oven, and the chives chopped into the sour cream. Top and tail the haricot-vert well in advance, and prepare the steaks ready for cooking.

CHILLED CONSOMMÉ WITH TIO PEPE

❀ ☆☆☆
CHILLING TIME: THE NIGHT BEFORE
PREPARATION TIME: 5 MINUTES

Ingredients:

5 tins of good quality beef consommé   *Tio Pepe*

Method:

Chill the tins of soup in the refrigerator overnight which will solidify the soup. Just before serving spoon the consommé into individual soup bowls and pour the Tio Pepe over it. Garnish with finely chopped parsley and chives.

STEAK AU POIVRE

❀ ☆☆☆☆☆
PREPARATION TIME: 20 MINUTES
COOKING TIME: 10 MINUTES

Ingredients:

10 fillet or rump steaks (approx 6 to 8 oz   *20 fl oz (570 ml) single cream*
(175/225 g) per steak)   *4 fl oz (110 ml) of brandy*
6 oz (175 g) of whole black peppercorns   *2 oz (50 g) of butter*

Method:

Trim the steaks. Break up the peppercorns by putting them in a plastic bag and crushing with a hammer. Press both sides of the steak into the peppercorns. Melt the butter in a frying pan, and heat until foaming. Add the steaks and fry for the desired amount of time. Pour the brandy over the steaks, and flambé. Add the single cream and bring slowly to just below boiling point. Serve immediately, garnished with watercress and grilled tomatoes.

GRAPES IN SAUTERNES

❀❀ ☆☆☆☆☆
Special Equipment: 10 Stemmed Wine Glasses or 10 Suitable Glass Dishes
PREPARATION TIME: 10 MINUTES
CHILLING TIME: 2 HOURS MINIMUM

Ingredients:

2 lbs (900 g) of seedless white grapes   *Sugar & lemon for frosting glasses*
2 bottles of Sauternes wine   *10 sprigs of mint to decorate (optional)*
2 oz (50 g) of powdered gelatine

Method:

Pour one bottle of wine into a saucepan and sprinkle the powdered gelatine over it. Leave to soak for 5 minutes and then gently heat until the gelatine has dissolved. Remove from the heat and allow to cool slightly.

Frost the top of the glasses by rubbing a piece of lemon around the rim and dipping into the sugar. Wash the grapes and fill each glass with the grapes. Add the second bottle of wine to the gelatine preparation and pour over the grapes in the glasses. Put to chill in the refrigerator and serve when set.

 **To complete this menu: Jacket Potatoes with Snipped Chives & Sour Cream, Haricots Verts & Purée Carrots**.

BIRTHDAY

We all anticipate the birthdays of friends and loved ones with great excitement. Do not be daunted by the thought of holding a party at home, even for a large number of persons. We have in this book compiled a selection of buffets which you can easily adapt to any birthday, at any time of the year, either indoors or outdoors.

Children's birthday parties are covered under 'Children's Parties'.

EIGHTEENTH & TWENTY-FIRST

They are usually celebrated with a large evening party. We recommend a knife-and-fork buffet, and of course a birthday cake is 'de rigueur'.

Note: Young people like discothèques. If you decide to have one, it is in our opinion of paramount importance that you vet it in advance for selection, programme and noise level!

EXTRAVAGANZA

We have chosen an extravaganza menu composed of 8 courses, for 6 persons. Each course can be prepared in advance. Clearly for such an extravaganza the courses need to be small in quantity and complement each other. The meal should be long and leisurely.

MENU FOR SIX PERSONS

French Onion Soup
Crab Claws with Herb Mayonnaise
Brochettes of Sole with Lemon
Orange Sorbet
Pigeon Bourgignon
Parmesan Duchess Potatoes, Brussels with Almonds,
Carrots
Pineapple & Raspberry Cups
Cheese Board with Dates & Port
Coffee & Petits Fours

White wine with the fish courses:

   Côtes-de-Provence

   Château-Fieuzal (Graves, Bordeaux)

   Auxey-Duresses (Côte de Beaune, Burgundy)

Red wine with the main course:

⊺ Fleurie (Beaujolais)

⊺⊺ Château-Lagrange (Medoc, Bordeaux)

⊺⊺⊺ Volnay-Les-Caillerets (Côte de Beaune, Burgundy)

Or Champagne throughout the meal.

FRENCH ONION SOUP WITH CHEESE CROUTES

❀ ☆☆☆
PREPARATION TIME: 15 MINUTES
COOKING TIME: 1 HOUR

Ingredients:

2 lbs (900 g) of onions finely sliced   *2 pts (1 ltr) of good chicken stock*
1 clove of garlic, crushed   *freshly ground black pepper, salt*
Cheese Croutes:
6 slices of French bread   *Oil for frying*
Grated Cheddar cheese

Method:
Sauté the onions with the garlic and add all the ingredients together and simmer gently for one hour. Fry the French bread on both sides until golden brown. Sprinkle the grated Cheddar cheese over one side of the bread and place under a hot grill until melted. Serve the soup with a cheese croûton in each portion.

CRAB CLAWS WITH HERB MAYONNAISE

❀ ☆☆☆☆☆
PREPARATION TIME: 20 MINUTES

Ingredients:

2 crab claws per person   *Finely chopped fresh herbs (parsley,*
Mayonnaise (see page 312)   *chives, fennel)*
Lemon wedges

Method:
Add the herbs to the mayonnaise and arrange the crab claws on individual serving plates and garnish.
Note: Supply your guests with a finger-bowl and paper napkins.

BROCHETTE OF SOLE WITH LEMON

❀ ☆☆☆☆
PREPARATION TIME: 15 MINUTES
COOKING TIME: 15 MINUTES
OVEN TEMP: 200C 400F M6
Special Equipment: Skewers

Ingredients:

3 lemon or Dover soles
½ pt (275 ml) of milk
3 oz (75 g) of butter
Juice of two lemons

1 lemon
1 tbs finely chopped parsley
Brown bread & butter

Method:

Ask your fishmonger to fillet and skin the soles. From each sole you should have four long fillets. Cut each length in half, crossways. Roll the fish up and arrange on the skewer, alternating with a slice of lemon. Place in an ovenproof dish and pour half milk-half water to cover the bottom up to one inch. Cook for 15 minutes. Melt the butter and add the lemon juice and chopped parsley. Serve one brochette per person, pouring the lemon butter over the fish. Serve with brown bread and butter.

ORANGE SORBET

You can buy sorbets which are presented in the orange shell. Take these out of the freezer approximately 15 minutes before serving to allow the shell to frost. Add a sprig of fresh mint to garnish.

PIGEON BOURGIGNON

❀ ☆☆☆☆
PREPARATION TIME: 30 MINUTES
COOKING TIME: 1½ HOUR
OVEN TEMP: 180C 350F M4

Ingredients:

1 pigeon per person
8 oz (225 g) of streaky bacon, chopped
2 oz (50 g) of butter
Seasoned flour
1 lb (450 g) of button onions

1 lb (450 g) of button mushrooms
1 pt (570 ml) of brown stock
½ pt (275 ml) of red wine
Bouquet garni
Seasoning

Method:

Melt the butter and fry the bacon until crispy. Roll the pigeon in the seasoned flour and brown in the pan. Arrange the pigeons in an ovenproof casserole and add the wine, stock, button onions, bouquet garni and seasoning. Cook for 1 hour in the oven. Add the button mushrooms and cook for another ½ an hour. When cooked, thicken the juice with cornflour. Serve.

BRUSSELS WITH ALMOND

Lightly sauté almonds slivers in hot butter and a little salt. Pour over cooked Brussels and serve.

PINEAPPLE WITH RASPBERRIES

❀ ☆☆☆☆
PREPARATION TIME: 1 HOUR

Ingredients:

6 individual small pineapples	*8 oz (225 g) of sugar*
1 lb (450 g) of fresh or frozen raspberries	*1 cup of grenadine*
½ pt (275 ml) of water	

Method:

Boil the water and sugar together until a light syrup is formed. Cool and add the grenadine. Cut the top of the pineapple and put aside, then scoop out the pineapple flesh leaving the shell intact. Mix the pineapple with the raspberries and add the syrup. Put back into the shell and refrigerate. Serve with their lids.

✍ **To complete this menu: Carrots, Duchess Potatoes (See Page 260). Add two tablespoons of grated Parmesan cheese to the hot potatoes during creaming.**

BAR MITZVAH

(Hebrew: son of the commandment)

The Bar Mitzvah is a celebration within the Jewish family. It is the ceremony marking the initiation of a Jewish boy into the adult community at the age of thirteen. He assumes his full religious responsibilities and it is customary for him to read publicly from the 'Torah' in the synagogue for the first time; in some communities he leads the singing. A parallel ceremony (Bat Mitzvah) exists for girls.

Food prepared according to Jewish law is termed 'kosher'. Under Jewish law, only cud-chewing animals and poultry may be eaten. Those must be ritually slaughtered. Such meat as pork, horse, deer and game is excluded from the diet. Rabbit is forbidden as it is considered verminous. Milk and meat dishes are separated, so that no one eats milk or a dairy product with a meat dish.

Preparation of kosher meat and poultry is a simple task. The meat or poultry should be placed in a bowl, submerged in cold water and left to soak for half an hour. Every particle of blood must be washed from the meat before removing from the water. Place the meat on a wooden board, with holes in it, and lightly sprinkle with salt. Leave to drain for one hour, then rinse thoroughly in cold water.

Kosher meat can be bought from Jewish butcher shops; if in doubt do not hesitate to enquire.

FULL ENGLISH BREAKFAST

Fresh Fruits

Fruit Juices

Porridge or Cereals

Smoked Fish or Kedgerre

Bacon, Sausages, Kidneys,
Black Pudding, Mushrooms
Fried Bread or Toast
Egg to your Choice

Toast or Croissants

Tea & Coffee

PORRIDGE

❀ ☆☆☆
PREPARATION TIME: 5 MINUTES
COOKING TIME: 10-15 MINUTES

Ingredients:

½ pt (275 ml) water   1 level tsp salt
2 oz (50 g) medium oatmeal

Method:

Bring the water to the boil in a saucepan, add the salt then sprinkle in the oatmeal keeping the water on the boil, stir all the time. Simmer gently for 10 to 15 minutes stirring occasionally. The water can be substituted for milk.

KEDGEREE

❀ ☆☆☆ **Serves 8 persons**
PREPARATION TIME: 30 MINUTES
COOKING TIME: 10 MINUTES

Ingredients:

8 oz (225 g) of flaked cooked finnan-   8 oz (225 g) of rice
haddock   4 oz (110 g) of butter

3 hard-boiled eggs
Seasoning & cayenne

½ beaten eggs or ²/₃ tbs cream
Chopped parsley

Method:

Boil the rice in salted water, drain thoroughly. Melt the butter in a pan and add the fish and chopped hard-boiled eggs. Season well, add the rice and stir with a fork until very hot. Just before serving, add the eggs or cream and cook for 1 minute. Serve sprinkled with parsley. Kedgeree should have a creamy texture.

To complete this menu: Grill or bake the bacon, sausages and tomatoes. Fry the kidneys, black pudding, bread, and last of all, when the rest of the cooking is completed, the eggs. Eggs can also be baked in the oven, coddled, poached or scrambled. Pop the toast in the toaster, the croissants in the oven to warm and tuck in.

BRUNCH

The word brunch is derived from breakfast and lunch and is exceedingly popular in America and Australia.

Brunch takes place at around 11.30 to 12 noon. It is an ideal time to entertain friends for a leisurely meal.

There are numerous recipes to choose from, bear in mind they should not be too heavy. Our suggestions are:

Fresh Fruit Salad

Piperade

Bacon & Chanterelle Toasties

Spanish Omelette
&
Green Salad

Savoury Jacket Potatoes

Beverages: Bucks Fizz: (See Page 18), Pussy Foot: (See Page 20), Tea or Coffee.

FRUIT SALAD PLATE

✹ ☆☆☆
PREPARATION TIME: 20 MINUTES

Ingredients:
Fresh fruits in season   *Natural yoghurt*

Method:
Choose a selection of brightly coloured fruits, prepare and arrange them on individual plates and serve with the yoghurt.

PIPERADE

✹ ☆☆☆
PREPARATION TIME: 10 MINUTES
COOKING TIME: 10 MINUTES

Ingredients:

2 red sweet peppers	*Seasoning*
½ lb (225 g) of ripe tomatoes	*4 eggs*
1 shallot finely chopped	*2 tbs of milk*
2 cloves of crushed garlic	*Garlic croutons*
2 oz (50 g) of butter	

Method:

Shred the peppers and blanch. Scald and skin the tomatoes and chop roughly. Heat a pan, add the butter and when frothing add the shallot and garlic. When the shallot changes colour add the peppers, and after 5 minutes the tomatoes. Season well and leave to simmer. Meanwhile beat the eggs with a fork and add the milk and seasoning. When the peppers and tomatoes are soft, add the eggs, cook for a further 4 minutes.

Turn the piperade on to a hot dish and decorate with garlic croutons, garnish with finely chopped parsley.

BACON & CHANTERELLE TOASTIES

❀ ☆☆☆
PREPARATION TIME: 10 MINUTES
COOKING TIME: 10 MINUTES

Ingredients:

4 slices of toast	*Lemon juice*
8 rashers of smoked back bacon	*4 slices of Brie or Cheddar*
8 chanterelle mushrooms	*Cayenne pepper*
Butter	

Method:

Grill the bacon slices until cooked. Sauté the mushrooms in the butter and lemon juice. Arrange the bacon on the toast with the mushrooms on top. Place slices of cheese over the mushrooms and sprinkle with cayenne. Place under a hot grill until the cheese melts. Serve hot.

SPANISH OMELETTE

❀ ☆☆☆
PREPARATION TIME: 10 MINUTES
COOKING TIME: 10 MINUTES

Ingredients:

4 eggs	*Salt & pepper*
1 tbs of mixed diced vegetables i.e.	*1 clove of crushed garlic*
potato, green & red peppers, peas, onions	*2 tbs of butter*
& roughly chopped tomatoes	

Method:

Heat the butter in the saucepan and add the vegetables, garlic and seasoning. Cook gently until the vegetables are tender.

Beat the eggs with a fork and season. Heat a large omelette pan and add a knob of butter. Add the vegetables and eggs and stir around. Leave to set on a gentle to moderate heat, after it has set, put the frying pan in a hot oven or under a hot grill to finish off cooking. Serve on a hot plate, cut into slices, with a green salad.

Note: This omelette is usually between a half to three quarter inches thick, and is not served folded but flat.

SAVOURY JACKET POTATOES

✹ ☆☆☆
PREPARATION TIME: 10 MINUTES
COOKING TIME: 1 HOUR
OVEN TEMP: 200C 425F MARK 7

Ingredients:

4 medium sized potatoes	*4 slices of smoked back bacon cooked*
Grated Cheddar cheese	*crisply*
2 oz (50 g) cream cheese	*Seasoning*

Method:

Cook the potatoes until soft. Cut in half lengthways, and scoop out the insides. Mix with the ingredients and pile into the shells. Place under a hot grill and brown. Garnish with finely chopped parsley and serve hot.

Note: If you so happen to have a jar of Beluga caviar lying around your kitchen, serve it along with sour cream on top of the jacket potato.

BUFFET LUNCH

T here are two types of buffet luncheons: **finger buffets** and **fork buffets**.
   All the cold food can be laid out in advance, naturally covered to keep fresh. Plates, knives, forks and napkins are arranged on the food table or nearby. Ensure there are ample serving utensils and cruets. When you are ready, serve the hot food, and encourage everyone to start eating. (When entertaining on any scale a hot plate is exceedingly useful to keep food warm.)

Offer red and white wine with a selection of soft drinks, set these and the glasses away from the food.

Throughout the buffet clear away discarded plates, empty bottles and ashtrays to keep a clear, tidy table.

Beef Carbonnade
Chilli Con Carne
Smoked Trout
Rice or
Jacket Potatoes
Selection of Salads
Fresh Fruits
Gateaux
Cheese Board

Each of the following recipes will serve approximately fifteen persons.

BEEF CARBONNADE

❀ ☆☆☆ **This recipe can be cooked in advance and frozen.**
PREPARATION TIME: 30 MINUTES
COOKING TIME: 3 HOURS

Ingredients:

4 lbs (1.8 kg) of lean stewing steak
3 lbs (1.35 kg) of finely sliced onions
2 lbs (900 g) of sliced carrots
4 sticks of celery finely sliced
1 pt (570 ml) of brown ale

1½ pts (850 ml) of brown stock
Bouquet garni
1 tbs of tomato purée
Seasoned flour
Seasoning

Method:

Cube the stewing steak and roll the meat in the seasoned flour. Heat some fat in a large heavy-based casserole and brown the meat. Remove from the pan and put aside. Fry the onions, carrots and celery for approximately 5 minutes, add the meat and the rest of the ingredients. Bring to the boil, turn down the heat and simmer on the hob or place in a very low oven for about 3 hours until the meat is tender. Thicken if necessary with cornflour at the end of cooking.

CHILLI CON CARNE

✿ ☆☆☆
PREPARATION TIME: 20 MINUTES
COOKING TIME: 2 HOURS

Ingredients:

4 lbs (1.8 kg) of minced beef   *2 tbs of tomato purée*
2 large onions   *2 large cans of kidney beans*
2 large green peppers   *Black pepper & salt*
3 cloves of crushed garlic   *Chilli powder to your own taste*
4 large cans of tomatoes   *3 tbs olive oil*

Method:
Heat the oil in a heavy-based pan. Fry the garlic and finely chopped onion and green pepper. Add the meat with the tomatoes and tomato purée and red kidney beans. Season and add the chilli powder.
Cook for approximately 1½ to 2 hours.

SMOKED TROUT

Serve either whole smoked trout or smoked trout fillets, accompanied with brown bread and horseradish.

RICE

Rice can be cooked in advance and heated by pouring boiling water through it just before serving.

SALADS

Bean sprouts with kidney beans: Mix the bean sprouts with the kidney beans. Dress with French dressing with crushed garlic in it. Allow to marinate for 2 to 3 hours.
Lettuce and watercress: Toss together and serve with a dressing of your choice.
Rice and apricot salad: Mix together cooked rice, finely chopped onion, apricots, raisins and chopped parsley. Dress with the apricot juice, oil and vinegar, a little dried mustard, salt and black pepper.

✿ **To complete this menu: Gateaux, Fresh Fruits, and Cheese Board of your choice.**

AFTERNOON TEA

In our previous chapter on Tea & Tisanes we have thoroughly covered the various types of tea and how to prepare and serve them.

A traditional English afternoon tea includes:
A round of delicate sandwiches per person.
A plain or fruit scone served with strawberry jam and clotted Devonshire cream or whipped double cream.
A slice of Dundee cake.

You may wish to substitute the scone on a winter's day for a toasted buttered tea cake or crumpet.

SCONES

❀ ☆☆☆ **Makes approximately 10 Scones**
PREPARATION TIME: 15 MINUTES
COOKING TIME: 15 MINUTES
OVEN TEMPERATURE: 220C 425F MARK 7

Ingredients:

12 oz (350 g) self-raising flour
½ tsp salt
1½ oz (40 g) butter
1½ oz (40 g) caster sugar

1½ oz (40 g) dried fruit optional
1 egg
Milk to bind

Method:
Sift the flour and salt into a bowl. Rub in the butter until you have a fine breadcrumb appearance. Mix in the dried fruit and sugar. Beat the egg and gradually add to the mixture with a little milk until the pastry is soft and pliable, but not sticky.

On a floured surface roll the scone mixture to half an inch thick, cut out your scones with a fluted pastry cutter. Place on a greased baking sheet, brush the tops with milk and sprinkle with caster sugar, cook in a pre-heated oven for approximately 12 to 15 minutes until risen and golden brown. Cool on a wire cooling rack.

HIGH TEA

High tea developed with the industrial revolution in the nineteenth century. Hungry families returned home from work and a heavy meal was prepared at around 6.00 p.m. Today, high tea is ideally suited for young children, or before going out for the evening. Savoury dishes such as cauliflower cheese, macaroni cheese, tagliatelles with a cream sauce, savoury stuffed potatoes, and Welsh rarebit are ideally suited for this meal.

CAULIFLOWER CHEESE

❀ ☆☆☆ **Serves 2 Persons**
PREPARATION TIME: 15 MINUTES
COOKING TIME: 15 MINUTES
OVEN TEMP: 200C 400F M6

Ingredients:

1 small to medium cauliflower   *Grated cheese*
1 pt of cheese sauce (see page 307)

Method:
Par-cook the cauliflower, in boiling salted water, drain well upside down. Make the cheese sauce and pour it over the cauliflower. Sprinkle grated cheese over the cauliflower and place in the oven to brown. Serve.
Note: Finely chopped ham can be added to the cheese sauce.

MACARONI CHEESE

❀ ☆☆☆ **Serves 2 Persons**
PREPARATION TIME: 5 MINUTES
COOKING TIME: 25 MINUTES
OVEN TEMP: 200C 400F M6

Ingredients:

4 oz (110 g) of macaroni   *2 slices of toast*
1 pt (570 ml) of cheese sauce   *Sprig of parsley*
Grated cheese   *4 slices of tomato*

Method:
Cook the macaroni, drain well. Make the cheese sauce, (see page 307). Mix the macaroni into the cheese sauce and pour into an ovenproof dish. Garnish with tomato slices and grated Cheddar cheese and put into the oven until browned. Garnish with finely chopped parsley and triangles of toast.

TAGLIATELLES WITH CHAMPIGNONS SAUCE

❀ ☆☆☆ **Serves 2 Persons**

PREPARATION TIME: 5 MINUTES
COOKING TIME: 20 MINUTES

Ingredients:

6 oz (175 g) of tagliatelle egg, or verdi
4 oz (110 g) of finely sliced sautéed
mushrooms

½ pt (275 ml) of Béchamel sauce
2 tbs of grated Parmesan cheese
Seasoning

Method:

Cook the tagliatelle, drain well. Make the Béchamel sauce (see page 304) adding 2 tablespoons of Parmesan and the sautéed mushrooms. Season and mix well with the tagliatelle. Serve on warm plates with finely chopped parsley to garnish.

SAVOURY STUFFED POTATOES

❀ ☆☆☆ **Serves 2 Persons**
PREPARATION TIME: 10 MINUTES
COOKING TIME: 1 HOUR
OVEN TEMP: 200C 400F M6

Ingredients:

2 medium size potatoes
4 oz (110 g) of cream cheese
Finely chopped fresh chives

Finely chopped stick of celery lightly
sautéed
Seasoning

Method:

Scrub and prick the potatoes and cook in the oven until soft. Sauté the celery. Cut the potatoes in half length ways and scoop out leaving the skins intact. Mix all the ingredients together and put back into the skins. Sprinkle finely chopped parsley over the top and put back into the oven until nicely brown, approximately 15 minutes.

WELSH RAREBIT

❀ ☆☆☆ **Serves 2 Persons**
PREPARATION TIME: 10 MINUTES
GRILLING TIME: 10 MINUTES - MEDIUM GRILL

Ingredients:

2 slices of bread toasted on one side only
4 oz (110 g) of grated Cheddar cheese
1 oz (25 g) of butter
A good dash of Worcestershire sauce

A good sprinkle of cayenne pepper
A heaped tsp of dry mustard
A dash of Tabasco if desired

Method:

Toast the bread. Mix all the remaining ingredients together and divide between the two slices of bread on the untoasted side. Place under the grill until melted.

Note: Never attempt to cook the cheese too quickly as it will go stringy.

LATE NIGHT SUPPER

After the theatre or the opera, a late night supper comes into its own. It is usually served between 10.00 p.m. and midnight. It should be a light meal as presumably one goes to bed shortly afterwards. The food can be prepared in advance.

Consommé with French Bread
Soufflé Omelette with Fine Herbs
Fresh Fruit

CONSOMMÉ WITH FRENCH BREAD

Purchase a superior brand of consommé. Heat gently with a tablespoon of small pasta shells or julienne strips of vegetables. Add some sherry before serving.

SOUFFLÉ OMELETTE WITH FINE HERBS

✿ ☆☆☆ **Serves 4 persons**
PREPARATION: 5 MINUTES
COOKING TIME: 15 MINUTES
HOT GRILL
Equipment Required: A Large Frying Pan

Ingredients:

6 eggs   *Black pepper & salt, oil*
4 tbs of water   *4 tbs of finely chopped fresh herbs*

Method:
Separate the eggs, putting aside the whites. Add the yolks with the water and beat, season and add the fresh herbs. Whisk the egg whites until stiff and fluffy, gently fold with a metal spoon into the yoke mixture.
Pre-heat the grill. Meanwhile heat the oil in the frying pan (make sure the pan can fit under the grill) and add the omelette mixture. Cook the omelette but do not fold in half to complete cooking, place the frying pan under the hot grill and you will find the omelette will rise like a soufflé and brown. Serve immediately with a tossed green salad.

SPRING

SPRING DINNER FOR FOUR PERSONS

Scallops with Champagne Vinegar

Individual Knuckle End of Lamb
Roasted with Rosemary & Garlic
Small Baby Turnips, Lemon Carrots, New Potatoes, Spinach
Red Currant & Mint Sauce

Crème Brulée

White wine with the scallops:

⬚ Sancerre (Loire)

⬚⬚ Montagny (Côte Chalonnaise)

⬚⬚⬚ Chablis Vaudésir Grand cru

Red wine with the Lamb:

🍷 Côtes-de-Provence

🍷🍷 Château-La-Tour-Carnet (Haut Médoc, Bordeaux)

🍷🍷🍷 Château-Trottevielle (Saint Emilion, Bordeaux))

SCALLOPS WITH CHAMPAGNE VINEGAR

✱ ☆☆☆☆☆
PREPARATION TIME: 5 MINUTES
COOKING TIME: 20 MINUTES

Ingredients:

4 large scallops, or 10 small scallops per person	*Olive oil*
	Endives
1 cup of white wine	*18 cherry tomatoes*
1 bay leaf	*Fried croutons*
Black peppercorns	*Glove of garlic*
Champagne vinegar	*Pine kernels*

Method:

146

Heat the white wine, a cup of water, bay leaf and peppercorns in a saucepan. Add the scallops and poach gently for about 5 minutes until opaque. Drain well. In a pan fry the croûtons, pine kernels, and garlic until golden brown. Add the Champagne vinegar and olive oil to the scallops and quickly toss in the dressing. Season. Arrange the endives on plates with the scallops, croutons, pine kernels and cherry tomatoes. Dress with the juices from the pan. Serve.

INDIVIDUAL KNUCKLE END OF LAMB

The season for baby lamb is short, eat it at Easter. The flavour of the animal's flesh varies with its grazing ground. In Provence the lamb is said to taste of wild thyme, as the Welsh lamb is said to taste of Wales!

Ask the butcher for the small knuckle ends of small legs of lamb. They should be about six to eight inches long, one is served per person, making an extravagant but novel presentation.

❀ ☆☆☆☆☆
PREPARATION TIME: 5 MINUTES
COOKING TIME: 1½ HOURS
OVEN TEMPERATURE: 200C 400F M6

Ingredients:

4 knuckle ends of leg of lamb	*Lard*
Fresh rosemary	*Salt*
Fresh garlic	

Method:
Pre-heat the oven. Cut the fresh garlic into slivers and insert with a sharp knife point into the lamb flesh. Melt the lard in the roasting dish and quickly roll the knuckle ends around in the hot fat to seal the meat. Sprinkle the rosemary over the lamb with a little salt. Cover and cook for 1¼ hours. Remove the cover to allow the meat to brown at the end of cooking. Leave to stand with the oven off for about 15 minutes before serving. Pour the juices over the meat.

GRAPES CRÈME BRULÉE

❀ ☆☆☆☆
PREPARATION TIME: 10 MINUTES
CHILLING TIME: 2 HOURS
Special Equipment: 4 Ramekins

Ingredients:

¾ lb (350 g) of seeded white or black	*5 fl oz (350 ml) double cream*
grapes	*8 oz (225 g) demerara sugar*

Method:
Place the grapes in the bottom of the ramekins or a large soufflé dish. Whip the cream until stiff and coat the grapes. Sprinkle the sugar in a thick layer over the cream so that no cream

can be seen. Chill for a couple of hours. Place under a very hot grill until the sugar melts, which takes approximately 3 to 4 minutes. Chill in the refrigerator until ready to serve.

✋ **To complete this menu: Baby Turnips (See Page 266), Lemon Carrots (See Page 247), New Potatoes, Spinach (See Page 264), Red Currant or Mint Sauce (See Page 315).**

SPRING LUNCH FOR SIX PERSONS

Hot Vegetable Brochette
with Fresh Tomato Sauce

Poached Salmon Trout
with Holandaise Sauce
New Potatoes Garden Peas
Chicory Salad with Walnut Dressing

Oranges with Grand Marnier

White wine throughout the meal:
🏺 Château Simone, Palette (Provence)
🏺🏺 Château-La-Louvière (Graves, Bordeaux)
🏺🏺🏺 Puligny-Montrachet Les Folatières (Côte de Beaune, Burgundy)

HOT VEGETABLE BROCHETTE

❀ ☆☆☆
PREPARATION TIME: 15 MINUTES
COOKING TIME: 15 MINUTES
Special Equipment: 6 Metal or Wooden Skewers

Ingredients:

3 medium size courgettes	*12 small sweetcorn*
12 tomatoes	*2 onions*
12 mushrooms	*Brocoli spears*
2 red peppers	*Fresh parsley & marjoram*
2 green peppers	

Method:

Cut the vegetables into bite-size pieces. Other than the tomatoes, mushrooms and herbs put all the vegetables into a pan of cold water and bring to the boil, allow to boil for 2 minutes, strain. Alternate the vegetables on the skewers, brush with oil and sprinkle with fresh herbs. Lay on a baking sheet and cook in a hot oven or under the grill turning frequently. Serve hot with tomato sauce and black pepper.

FRESH TOMATO SAUCE

The sauce can be prepared in advance. **Never leave tomatoes in an aluminium pan as the acid will pick up the flavour of metal.**

❀ ☆☆☆
PREPARATION TIME: 15 MINUTES
COOKING TIME: 30 MINUTES

Ingredients:

1½ lbs (700 g) of fresh tomatoes	*1 stick of celery*
or 2 medium size tins of tomatoes	*1 mushroom*
1 large onion	*1 level tbs tomato purée*
4 rashers of streaky bacon	*Fresh parsley & majoram*
1 carrot	*Salt & black pepper*

Method:
Chop the bacon finely and fry. Chop the carrot, celery, mushroom and onion finely and add to the pan and fry gently until cooked, approximately 7 minutes. Add the skinned fresh or tinned tomatoes, tomato purée, fresh herbs and seasoning. Simmer gently for about 15 minutes. Sieve or liquidise the sauce if preferred.

CHICORY SALAD WITH NUT DRESSING

❀ ☆☆☆
PREPARATION TIME: 10 MINUTES

Ingredients:

6 heads of chicory	*20 walnut halves*
1 bunch of watercress	*2 oranges*

Method:
Discard any damaged outer leaves of the chicory and separate the leaves of the spears. Wash the watercress. Roughly chop the walnuts. With a sharp knife cut the skin and pith from the oranges, cut out the fleshy segments. Arrange the chicory leaves in a fan shape (either on one large serving plate or six individual side plates), lightly cover with the watercress and some orange segments. Sprinkle the chopped walnuts over the salad. Dress with French dressing, (see page 315) using a walnut oil.

✌ **To complete this menu: Poached Salmon Trout (See Page 97), Holandaise Sauce (See Page 311), Grand Marnier Oranges (See Page 283).**

SPRING DINNER FOR FOUR PERSONS

Artichokes Vinaigrette

Pork Fillet with Apricot & Walnut Stuffing
with Apricot Sauce
Broccoli, New Potatoes, Squashes

Compote of Summer Fruits

White or rosé wine throughout the meal:

Château de Fonscolombe (Provence)

Château-Vrai-Caillou (Entre-deux-Mers, Bordeaux))

Vougeot (Côte de Nuits, Burgundy)

STUFFED PORK FILLETS

✾✾ ☆☆☆ **The pork fillets can be prepared in advance.**
PREPARATION TIME: 20 MINUTES
COOKING TIME: 1 HOUR
OVEN TEMPERATURE: 200C 400F M6

Ingredients:

4 pork fillets
2 oz (50 g) of walnuts
4 oz (100 g) of apricots
4 oz (100 g) of fresh white breadcrumbs
Apricot Sauce:
1 large tin of apricot halves
1 chicken stock cube

2 oz (50 g) of margarine
1 medium onion finely chopped
1 tbs of finely chopped parsley
Salt & black pepper

Apricot brandy (optional)

Method:

Remove any muscle and fatty tissue from the pork fillets. With a sharp knife, carefully cut an incision into the pork fillets in half but not going right through, then cut sideways and open the pork fillet out. Lay on a board and with a meat tenderiser flatten the meat. Melt the margarine and sauté the onions until clear. Add the bread crumbs, finely chopped walnuts, parsley and apricots, season and bind together. Divide and spread the mixture between the fillets. Roll the fillets up and secure with cocktail sticks or string. Put into a roasting tin with some butter, cover and cook in the oven for approximately 1 hour.

Sauce:

Simmer together the apricots and chicken stock cube for about 10 minutes. Liquidise or sieve the sauce. Add the juices from the pan and brandy after the pork fillets are cooked.

Serving:

Slice the pork fillets into rounds and arrange on a plate. Pour the apricot sauce over them and garnish with apricot halves and watercress.

✍**To complete this menu: Artichokes Vinaigrette (See Page 240), Brocolli (See Page 245), Squashes (See Page 263), Summer Fruit Compote (See Page 272).**

SPRING MENU FOR FOUR PERSONS

Mushrooms with Pine Kernels

Stuffed Roast Veal
Braised Celery, Lemon Carrots, Brocoli

Lemon Poached Peaches

White or rosé wine throughout the menu:

🍶 Rosé d'Anjou

🍶🍶 Hermitage Blanc (Côtes du Rhone)

🍶🍶🍶 Chablis Montée de Tonnerre Premier Cru

STUFFED ROAST VEAL

✿ ☆☆☆☆☆
PREPARATION TIME: 30 MINUTES
COOKING TIME: 2 HOURS
OVEN TEMP: 220C 425F M7

Ingredients:

2½ lbs (1.15 kg) joint of best end neck of veal (boned)

Apricot & Walnut Stuffing:

12 oz (350 g) of fresh white bread crumbs	*2 tbs of finely chopped sultanas*
8 oz (225 g) of apricot halves (tinned)	*Salt & black pepper*
2 tbs of finely chopped parsley	*2 oz (50 g) of margarine*
2 tbs of finely chopped walnuts	*1 small onion finely chopped*

Method:

Ask the butcher to bone the veal joint. With a meat tenderiser flatten the meat as much as you can. Fry the onions in the margarine and then mix all the ingredients together. Spread the stuffing evenly over the inside of the meat. Roll the joint up tightly securing with string. Cover and roast in the oven until cooked, approximately 2 hours. Serve with gravy (see page 306).

✋ **To complete this menu: Mushrooms with Pine Kernels (See Page 255), Braised Celery (See Page 249), Lemon Carrots (See Page 247), Brocolli (See Page 245), Lemon Poached Peaches (See Page 286).**

SPRING MENU FOR FOUR PERSONS

Pears with Stilton

Guard of Honour
Deep Fried Courgettes, Roast Potatoes
Julienne of French Beans, Carrots

Lime Possett

Red wine throughout the meal:

🍷 Côtes-de-Blaye (Bordeaux)

🍷🍷 Château-Haut-Batailley (Pauillac, Bordeaux)

🍷🍷🍷 Château-Margaux (Bordeaux)

PEARS WITH STILTON

✿ ☆☆☆
PREPARATION TIME: 10 MINUTES
COOKING TIME, HOT GRILL: 10 MINUTES

Ingredients:

4 slices of white or brown bread	*Watercress*
2 ripe dessert pears	*Cayenne*
8 oz (225 g) of Stilton	

Method:

Toast one side of the bread. On the untoasted side arrange slices of Stilton to cover the bread completely. Peel, core, and halve the pears, slice finely lengthways and arrange in a fan on top of the Stilton. Put under a hot grill until the cheese has melted. Garnish with a sprinkle of cayenne and a sprig of watercress. Serve hot.

GUARD OF HONOUR

❀❀ ☆☆☆☆
PREPARATION TIME: 15 MINUTES
COOKING TIME: 1 HOUR
OVEN TEMP: 200C 400F M6

Ingredients:
Guard of honour: Give the butcher ample notice if you require him to prepare a guard of honour for you. I suggest three chops per person. Some butchers stuff the guard of honour, but it is better to make your own stuffing.

Stuffing:
12 oz (350 g) of fresh white bread crumbs	*Salt & black pepper*
1 large onion finely chopped	*3 oz (75 g) of butter*
1 heaped tbs of finely chopped parsley	*1 egg*
2 oz (50 g) of chopped dried mixed fruits	

Method:
Melt the butter and sauté the onion. Mix all the ingredients together until combined. Spoon the stuffing into the cavity of the guard of honour. Cover the tops of the bones with tin foil and the stuffing, roast in the oven.

Cook for approximately 1 hour, remove from the oven and take away the foil. The butcher will have supplied white hats for the bone tops and these should be put back on to serve. You may alternate the hats with small button onions or tomatoes. Garnish the guard with fresh watercress and pear boats filled with either mint or redcurrant jelly. Serve with fresh mint sauce (see page 315) or onion sauce (see page 308).

🖐 **To complete this menu: Deep Fried Courgettes (See Page 254), Julienne of French Beans & Carrots (See Page 243), Roast Potatoes (See Page 260), Lime Possetts (See Page 280).**

SUMMER

SUMMER LUNCH FOR FOUR PERSONS

Salade Niçoise

Chicken Breasts with Sage
New Potatoes, Baby Courgettes
Baby Carrots

Fruit Brochettes with Brandy Cream & Caramel
or Raspberry Sauce with Cream

White wines throughout the meal:

 Coteaux d'Aix-en-Provence

Saint-Véran-Les-Terres-Noires (Maconnais)

Criots-Bâtard-Montrachet (Côte de Beaune, Burgundy)

CHICKEN BREASTS WITH SAGE

❀ ☆☆☆
PREPARATION TIME: 10 MINUTES
COOKING TIME: 30 MINUTES

Ingredients:

8 boned skinned chicken breasts   ½ pt (275 ml) of water
16 fresh sage leaves   Seasoned flour
1 chicken stock cube   1oz (25g) butter
½ pt (275 ml) of white wine   2 tbs oil

Method:

Coat the chicken breast in the seasoned flour. Dissolve the stock cube in the water. Heat the butter and oil in a frying pan and lightly brown the breasts, add the stock, white wine and sage leaves. Simmer for 30 minutes. Serve the chicken breasts with the juices from the pan. Garnish with fresh sage leaves or watercress.

FRUIT BROCHETTES

❀ ☆☆☆☆
PREPARATION TIME: 30 MINUTES
Special Equipment: Skewers

Ingredients:
A selection of fresh fruits in season: kiwi, pineapple, strawberries, bananas, apple, orange, grapefruit, apricot, nectarine or peaches, star fruits, lychees, pear or any fruits that are easy to secure on the skewer. Remember when using banana, apple or pear to sprinkle the fruits with lemon to prevent discoloration.
4 oz (100 g) of caster sugar

Method:
Peel the fruits if necessary, and cut into bite size pieces. Arrange on the skewers. Melt the sugar in a pan over a gentle heat until it has turned golden brown. Lay the skewered fruits on a large plate and pour the caramel over them, this will create a hard crust. Chill in the refrigerator. Serve with fresh cream, brandy cream or fresh raspberry sauce.

BRANDY SAUCE

❀ ☆☆☆☆☆
PREPARATION TIME: 5 MINUTES

Ingredients:
10 fl oz (300 ml) of single cream   *2 fl oz (55 ml) of brandy*
2 oz (50 g) of demerara sugar

Method:
Gently heat the above ingredients together and serve warm. **Do Not Boil**.

FRESH RASPBERRY SAUCE

❀ ☆☆☆
COOKING TIME: 15 MINUTES

Ingredients:
1 lb (450 g) of fresh raspberries or frozen   *Squeeze of lemon juice*
2 oz (50 g) of icing sugar
1 cup of water

Method:
Heat the above ingredients together in a pan and gently simmer for about 15 minutes. Sieve the sauce, serve hot or cold.

✌ **To Complete this menu: Salade Niçoise (See Page 243), Boiled Baby Carrots (See Page 247), Boiled Baby Courgettes (See Page 254), Boiled New Potatoes.**

SUMMER MENU FOR FOUR PERSONS

Guacamole

Grilled Steak with Cranberry Sauce
Fried Potato Balls & Side Salad

Melon with Port

Dry White wine for the first course:
Bordeaux Blanc de Blanc
Château-Tanesse (Bordeaux)
Chablis Bougros Grand Cru

Red wine for the main course:
Beaujolais Villages
Lalande de Pomerol, Domaine de Caselis (Bordeaux)
Château-Nenin (Pomerol, Bordeaux)

GRILLED STEAK WITH CRANBERRY SAUCE

✿ ☆☆☆☆
PREPARATION TIME: 5 MINUTES
COOKING TIME: 20 MINUTES

Ingredients:

4 steaks	*Juice & zest of one orange*
8 oz (225 g) of cranberries	*Juice of one lemon*
3 oz (75 g) of sugar	*½ beef stock cube*
1 glass of port	*Watercress*

Method:
Grill or fry the steaks to your preference. Add the rest of the ingredients together in another pan, boil for about 10 minutes. Serve with the steak. Garnish with watercress.

To Complete this menu: Guacamole (See Page 269), Fried Potato Balls (See Page 261), Melon With Port (See Page 283).

SUMMER LUNCH FOR FOUR PERSONS

Sliced Avocado & Egg Salad

Baked Halibut
Hollandaise Sauce
French Beans with Hazelnuts, Stuffed Tomatoes
New Potatoes with Chive Cream

Fruit Salad with Champagne

White wine throughout the meal:

⚏ Bourgogne Blanc

⚏⚏ Coteaux-du-Lyonnais

⚏⚏⚏ Corton Clos du Roi (Côte de Beaune, Burgundy)

SLICED AVOCADO & EGG SALAD

✹ ☆☆☆
PREPARATION TIME: 10 MINUTES

Ingredients:

2 ripe avocados
4 hard boiled eggs

French dressing (see page 315)
Endives & salad leaves

Method:
Finely slice the hard boiled eggs. Peel the avocados and slice crossways. Arrange the salad leaves on a plate and fan the advocados and egg alternately. Dress.

BAKED HALIBUT

✹ ☆☆☆☆☆
PREPARATION TIME: 10 MINUTES
COOKING TIME: 20 MINUTES

Ingredients:

4 halibut steaks
¼ pt (150 ml) of milk
¼ pt (150 ml) of water
Seasoning

Parsley
1 shallot
1 small carrot

Method:

Butter an ovenproof dish large enough to hold the four halibut steaks. Add the rest of the ingredients and cover. Bake in the oven until cooked approximately 25 minutes, the juices from the fish will have the appearance of buttermilk. Drain, garnish with parsley, and serve.

FRUIT SALAD WITH CHAMPAGNE

❀ ☆☆☆☆☆
PREPARATION TIME: 30 MINUTES

Ingredients:
Any fruit of your choice.

Syrup:

6 oz (175 g) of sugar	*2 glasses of champagne*
1 pt (570 ml) of water	*2 tbs of brandy*
Juice of one lemon	

Method:

Boil the above ingredients (excluding the brandy and Champagne) until a light syrup has formed. When the syrup has cooled add the fruits of your choice, Champagne and brandy.

✍ **To complete this menu: Hollandaise Sauce (See Page 311), French Beans with Hazelnuts (See Page 244), Stuffed Tomatoes (See Page 292), New Potatoes with Snipped Chives & Soured Cream.**

SUMMER MENU FOR FOUR PERSONS

Melon Balls with Parma Ham

Lasagna
Orange Avocado & Endive Salad

Branded Figs

Rosé or red throughout the meal:

♉ Tavel Rosé (Provence)

♉♉ Château-Laville-Bertrou (Minervois, Languedoc)

MELON BALLS WITH PARMA HAM

❀ ☆☆☆
PREPARATION TIME: 15 MINUTES
Special Equipment: Melon Baller

Ingredients:

2 ripe melons   *Endive leaves*
6 oz (175 g) Parma ham

Method: Arrange the endive leaves on individual plates. Scoop melon balls and divide between the plates. Chill. **Just before serving:** cut the ham into fine strips and lay over the melon

LASAGNA

❀ ☆☆☆
PREPARATION TIME: 15 MINUTES
COOKING TIME: 1½ HOURS
OVEN TEMP: 200C 400F M6

Ingredients:

Lasagna sheets (verdi or egg)   *1 green pepper finely chopped*
l pt (570 ml) cheese sauce (see page 307)   *1 tbs of tomato purée*
1 lb (450 g) of ground beef   *4 oz (110 g) of mushrooms finely sliced*
1 x 15 oz (500 g) tin of chopped tomatoes   *Salt & black pepper*
1 clove of crushed garlic   *Fresh or dried mixed herbs*
1 medium onion finely chopped

Method:
Sauté the onions and garlic in a tablespoon of oil. Add the green pepper and ground beef, fry gently until brown. Add the tomatoes, tomato purée, mushrooms, seasoning and herbs and simmer for 30 minutes. Butter an oblong ovenproof dish and pour a layer of sauce over the bottom. Lay sheets of lasagna to cover this. Arrange alternate layers of meat sauce, lasagana and cheese sauce, finish off with a cheese sauce layer, sprinkle grated cheese over the top. Cook in the oven for about 30 minutes until browned. Serve.

ORANGE AVOCADO & ENDIVE SALAD

❀ ☆☆☆
PREPARATION TIME: 15 MINUTES

Ingredients:

4 oranges   *Endive leaves*
1 avocado   *French dressing (see page 315)*

Method:

Cut the skin, pith and membrane away from the oranges and remove the segments. Arrange on individual plates the endive leaves, avocado and oranges. Dress.

BRANDIED FIGS

❀ ☆☆☆☆☆
PREPARATION TIME: 10 MINUTES
CHILLING TIME: 1 HOUR

Ingredients:

1 large tin of figs in syrup
¼ tsp ground cinnamon
1 tbs of grated orange zest
4 tbs of brandy

2 tbs of dry sherry
Whipped cream
Flaked toasted almonds to garnish

Method:

Heat gently the cinnamon, orange zest, brandy and dry sherry, do not boil. Drain the figs, arrange them in a shallow serving dish. Pour the hot marinade over them along with 6 tablespoons of syrup. Allow the figs to cool for at least 1 hour. Immediately before serving spoon a little whipped cream over the figs and garnish with the toasted almonds.

SUMMER MENU FOR SIX PERSONS

Gazpacho Soup

Grilled Fillet Steak
with *Maître d'Hôtel Butter*
Tossed Green Salad with Artichokes & Avocado

Hot Strawberries with Green Peppercorn

We do not recommend wine with the first course. Red wine for the main course:

Ⅰ Côte-de-Beaune-Village (Burgundy)

ⅠⅠ Chassagne-Montrachet (Burgundy)

ⅠⅠⅠ La Tâche, Domaine Romanée-Conti (Côte de Nuits, Burgundy)

GAZPACHO SOUP

❀ ☆☆☆
PREPARATION TIME: 10 MINUTES

CHILLING TIME: 2 HOURS OR MORE
Special Equipment: Liquidiser or Food Processor

Ingredients:

1 cup of fresh white bread crumbs	*1 green pepper*
1 tbs red wine vinegar	*1 medium sized onion*
2 cloves of garlic	*4 tbs of salad oil*
Salt & black pepper	*½ pt (275 ml) of tomato juice*
½ cucumber	*1 lb (450 g) of tomatoes skinned*

Method:

Place all the ingredients in a liquidiser or food processor and blend. Check the seasoning, add a little more tomato juice if you feel the consistency is not quite to your liking. It is optional at this stage whether or not you sieve the soup. Chill in the refrigerator. Garnish with croutons of toasted bread or finely snipped fresh chives.

GRILLED FILLET STEAK

❀ ☆☆☆☆
PREPARATION TIME: 5 MINUTES
COOKING TIME: STEAK CHART (See Page 211)

Ingredients:

4 x 6/8 oz (175-225 g) fillet steaks	*Garnish with watercress & grilled*
Clarified butter (see page 299)	*tomatoes*
Maître d'hôtel butter (see page 299)	

Method:

Grill the steaks and when they are piping hot from the grill, arrange two to three slices of maître d'hôtel butter on the top. Garnish and serve.

TOSSED GREEN SALAD WITH ARTICHOKES & AVOCADOS

❀ ☆☆☆
PREPARATION TIME: 10 MINUTES

Ingredients:

1 ripe avocado	*1 lettuce heart*
Juice of one lemon	*Endive leaves*
1 tin of artichoke hearts	*French dressing (see page 315)*

Method:

Peel and halve the avocados, slice thinly and cover with lemon juice. Drain and rinse the artichoke hearts. Arrange in a bowl with the lettuce and endives. Dress.

✤ **To complete this menu: Hot Strawberries with Green Peppercorns (See Page 291).**

LATE SUMMER MENU FOR TWO PERSONS

Cheese Choux Agriette
with Horseradish Sauce

Roast Grouse
Salsify, Roast Potatoes, Crispy Fried Leeks

Star Fruits & Kiwis with Cointreau

Red wine for the main course:

Hautes-Côtes-de-Nuits (Burgundy)

Chevrey-Chambertin (Côte de Nuits, Burgundy)

Chambertin Clos de Bèze (Côte de Nuits, Burgundy)

CHEESE CHOUX AGRIETTE

❀ ☆☆☆
PREPARATION TIME: 10 MINUTES
DEEP FAT FRYING: 5 MINUTES
FAT TEMPERATURE: 190C

Ingredients:

7½ fl oz (220 ml) of water	*1 oz (25 g) of Parmesan cheese or grated*
3 oz (75 g) of butter or margarine	*gruyère*
3 oz (75 g) of flour	*3 eggs*

Horseradish Sauce:

4 tbs of creamed horseradish	*10 fl oz (300 ml) of single cream*

Method:
Put the water and fat into a saucepan and bring to a rapid boil. Draw aside and immediately add the sifted flour. Beat vigorously until a smooth paste has formed and it leaves the side of the pan clean. Beat in the cheese, and leave to cool until you can lay your hand against the side of the pan without burning it. Whip the eggs, adding a little at a time, beating thoroughly. You may not need to add all the egg, the mixture should be glossy and able to hold its shape. Heat the fat and add two to three large teaspoons of mixture at a time until they swell and are cooked. They should be golden brown and have trebled in size. Place on absorbent kitchen paper and keep warm. Add the horseradish and cream together heating gently, serve with the aigrettes.

ROAST GROUSE

✾ ☆☆☆☆☆
PREPARATION TIME: 10 MINUTES
COOKING TIME: 30 MINUTES
OVEN TEMP: 200C 400F M6

Ingredients:

1 grouse per person   *Butter*
4 slices of streaky bacon   *Lemon juice & cayenne pepper*

Method:

Cover the birds with bacon slices and arrange in a roasting tin. Spread butter over the breast, sprinkle lemon juice and cayenne pepper. Cover and roast in a preheated oven for 20 minutes. Remove the cover and roast for a further 10 minutes allowing the breast to brown. Serve the grouse on a fried croûte, slitting each side of the breast bone, pour game gravy in and around. Garnish with crumbs and watercress. Serve with cranberry sauce or redcurrant jelly.

CRUMBS

Ingredients:

12 oz (350 g) of fresh white crumbs   *4 oz (100g) of butter*
Salt & black pepper

Method:

Melt the butter in an ovenproof dish, add the crumbs and seasoning and give them a good stir. Put back in the oven and allow to brown and become crisp. Keep stirring the crumbs to make sure they are evenly browned. Cook until golden brown and crisp.

STAR FRUIT & KIWI WITH COINTREAU

✾ ☆☆☆☆
PREPARATION TIME: 10 MINUTES

Ingredients:

1 star fruit, 2 kiwis   *¾ pt of water*
3 oz of sugar   *2 tbs of Cointreau*

Method:

Dissolve the sugar in the water to form a syrup, leave to cool and add the Cointreau. Peel and thinly slice the kiwis. Slice the star fruit and arrange alternately with the kiwis slightly overlapping each other around the perimeter of the dessert plate. Pour the syrup over the fruits and serve.

✍ **To complete this menu: Salsify With Mousseline Sauce (See Page 263), Crispy Fried Leaks (See Page 252), Game gravy (See Page 306).**

AUTUMN

AUTUMN MENU FOR FOUR PERSONS

Devilled Whitebait

Roast Partridge
Crumbs & Bread Sauce
Root Vegetable Purée, Brussels with Chestnuts
Roast Potatoes

Figs Cléopatra

White wine with the first course:

Bourgogne-Aligoté (Burgundy)

Château-La-Tour-Martillac (Graves, Bordeaux)

Corton, Clos des Cortons Faiveley (Côte de Beaune, Burgundy)

Red wines for the main course:

Bourgogne-Passetoutgrains (Burgundy)

Château-Grand-Puy-Lacoste (Pauillac, Bordeaux)

Château-Bel-Air-Marquis-d'Aligre (Margaux, Bordeaux)

DEVILLED WHITEBAIT

❀ ☆☆☆
PREPARATION TIME: 5 MINUTES
COOKING TIME: 5 MINUTES
Special Equipment: Deep Fat Frying Equipment

Ingredients:

16 oz (550 g) of whitebait	*Parsley*
Seasoned flour	*Lemon*
Cayenne pepper	

Method:
Season the flour and add cayenne. Toss the whitebait in the flour until evenly coated. Heat the fat so that it browns a piece of bread within 20 seconds, or if you are using a electric fryer follow the manufacturer's instructions. Submerge the whitebait in the fat and cook for

approximately 4 to 5 minutes until crispy and golden. Drain on absorbent kitchen paper.
Deep fry some parsley sprigs for about 2 seconds, serve with a lemon wedge and parsley.

ROAST PARTRIDGE

❀❀ ☆☆☆☆☆
PREPARATION TIME: 10 MINUTES
COOKING TIME: 30 MINUTES
OVEN TEMP: 200C 400F M6

Ingredients:
1 partridge per person   *Butter*
4 slices of bacon
Crumbs:
12 oz (350 g) of fresh white bread crumbs   *Salt & black pepper*
4 oz (100 g) of butter

Method:
Arrange the birds in a roasting tin and lay the bacon slices over the breasts. Cook in the oven
basting with butter. Serve with bread sauce (see page 314), crumbs, and game gravy (see
page 306). Whilst the birds are roasting melt the butter in an oven proof dish, add the
crumbs and seasoning and give them a good stir. Put back in the oven and allow to brown
and become crisp. Keep stirring the crumbs every 5 minutes to make sure they are evenly
browned. Cook until golden brown and crisp. Garnish the partridge with the crumbs and
some watercress.

✍ **To complete this menu: Brussels with Chestnust (See Page 245), Root Vegetable
Purée (See Page 265), Figs Cleopatra (See Page 276).**

AUTUMN LUNCH FOR FOUR PERSONS

Warm Chicken Liver Salad

Dover Sole with Salmon Mousseline
Spinach, Baked Celery, Duchess Potatoes

Poached Pears with Almonds

White wine throughout the meal:
🍶 Anjou Blanc
🍶🍶 Château Olivier (Graves, Bordeaux)
🍶🍶🍶 Château Fieuzal (Graves, Bordeaux)

WARM CHICKEN LIVER SALAD

❀ ☆☆☆ **This menu can be prepared in advance.**
PREPARATION TIME: 10 MINUTES
COOKING TIME: 15 MINUTES

Ingredients:

1 lb (450 g) of chicken livers   *Endives or salad leaves*
Oil & butter for frying   *Cherry tomatoes*
1 glove of crushed garlic   *Finely chopped parsley*
Seasoned flour   *Champagne vinegar*

Method:
Clean the chicken livers and remove any muscle tissue, toss in the seasoned flour. Heat the oil and butter in a frying pan large enough to accommodate the livers, add the crushed garlic and the chicken livers, sauté until cooked, approximately 7 minutes. Add a couple of tablespoons of Champagne vinegar and heat quickly. Arrange the salad leaves on individual plates with the chicken livers and garnish with cherry tomatoes and parsley. Divide the liquid from the pan equally between the plates. Serve warm.

DOVER SOLE WITH SALMON MOUSSELINE

❀❀ ☆☆☆☆☆
PREPARATION TIME: 20 MINUTES
COOKING TIME: 25 MINUTES
OVEN TEMP: 180C 350F M4
Salmon mousseline has to be made at least 12 hours before use. Ask the fishmonger to fillet and skin the sole. This menu does require advanced preparation.

Ingredients:

4 Dover soles (filleted)   *¼ pt (150 ml) of milk*
¼ pt (150 ml) of white wine
Salmon Mousseline:
8 oz (225 g) of fresh salmon skinned &   *1 egg white*
bonned   *A pinch of grated nutmeg*
5 fl oz (150 ml) of double cream   *Seasoning*

Method:
Liquidise the salmon, then add the double cream, egg white and seasonings and liquidise further to a smooth mixture. Place in the refrigerator to chill overnight.
Divide and spread the mousseline between the sole fillets. Roll up the sole fillets and place in a buttered ovenproof dish. Pour the white wine and milk over the sole, cover and cook in a preheated oven for 20 minutes.
Drain the fillets from the stock and thicken the remaining juices with cornflour to a coating consistency. Arrange the fillets on warm individual serving plates and pour the sauce over the fish. Garnish with a sprig of parsley and a lemon wedge. Serve immediately.

✍ **To complete this menu: Spinach (See Page 264), Baked Celery (See Page 249), Duchess Potatoes (See Page 260), Poached Pears With Almonds (See Page 288).**

AUTUMN DINNER FOR FOUR PERSONS

Flambé Prawns with Fennel

Beef Wellington
**Lemon Carrots, Cauliflower Polonaise,
Red Wine Sauce**

Ginger & Melon Baskets

Dry white wine for the first course:

Ⓧ Cassis Blanc

ⓍⓍ Château-de-la-Roche-aux-Moines-Savennières (Loire)

ⓍⓍⓍ Domaine de Chevalier (Graves, Bordeaux)

Red wine for the main course:

Ⓨ Beaujolais Nouveau

ⓎⓎ Morgon (Beaujolais)

ⓎⓎⓎ Romanée-St-Vivant (Côte de Nuits, Burgundy)

FLAMBE PRAWNS WITH FENNEL

❀ ☆☆☆☆☆
COOKING TIME: 5 MINUTES

Ingredients:
12 oz (350 g) peeled prawns   *1 glove of garlic (crushed)*
2 oz (50 g) butter   *Brandy*
1 heaped tbs finely chopped fennel

Method:
Melt the butter, add the garlic and prawns and quickly heat through. Add the fennel and brandy, flambé. Serve immediately with crusty French bread.

BEEF WELLINGTON

❀❀❀ ☆☆☆☆☆ **Beef Wellington is served rare.**
PREPARATION TIME: 1 HOUR
RESTING TIME: 1 HOUR
COOKING TIME: ¾ HOUR

Ingredients:
2 lbs (900 g) of fillet of beef   *1 lb (450 g) puff pastry*
1 medium sized onion   *1 egg*
8 oz (225 g) mushrooms

Advanced Preparation:
Chill the pastry. Trim the fat from the fillet and cook in a preheated oven at 220C/425F/Gas mark 7 for approximately 10 minutes. Ensure the meat is cool (warm meat will cause the pastry to melt when preparing). Finely chop the onions and mushrooms and sauté in a knob of butter, leave to cool. Roll the pastry to an oblong three and a half times the width of the fillet and 7" (18 cm) longer in length. Leave the pastry to rest in the refrigerator for approximately 1 hour.

Method:
Lay the pastry on a floured surface and lay the cold pre-cooked fillet in the centre of the pastry. Carefully drain any liquid from the mushrooms and onions, (put to one side for use in the sauce) and place evenly on the fillet. Lightly beat the egg and with a pastry brush dampen the edges of the pastry. Make a neat parcel ensuring that the fillet is totally encased. Put on a damp baking sheet making sure that the seam is underneath. Do not be afraid to trim any excess pastry to make it look presentable. Glaze the pastry and decorate. Cook in a preheated oven at 425F/220C/M7 for 35 minutes until the pastry is golden brown. Garnish with watercress, baked whole tomatoes, or lightly sautéed button mushrooms.

✍ **To complete this menu: Lemon Carrots (See Page 247), Cauliflower Polonaise (See Page 248), Red Wine Sauce (See Page 305), Ginger & Melon Baskets (See Page 282).**

AUTUMN MENU FOR FOUR PERSONS

Grapefruit & Watercress Salad

Wild Duck with Orange Salad
Jerusalem Artichokes, Courgettes, Baby Carrots
Roast Potatoes

Paris-Brest

White wine for the first course:

🍷 Premières Côtes-de-Bordeaux (Bordeaux)
🍷🍷 Chablis Vaillons Premier Cru
🍷🍷🍷 Meursault Charmes (Côte de Beaune, Burgundy)

Red wine for the main course:

Ṭ Crozes Hermitage (Côtes du Rhône)

ṬṬ Château-Patache-d'Aux (Medoc, Bordeaux)

ṬṬṬ Château-du-Tertre (Margaux, Bordeaux)

GRAPEFRUIT & WATERCRESS SALAD

❀ ☆☆☆
PREPARATION TIME: 20 MINUTES

Ingredients:

2 pink grapefruits
1 bunch of watercress
8 oz (225 g) of shelled prawns

Seafood dressing (Marie Rose dressing)
(see page 313)

Method:
Prepare the grapefruit removing the skin, pith and membrane. Arrange on a plate with the prawns and watercress. Dress.

WILD DUCK

❀ ☆☆☆☆
PREPARATION TIME: 15 MINUTES
COOKING TIME: 45 MINUTES
OVEN TEMP: 400F 200C M6

Ingredients:

One wild duck for two persons
Butter, cayenne pepper
Orange Salad:
4 oranges
2 tbs finely chopped parsley

Lemon juice
Watercress to garnish

French dressing (see page 315)

Method:
Arrange the duck in a roasting tin and cover with butter, sprinkle with cayenne and lemon juice. Loosely cover and put into the oven for 30 minutes. Remove the cover for the last 15 minutes. Wild duck is served rare, when skewered breast blood will appear. Garnish with watercress.
Orange salad:
Remove the skin, pith and membrane from the oranges and dissect the segments from the membrane. Mix with the parsley and French dressing, chill in the refrigerator.

✌ **To complete this menu: Jerusalem Artichokes (See Page 240), Courgettes (See Page 254), Paris-Brest (See Page 123).**

AUTUMN MENU FOR FOUR PERSONS

Eggs Provençale Style

Stir-Fry Chicken
Egg Fried Rice

Flambée Bananas

Rosé throughout the meal:

Côtes-du-Rhône, Rosé

Lirac, Rosé

EGGS PROVENÇALE

✹ ☆☆☆
PREPARATION TIME: 15 MINUTES
COOKING TIME: 10 MINUTES
OVEN TEMP: 200C 400F M6
Special Equipment: Ramekins

Ingredients:
4 eggs
Provençale Sauce:
1 small onion finely chopped   *1 tsp of tomato purée*
1 clove of garlic crushed   *Finely chopped parsley*
8 oz (225 g) of chopped tomato   *Basil & thyme*

Method:
Lightly sauté the onion and garlic in olive oil, add the rest of the ingredients and simmer for about 10 minutes. Meanwhile butter the ramekins and break an egg into each one, bake in the oven for about 4 minutes. Pour a little of the sauce over each egg and put back in the oven until the egg is set. Garnish with parsley. Serve hot with French bread.

STIR FRY CHICKEN

✹ ☆☆☆
PREPARATION TIME: 10 MINUTES
MARINADING TIME: 2 HOURS
COOKING TIME: 7 MINUTES

Special Equipment: Wok

Ingredients:

3 chicken breasts   1 red pepper cut in half inch cubes
16 button mushrooms halved   2 oz (50 g) of fresh bean sprouts
1 green pepper cut in half-inch cubes   4 spring onions cut in quarter inch length

Marinade:

1 tbs of oil   1 tbs of soya sauce
2 tbs of white wine   1 tbs of oyster sauce
1 tbs of honey   Sprinkle of cayenne pepper
1 medium finely chopped onion

Method:

Combine all the marinade ingredients together. Cut the chicken breasts into 1" (2.5cm) cubes and marinate for at least 2 hours. Heat one tablespoon of oil in the wok. Cook half of the chicken for 5 minutes, remove from the wok, put aside, then add the remaining chicken and cook for 5 minutes. Remove the chicken from the wok and keep warm. Add one more tablespoon of oil to the wok and stir-fry the peppers for 2 minutes. Add the mushrooms and cook for 1 minute then the bean sprouts and spring onions and cook for a further minute. Add the chicken and remaining marinade. Bring to the boil and serve.

EGG FRIED RICE

❀ ☆☆☆
PREPARATION TIME: 5 MINUTES
COOKING TIME: 10 MINUTES

Ingredients:

8 oz (225 g) of cooked rice   2 spring onions finely chopped
1 egg   1 tbs of oil
1 tbs of peas   ½ oz (10 g) of butter

Method:

Heat the oil and butter in a frying pan until foaming. Break the egg into the pan and break up with a spatula. Allow the egg to cook, browning slightly (it should have the appearance of a fried egg but broken up). Add the rice and stir letting the bottom stick so that it browns lightly between each stir. Add the peas and onions and keep browning and stirring. Serve.

FLAMBÉE BANANAS

❀ ☆☆☆
PREPARATION TIME: 10 MINUTES
COOKING TIME: 15 MINUTES
OVEN TEMPERATURE: 200C 400F M6

Ingredients:

4 bananas   4 tbs brandy
2 tbs brown sugar   2 oz (50 g) butter
Lemon juice

Method:

Heat the butter in a frying pan until foaming, add the sugar and lemon juice. Peel the bananas and add to the pan, heat quickly. When they are warmed through add the brandy. Flambé, serve immediately with single cream.

AUTUMN DINNER FOR FOUR PERSONS

Deep Fried Camembert

Poussins en Papillote
Sir Fry Mixed Vegetable, Jacket Potatoes

Green Fruit Salad

Light dry white wine throughout the meal:

Riesling Reserve (Alsace)

Château d'Arlay (Jura)

Morey-Saint-Denis (Côte de Nuits, Burgundy)

DEEP FRIED CAMEMBERT

❀ ☆☆☆
FREEZING TIME: 1 HOUR
COOKING TIME: 6 MINUTES

Ingredients:

8 x 1 oz (25 g) portions of firm Camembert
2 tbs flour, pinch cayenne pepper
2 eggs beaten

2 oz (50 g) breadcrumbs
Oil for deep frying
4 dessert apples (cored & quartered)

Method:

Freeze the portions of Camembert for one hour. Add the cayenne to the flour and roll each Camembert portion in the flour, then the beaten egg and then the breadcrumbs. Heat the oil in a deep fryer to 180C/350F or until a bread cube browns in 60 seconds. Fry the Camembert portions for 30 seconds or until golden brown. Drain on absorbent kitchen paper and garnish with the apple. Serve immediately.

POUSSINS EN PAPILLOTE

❀❀❀ ☆☆☆

MARINATING TIME: 2 HOURS
PREPARATION TIME: 20 MINUTES
COOKING TIME: 40 MINUTES
OVEN TEMP: 180C 350F M4

Ingredients:

4 poussins
4 tbs of olive oil
Ground black pepper
8 oz (225 g) thinly slice mushrooms
Juice of half a lemon
4 oz (110 g) finely chopped onions
3 tbs of finely chopped chives

3 tbs of finely chopped parsley
¼ tsp dried sage
½ tsp of dried basil
2 tbs of brandy
Salt
1 oz (25 g) of butter
8 slices of streaky bacon

Method:

Rub each poussin with olive oil and season with the black pepper. In a bowl mix the mushroom, lemon juice, onion, chives, sage, basil and parsley. Moisten with the remaining olive oil and the brandy. Mix well and season to taste. Arrange the poussin in a shallow dish and spoon the mixture over them and marinate for 2 hours. Cut four circles of foil each large enough to hold a poussin. In a frying pan melt the butter and sauté the poussin for 2 to 3 minutes until evenly brown all over. Place in the centre of the foil, lay two slices of bacon over each poussin and divide the marinade between the four poussins. Seal the foil carefully around the poussin and place the papillotes on baking sheets and bake for 30 minutes until tender. Arrange on a heated serving dish opening the foil a little to reveal the poussin, garnish with watercress and tomato wedges.

GREEN FRUIT SALAD

❀ ☆☆☆
PREPARATION TIME: 20 MINUTES

Ingredients:

1 lb (450 g) of seedless green grapes
1 olga melon
2 grapefruits
1 star fruit, 4 firm kiwis
Syrup:
6 oz (175 g) of sugar
1 pt (570 ml) of water

8 halves greengages
½ lb (225 g) of ripe gooseberries, topped
& tailed
Any green coloured fruits

Juice of lemon

Method:

Boil the sugar, water and lemon juice until a light syrup has formed. Set aside to cool. Prepare the fruits, removing any stones and chopping into bite-size pieces. Add to the syrup and serve.

✎ **To complete this menu: Stir fry mixed vegetables of your choice.**

WINTER

WINTER LUNCHEON FOR FOUR PERSONS

King Prawns with Mayonnaise

Roast Beef
Baby Turnips, Roast Potatoes, Braised Cabbage with Bacon

Pears in Grenadine

White wine for the first course:

Entre-deux-Mers, Haut-Benauge (Bordeaux)

Pouilly-Fuissé, Vieilles Vignes (Maconnais)

Ladoix (Burgundy)

Red Wine for the main course:

Château-Potensac (Medoc, Bordeaux)

Château-Camensac (Haut-Medoc, Bordeaux)

Château-Latour (Pauillac, Bordeaux)

KING PRAWNS WITH MAYONNAISE

✿ ☆☆☆☆☆
PREPARATION TIME: 20 MINUTES

Ingredients:

4 king prawns per persons   *Mayonnaise*
Crushed ice   *Caviar or lumpfish*

Method:
Peel the prawns being careful to leave the head on and a small portion of the tail. Make the mayonnaise (see page 312). Arrange the prawns on a bed of crushed ice, and serve with mayonnaise mixed with caviar or lumpfish.

ROAST BEEF

❀ ☆☆☆☆☆
PREPARATION TIME: 5 MINUTES
COOKING TIME: SEE CHART ON PAGE 211

Ingredients:
2½-3 lbs (1.15-1.35 kgs) joint sirloin beef

PEARS IN GRENADINE

❀ ☆☆☆
PREPARATION TIME: 10 MINUTES
COOKING TIME: 20 MINUTES

Ingredients:

1 pear per person	*¼ pt (150 ml) of grenadine syrup*
1 pt (570 ml) of water	*Juice of half a lemon*
8 oz (225 g) of granulated sugar	*Juice of one orange*

Method:
Boil the water, sugar, lemon and orange juice together. Add the grenadine syrup, peeled pears and simmer gently until tender. Serve hot or cold.

☝ **To complete this menu: Baby Turnips (See Page 266), Roast Potatoes (See Page 260), Braised Cabbage With Bacon (See Page 246).**

WINTER DINNER FOR FOUR PERSONS

Pears with Roquefort

Roast Pheasant
Leeks Béchamel, Carrots à la Forcalquier,
Brussels Sprouts, Game Chips

Armoretti Biscuits in Red Wine

Red wine throughout the meal:

❦ Côtes-du-Vivarais (Côtes du Rhône)
❦❦ Carruades (Pauillac, Bordeaux)
❦❦❦ Vosne-Romanée-Suchots (Côte de Nuits, Burgundy)

PEARS WITH ROQUEFORT

❀ ☆☆☆ **The dressing can be made in advance.**
PREPARATION TIME: 30 MINUTES

Ingredients:

4 ripe dessert pears   Watercress
8 oz (225 g) of Roquefort cheese   1 tomato
10 fl oz (300 ml) of single cream

Method:
Blend the Roquefort cheese with the single cream until a smooth coating consistency is achieved. Peel and core the pears and cut in half lengthways. Arrange on a plate and coat with the Roquefort dressing. Garnish with watercress and tomato wedges.

ROAST PHEASANT

❀❀ ☆☆☆☆☆
PREPARATION TIME: 10 MINUTES
COOKING TIME: 45 MINUTES
OVEN TEMP: 200C 400F M6

Ingredients:

1 pheasant for every two persons   Butter
Bacon rashers   Seasoning

Method:
Cover the breast of the birds with the bacon rashers and put in a roasting tin with a little butter, season. Cover loosely and place in the oven. Fifteen minutes before the end of cooking remove the cover and bacon rashers to allow the birds to brown. For older birds, add water to the bottom of the pan to give moisture whilst cooking. Baste the birds during cooking with the juices from the pan. A pheasant only serves 2 persons, and is hard to carve, one idea is to serve half a pheasant per person on the bone as is done with duck. Garnish with watercress.
Serve roast pheasant with redcurrent jelly, bread sauce (see page 314) and game chips.

ARMORETTI BISCUITS IN RED WINE

❀ ☆☆☆☆
PREPARATION TIME: 10 MINUTES

Ingredients:

8 oz (225 g) of armoretti biscuits (small)   8 fl oz (225 ml) of single cream
8 fl oz (225 ml) of red wine

Method:

Frost 4 glasses. Divide the biscuits between the glasses, pour over the wine and then the single cream. Serve immediately.

 To complete this menu: Leeks Béchamel (See Page 253), Carrots à la Forcalquier (See Page 247), Roast Potatoes (See Page 260), Brussels Sprouts With Nutmeg (See Page 246), Game Gravy (See Page 306).

WINTER MENU FOR SIX PERSONS

Cucumber Cheese Mould

Beef Curry
Aubergines Baghee, Saffron rice

Figs in Greek Yoghurt

Wine is not recommended to accompany curry.

BEEF CURRY

✻ ☆☆☆ **Ideally made the day before to let the flavour penetrate the ingredients.**
PREPARATION TIME: 30 MINUTES
COOKING TIME: 4 HOURS
OVEN TEMP: 180C 375F M4

Ingredients:

2 lb (900 g) of lean stewing steak	*3 carrots (sliced)*
Oil	*2 x 15oz (55 g) tin of tomatoes*
1 lb (450 g) of sliced onions	*1 tbs of tomato purée*
2 cloves of crushed garlic	*Curry powder*
1 aubergine (cubed)	*Any vegetables chopped to the size you*
3 potatoes (cubed)	*desired depending whether you want the*
2 cooking apples (cubed)	*sauce to be puréed or chunky*

Method:

Cube the meat. Heat the oil in a heavy based pan, add the onions and garlic, fry quickly. Add all of the ingredients and stir, place in a slow oven and cook for approximately 3 to 4 hours.

Note: Use the same method for vegetable curry but reduce the cooking time. (It can be puréed and served as a curry sauce). Use left over cold chicken in the vegetable curry and gently heat. If you cook the chicken for a long time it will become stringy. If you use raw chicken cook the curry for about 1½ hours. Prawns should be added to the vegetable curry and very quickly heated through. An other way is to leave the prawns in the curry mixture for 2 to 3 hours and then gently heat through.

SAFFRON RICE

Boil the rice with a strand of saffron (powdered tumeric will add colour), whole cardaman seeds and a whole clove.

AUBERGINE BAGHEE

❀ ☆☆☆
PREPARATION TIME: 10 MINUTES
COOKING TIME: 30 MINUTES

Ingredients:

2 aubergines	*Oil*
1 lb (450 g) of onions	*Curry powder*
2 gloves of garlic	

Method:
Heat the oil, add the garlic and sliced onions and fry until soft. Add the cubed aubergines and curry powder. Allow to simmer gently for about 30 minutes. Serve garnished with chopped chervil.

✍ **To complete this menu: Figs In Greek Yoghurt (See Page 275), Cucumber Cheese Mould (See Page 250).**

WINTER DINNER FOR SIX PERSONS

Carrot & Orange Soup

Roast Pork with Apple & Calvados Cream Sauce
Forcemeat Balls, Kohlrabi, Ratatouille, Roast Potatoes

Pineapple with Fresh Mint Syrup

White wine for the main course:

☖ Entre-deux-Mers, Château d'Arzac (Bordeaux)

☖☖ Château-La-Jalgue (Bordeaux)

☖☖☖ Puligny-Montrachet, Les Pucelles (Côte de Beaune, Burgundy)

CARROT & ORANGE SOUP

❀ ☆☆☆
PREPARATION TIME: 10 MINUTES
COOKING TIME: 1 HOUR

Ingredients:

2 lbs (1 kg) of carrots sliced	*2 pts (1 ltr) of white stock*
4 oranges	*5 fl oz (150 ml) single cream*
1 large onion finely chopped	*Caraway seeds (optional)*

Method:

Sauté the onion and carrots, add the stock, caraway seeds, zest and juice of the oranges. Season. Simmer for 1 hour then liquidise. Stir in the single cream just before serving.

ROAST PORK WITH APPLE & CALVADOS CREAM SAUCE

❀ ☆☆☆☆
PREPARATION TIME: 15 MINUTES
COOKING TIME: 2½ HOURS
OVEN TEMP: 190C 375F M5

Ingredients:

4 lbs (1.8 kgs) joint of pork
Sauce:

2 cooking apples	*Seasoning*
10 fl oz (300 ml) of single cream	*Calvados liqueur (optional)*

Method:

Sprinkle salt over the pork, sear in hot fat and roast in the oven allowing the crackling to crisp. Meanwhile make the sauce. Peel and core the cooking apples and cook in a saucepan with 2 tablespoons of water and a little sugar if required. Season, and add the single cream. Heat very gently. At the end of roasting, pour the juices from the tin into the sauce along with the calvados. Carve the pork and serve with the sauce.

FORCEMEAT BALLS

❀ ☆☆☆
PREPARATION TIME: 20 MINUTES
COOKING TIME: 20 MINUTES

Ingredients:

12 oz (350 g) of fresh white bread crumbs	*Finely chopped parsley*
1 onion finely chopped	*Finely chopped thyme or sage*

Salt & black pepper   *2 oz (50 g) of margarine*
1 egg

Method:
Fry the onions in the margarine and mix all the ingredients together and bind well. Shape into golf ball sized balls and roast around the joint for approximately 20 minutes.

✌ **To complete this menu: Pineapple With Mint Syrup (See Page 289), Kohlrabi (See Page 251, 252), Ratatouille (See Page 242).**

WINTER LUNCH FOR FOUR PERSONS

La Soupe au Deux Ognions

Fillet Mignon
Red Wine Sauce
Buttered New Potatoes, Cauliflower Polonaise, Lemon Carrots

Crèpes Suzette

Red wine for the main course:

🍷 Bordeaux Supérieur

🍷🍷 Château-Plagnac (Medoc, Bordeaux)

🍷🍷🍷 Château-Pétrus (Pomerol, Bordeaux)

LA SOUPE AUX DEUX OGNIONS

✻ ☆☆☆
PREPARATION TIME: 20 MINUTES
COOKING TIME: 1 HOUR

Ingredients:

1½ lbs (700 g) of medium sized onions   *1 pt (570 ml) of chicken stock*
sliced finely in rings   *Juice of one lemon*
4 large clove of garlic (sliced)   *1 bunch of spring onions, chopped finely*
4 whole clove of garlic   *16 fl oz (440 ml) of natural yoghurt*
½ pt (275 ml) of orange juice   *salt & black pepper*
(unsweetened)   *Cayenne pepper*

Method:

Put the sliced onions, sliced garlic and the gloves of garlic in a saucepan with the orange juice and chicken stock. Bring to the boil, cover the pan and simmer very gently for 1 hour. Add the lemon juice, seasoning and cayenne. Add the chopped spring onions to the soup and simmer for a further 5 minutes. Just before serving, stir the yoghurt into the soup with a fork to create a marble effect.

FILLET MIGNON

✿ ☆☆☆☆☆ **It is not necessary to use truffle and paté de foie for this recipe, you can improvise with a good mock paté de foie and garnish the top of the steaks with lightly fried mushrooms.**
PREPARATION TIME: 10 MINUTES
COOKING TIME: 10 MINUTES

Ingredients:

4 fillet steaks   *4 slices of truffle or 4 mushrooms*
4 round croûtes of fried bread   *Butter for frying*
Paté de foie gras   *Watercress*

Method:

Spread the paté on the fried bread croutes and keep warm. Cook the steaks (according to the chart on page 211). Place one steak on top of a croûte and garnish with the truffle or mushroom and watercress. Serve with red wine sauce (see page 305).

✍ **To Complete this menu: Buttered New Potatoes, Lemon Carrots (See Page 247), Cauliflower Polonaise (See Page 248), Crèpes Suzette (See Page 284).**

COCKTAIL PARTIES

A cocktail party is great fun, you might wish to experiment with all the cocktails listed in the earlier chapter. Morning cocktails are served from 11.00 a.m. Evening cocktails are held at approximately 6.00 p.m., often preceding dinner. The dress can be formal or informal.

Stuffed Grapes
Smoked Salmon Rolls
Asparagus Rolls
Devils on Horseback
Cocktail Sausages

STUFFED GRAPES
Wash and carefully slit the grapes lengthways. Remove the pips. Mix cream cheese with an ingredient of your choice and carefully insert a small amount into the grape.

SMOKED SALMON ROLLS
Use brown or white sliced bread. Remove the crust and roll with a rolling pin until thin. Butter one side of the bread, lay a slice of smoked salmon on the bread, sprinkle with cayenne and lemon juice, roll up tightly. These can be cut in half, or into six to give the appearance of Catherine wheels.

ASPARAGUS ROLLS
Use brown sliced bread. Remove the crust and roll with a rolling pin until thin. Butter one side of the bread, lay an asparagus spear at the edge and roll tightly. Cut into half and serve.

DEVILS ON HORSEBACK
Purchase prunes that have been already soaked and stoned. Cut the rind off, of the streaky bacon slices. Cut the bacon in half and wrap around the prune. Cook in the oven until the bacon is crisp. Insert a cocktail stick and serve.

COCKTAIL SAUSAGES
Purchase cocktail sausages. Remove the rind from the streaky bacon and cut in half, wrap around the sausages and cook for approximately 20 minutes in a hot oven.

BARBECUE

A barbecue party relies heavily on the weather. It is advisable to have an alternative plan should the heavens open up! Always plan in accordance with the cooking capacity of your barbecue, nothing is worse than having a great queue of people waiting for their food.

**Barbecue
for Twelve Persons**

Spit-Roasted Poussins
Pork Fillet Brochettes
Vegetable Brochettes
Barbecue Steaks
Sausages
Lamb Chop
Sardines
Tuna Steak
Barbecue Sauce
Selection of Salads
Baked Bananas
Fresh Fruit Brochettes

SPIT-ROASTED POUSSINS

❀ ☆☆☆
MARINADE: SIX HOURS
COOKING TIME: 1 HOUR

Ingredients:
6 poussins (½ per person)
Marinade:

¼ pt (150 ml) of oil	*1 tbs of tomato purée*
¼ pt (150 ml) of vinegar	*1 bay leaf*
¼ pt (150 ml) of white wine	*2 cloves of garlic crushed*
Black pepper, salt	

Method:
Mix the ingredients together, pour over the chickens, cover and leave to marinade for 6 hours. A good tip for barbecuing chickens is to par-cook them for ¾ of the time in your oven and then to finish the cooking time on the barbecue. Baste the chickens whilst cooking with the marinade. Some barbecues have a spit-roast attachment. If you have one of these, pierce the chickens lengthways onto the spit and cook in this way. Baste with the marinade. Chicken joints can be marinated in Tandoori mixture and cooked in the same way.

PORK FILLET BROCHETTES

❋ ☆☆☆
PREPARATION TIME: 30 MINUTES
Equipment Required: Skewers

Ingredients:

6 pork fillets trimmed & cubed   *1 tbs tomato purée*
Oil & crushed garlic   *Streaky bacon (optional)*

Method:
Skewer the meat, alternate with rolled-up streaky bacon (optional). Cook on the barbecue basting with the mixed oil, garlic and tomato purée. Herbs of your choice can be added to the oil.

VEGETABLE BROCHETTES

❋ ☆☆☆
PREPARATION TIME: 30 MINUTES
Equipment Required: Skewers

Ingredients:

Onions, red & green peppers, courgettes,   *Baby corns or cubed sweet corn.*
mushrooms, tomatoes,   *Oil mixture for cooking.*

Method:
Vegetable brochettes take less time to cook than the meat, therefore take this into consideration before cooking.
Note: There are various alternatives: liver and kidneys with bacon, vegetables mixed with meat, cubed fish and shellfish

BARBECUED STEAK

The heat of a barbecue varies dramatically, and so timing is difficult to predict for cooking each and every one. For this reason we suggest that you use tender meat. A steak should not be more than 1½ " (2.54 cm) thick, baste with oil whilst cooking.

SAUSAGES

Always cook sausages thoroughly, but remember to put them on a cooler part of the barbecue to prevent blackening and splitting.

LAMB CHOPS

Cook thin chops or cutlets. Marinade if desired, and cook with fresh rosemary.

SARDINES

Special Equipment Required: Skewers

Ingredients:

3-4 sardines per person   *Seasoning*
Oil for basting   *Fresh crushed garlic*
Cayenne

Method:
Gut and wash the sardines. Skewer three or four sardines for each person. Brush with oil flavoured with garlic, salt and black pepper. Cook on the barbecue for about 10 minutes turning once.

TUNA STEAKS

Brush with oil. Season the steaks and cook for approximately 10 to 15 minutes, turning once.

SELECTION OF SALADS

Tomato & spring onion:
Slice firm ripe tomatoes and sprinkle with chopped spring onions and marjoram. Dress with French dressing.
Potato salad:
Cube or slice cooked new potatoes and mix with fresh chopped chives and stoned black olives. Either dress with mayonnaise or French dressing.
Green salad:
Toss any seasonal green salad ingredients together, choose a dressing of your choice.

BAKED BANANAS

In individual pieces of tin foil place a banana with a tablespoon of honey, lemon juice, brandy or rum and brown sugar. Wrap securely. Cook for approximately 10 to 15 minutes, serve with cream.

FRESH FRUIT BROCHETTES

Skewer a selection of fresh fruits, and cook on the barbecue basting with a syrup of sugar and water. Serve with cream.

✌ **To complete this barbecue: Barbecue Sauce (See Page 103).**

CHILDREN'S PARTIES

A children's party is great fun for the children but can cause stress to the parents. Planning and organisation is of the **upmost** importance both for the children's safety and the smooth running of the party. Bear in mind that a large group of children can get out of hand, particularly if the weather is bad and they cannot go out in the garden to play. Enlist the help of other adults to help mind them. Clear your rooms of any ornaments to avoid regrettable incidents and push furniture out of the way.

Children get very excited, and tend to eat and drink more than usual, in a great hurry, which can cause upset tummies. Try to avoid too much rich food and fizzy drinks.

Purchase party packages which includes paper cups, plates, napkins and tablecloth, featuring children's favourite characters. Party hats, balloons, poppers and streamers create a jolly atmosphere. If a child's birthday is being celebrated, balloons can be tied to the front door or gate, to indicate where the party is being held. Plan several games for example: oranges and lemons, musical chairs, pass the parcel, postman's knock, sardines and hide-and-seek. Conjurors, or puppet shows are a great favourite.
Children adore playing games where a small prize is awarded to the winner. It is a good idea to give each child a small present to take home, thus avoiding tantrums and tears.
At the end of the party, the birthday child, makes a wish whilst blowing out the candles on the cake, and the guests sing 'Happy Birthday'.

Savoury & Sweet Sandwiches
Bridge Rolls
Sausages on Sticks
Pineapple & Cheese on Sticks
Animal Shapes Biscuits
Jelly with Fruits
Crisps

SAVOURY & SWEET SANDWICHES

Cut the sandwiches into small shapes, either fingers, triangles or rounds, removing the crusts.
Suggested fillings:
Cheese and tomato, egg, tuna fish, peanut butter, Marmite, fish and meat paste, jam or mashed banana. Do not try exotic fillings for children.

BRIDGE ROLLS

As above

SAUSAGES ON STICKS

Buy cocktail sausages or chipolatas which you twist in half. Spread a small amount of Marmite on the sausages before cooking.

CHEESE & PINEAPPLE STICKS

Cube Cheddar cheese and pineapple and put a piece of each on a stick. Cover half a melon with tin foil and skewer the sticks into it to make it look like a hedgehog.

JELLY WITH FRUIT

Set the jelly in exciting moulds with a variety of fruits.

POOL PARTIES

ool parties are fun! However be mindful of guests' safety both in and around the water. Wear suitable shoes and clothing, use plastic glasses and paper plates around the pool area. We have chosen a Caribbean theme for this party. To create the atmosphere arrange exotic flowers and plants and play steel band or Latin American music.

MENU FOR TWENTY PERSONS
All the dishes on this menu can be prepared well in advance.

Prawn & Pineapple Salad
Chicken in Mango Mayonnaise
Kiwi & Cream Cheese
Shredded Beef & Kidney Beans
Green Salad, Tomato Salad & Russian Salad
Alabama, Mexican & Guacamole Dips with Tortilla Chips
Exotic Fruit Salad

PRAWN & PINEAPPLE SALAD

❀ ☆☆☆☆☆
PREPARATION TIME: 1 HOUR

Ingredients:
2 large fresh pineapples
2 lbs (900 g) of peeled prawns

Pulp of 10 passion fruits
1 pt (570 ml) of mayonnaise, seasoning

Method:
Prepare the pineapple and cut into small cubes. Mix all the ingredients and coat with mayonnaise. Season to taste.

CHICKEN IN MANGO MAYONNAISE

❀ ☆☆☆☆
PREPARATION TIME: 45 MINUTES

Ingredients:

Cooked meat of 4 large chickens   1 pt (570 ml) of mayonnaise
1 lb (450 g) of sweetcorn kernels   4 mangoes
12 oz (350 g) of chopped red peppers

Method:

Chop the chicken, mix with the sweet corn and pepper. Peel, remove the stone from the mangoes and purée the flesh. Mix the mango with the mayonnaise, season to taste and mix with the salad ingredients.

KIWI & CREAM CHEESE

❀ ☆☆☆☆
PREPARATION TIME: 1 HOUR

Ingredients:

Chopped watercress, 10 kiwi fruits   1 lb (450 g) of cream cheese

Method:

Peel the kiwis and cut in half lengthways. Mix the watercress with the cream cheese, season to taste. With a teaspoon carefully remove the centre of the kiwi, fill with the cream cheese.

SHREDDED BEEF & KIDNEY BEANS

❀ ☆☆☆
PREPARATION TIME: 30 MINUTES

Ingredients:

3 lbs (1 kg 350 g) of cooked rare beef   French dressing (see page 315)
4 x 14 oz (380 g) cans of kidney beans   Tabasco, Worcestershire & chilli sauce
12 oz (350 g) shredded green peppers

Method:

Cut the beef into thin strips, mix the beef, kidney beans and green pepper together. Make French dressing, mix with chilli sauce, Tabasco and Worcestershire sauce.

TOMATO SALAD

❀ ☆☆☆
PREPARATION TIME: 30 MINUTES

Ingredients:

30 tomatoes   2 tbs of finely chopped fresh chives
1 lb (450 g) of stoned black olives   Garlic salt, black pepper,
2 large finely sliced onions   French dressing
4 tbs of finely chopped fresh parsley

Method:

Skin the tomatoes and slice, place in a shallow dish with the onion slices and olives, sprinkle the parsley, chives, garlic salt and French dressing over it.

RUSSIAN SALAD

❀ ☆☆☆
PREPARATION TIME: 1 HOUR

Ingredients:

1 lb (450 g) of cubed cooked carrots
1 lb (450 g) of cubed cooked potatoes
1 lb (450 g) of cooked peas

2 large onions finely chopped,
Mayonnaise

Method:
Mix all the ingredients together.

MEXICAN DIP

❀ ☆☆☆
PREPARATION TIME: 10 MINUTES
COOKING TIME: 30 MINUTES

Ingredients:

2 green peppers, finely chopped
2 fresh green chillies, finely chopped
1 large onion, finely chopped
3 tbs of tomato chilli sauce

2 gloves of crushed garlic
2 x 14 oz (380 g) cans of chopped
tomatoes, 2 tbs of oil
Tabasco, Worcester sauce, seasoning

Method:
Heat the oil and lightly fry the garlic, onions, pepper and chilli. Add the tomatoes and seasoning. Cook for approximately 30 minutes. Leave to cool. Serve the dips with tortilla chips.

EXOTIC FRUIT SALAD

❀ ☆☆☆☆☆
PREPARATION TIME: 1 HOUR

Ingredients:

1 large pineapple, lychees, strawberries
Mangoes, kiwis, passion fruit, bananas
Syrup:
l pt (750 ml) of water with 8 oz (225 g) of
sugar dissolved in it

Pawpaws, apricots, nectarines
Any fresh fruit with a tropical taste.

Juice of a lemon
1 pt of tropical fruit juice.

Method:
Prepare all the fruits and mix with the syrup.

☝ **To complete this menu: Alabama Dip (See Page 314), Guacamole Dip (See Page 203).**

THE PICNIC HAMPER

Whether it is Henley, Ascot, The Derby or eating 'al fresco' on a hot summer's day, a picnic can be a simple or extravagant affair. A little forward planning is essential. Be prepared for all weathers. A golfing umbrella is excellent for shading from the hot sun and also can come in handy should the heavens open up. You will need a ground sheet or a rug to sit on, and folding chairs for any members of the party who cannot sit on the ground.

A picnic hamper should be of manageable weight, food and drink must be well packed to prevent spillages. Remember to take a damp flannel or moist tissues, and a small first aid box for cuts and grazes. Do not forget to take a dustbin liner to dispose of the rubbish.

Picnic food can be prepared on the same day or made and frozen in advance. The other option is to purchase pre-cooked foods such as game or pork pies, quiches, cooked chicken, sandwiches and rolls, salads, and various deserts.

Baguettes
Babs
Quiches Slices
Chicken Drumsticks
Sausage Rolls
Spanish Omelette Wedges
Sweet Cheese Cake
Trifle

AUSTRALIAN NIGHT

MENU FOR FOUR PERSONS

Stuffed Kiwi Fruits

Baked Barramundi
Haricots Verts, New Boiled Potatoes

Hot Spiced Apricots

STUFFED KIWI FRUITS

❀ ☆☆☆
PREPARATION TIME: 20 MINUTES

Ingredients:

4 large kiwi fruits, peeled
4 oz (100 g) cream cheese
Vinaigrette:
3 tbs of white wine vinegar
½ tbs of olive oil

2 rashers of bacon, rind removed
1½ oz (40 g) of walnuts, finely chopped

Salt
Freshly ground black pepper

Method:

Remove the central core of the kiwi and keep it to one side. In a bowl pound the cheese until soft. Grill the bacon until brown and crispy and chop it finely. Add the bacon and walnuts to the cheese and stir well. Place each kiwi on a plate and fill it with the mixture. Liquidise the kiwi core together with the vinegar and oil. Season. Pour a little vinaigrette around each kiwi and garnish with salad.

BAKED BARRAMUNDI

❀❀ ☆☆☆☆
PREPARATION TIME: 20 MINUTES
COOKING TIME: 45 MINUTES
OVEN TEMPERATURE: 180C 350F M4

Ingredients:

3-3½ lbs (1.3-1.5 kgs) whole barramundi,
hake or bream
1 lemon cut in halves
1 large green pepper cut in halves
2-4 oz (50-100 g) of cooked rice
1 stalk celery, finely chopped
1 tsp of finely chopped fresh sage leaves

Salt & fresh ground black pepper
Melted butter for greasing
2 tsp of chilled butter, cut into flakes
1 large tomato, sliced
1 tbs chopped parsley
Sprigs of fresh sage to garnish

Method:

Cut the head and fins from the fish and clean under cold water, dry with absorbent paper. Rub the fish inside and out with one half of the lemon, then squeeze and reserve the juice of the other half.

Slice one half of the pepper thinly and reserve, and chop the second half. Mix the chopped pepper, rice, celery, chopped onion, lemon juice and sage together. Season well with salt and pepper. Grease a baking dish and put the fish in it then brush with the melted butter. Arrange the pepper and tomato slices alternately in a line on the top of the fish. Place the chilled butter flakes on the top. Cook in the oven, basting with butter occasionally. Cut the remaining lemon half into small wedges.

Serve the fish garnished with the parsley, sprigs of sage and lemon wedges.

HOT SPICED APRICOTS

✾ ☆☆☆

PREPARATION TIME: 10 MINUTES
COOKING TIME: 15 MINUTES
OVEN TEMPERATURE: 180C 350F M4

Ingredients:

4 fresh apricots per person	*2 tsp of ground cinnamon*
1 pt of orange & apricot fruit juice	*Single cream*

Method:

Cut the apricots in half and stone. Arrange in an oven-proof dish and pour the fruit juice over the apricots, sprinkle with cinnamon. Bake in the oven, serve with single cream.

✋ **To complete this menu: Boiled Haricots Verts, New Boiled Potatoes.**

CHINESE NIGHT

MENU FOR FOUR PERSONS

Wun Tun Soup

Sweet & Sour Chicken Drumsticks
Bean Sprouts with Spring Onion
Prawns & Egg Fried Rice

Caramel Apples

WUN TUN SOUP

Wun Tuns: A noodle paste rolled out very thinly and cut into 2-3" (5-7 cm) squares. To make the paste sift 8 oz (200 g) of plain flour with a pinch of salt. Mix in one egg with water to make a stiff dough. Knead the dough very thoroughly. Roll out very thinly on a floured surface and cut as required.

❀ ☆☆☆
PREPARATION TIME: 10 MINUTES
COOKING TIME: 20 MINUTES

Ingredients:

1½ pt (845 ml) of chicken stock
2 spring onions
8 wun tun skins (bought from Chinese groceries)
Salt & pepper
1 egg white

4 oz (110 g) of chicken, cooked & chopped
4 oz (110 g) of peeled prawns
Snipped green tops of spring onions

Method:
Slowly heat the stock in a large saucepan until boiling and season. Chop the chicken, prawns and spring onions very finely and mix them together. Place some of this mixture on the top of each wun tun skin, brush the edges with a little egg white and roll. Press the edges together and drop it into the boiling stock and cook for about 10 minutes. Serve sprinkled with snipped green spring onion tops.

SWEET & SOUR CHICKEN DRUMSTICKS

❀❀ ☆☆☆
PREPARATION TIME: 20 MINUTES
COOKING TIME: 15 MINUTES
DEEP FAT FRYING TIME: 10 MINUTES

Ingredients:

6 chicken drumsticks	*¾ pt (425 ml) of chicken stock*
1 egg	*4 tbs vinegar*
4 tbs of cornflour	*4 tbs of soft brown sugar*
Salt & pepper	*1 tbs of cornflour*
Onion	*1 tbs of soy sauce*
1 small pepper	*1 tbs of sherry*
1 carrot	*Oil for deep frying*

Method:

Beat the egg with 1 tablespoon of water. Mix the cornflour with the salt and pepper. Dip the drumsticks in the egg, then in cornflour and put aside. Cut the onion in eighths and the pepper and carrot into wedges, boil for 5 minutes, drain. Mix together in a saucepan, the chicken stock, vinegar, sugar, remaining cornflour, soya sauce and sherry. Bring to the boil, stirring constantly, simmer for 2-3 minutes.

Deep fry the chicken until golden brown. Drain on absorbent kitchen paper. Add the vegetables and chicken to the sauce, reheat and serve.

BEAN SPROUTS WITH SPRING ONIONS

❀ ☆☆☆
PREPARATION TIME: 5 MINUTES
COOKING TIME: 5 MINUTES

Ingredients:

1 packet bean sprouts	*1 clove of garlic*
2 spring onions	*Pinch of monosodium glutamate*
¼ pt (150 ml) of chicken stock	*Salt & pepper*
1 tbs of peanut oil	

Method:

Rinse sprouts under cold water and drain. Slice the spring onion into ½" (1 cm) lengths. Fry the garlic in the oil until golden, remove. Add the bean sprouts and onions to the pan and fry for 3-4 minutes. Add the chicken stock, season to taste. Bring to the boil and simmer for 2 minutes. Serve.

PRAWN & EGG FRIED RICE

❀ ☆☆☆
PREPARATION TIME: 10 MINUTES
COOKING TIME: 20 MINUTES

Ingredients:

8 oz (200 g) of rice	*2 eggs*
1 cup of cooked peas	*Soya sauce*
1 cup of cooked prawns	*Salt & pepper*
2 spring onions finely chopped	*Oil & butter*

Method:

Cook the rice and drain. Melt 1 tablespoon of oil and butter in the frying pan. Break the eggs into the pan and break up with a spatula and allow to brown. Add the remaining ingredients, stir periodically allowing the rice to brown. Add 2 tablespoons of soya sauce, season and serve.

CARAMEL APPLES

❋ ☆☆☆ **Bananas, pears and plums can be served this way.**
PREPARATION TIME: 10 MINUTES
DEEP FAT FRYING TIME: 5 MINUTES

Ingredients:

6 apples	*Oil for deep frying*
1½ oz (40 g) of plain flour	*4 oz (110 g) of granulated sugar*
½ oz (10 g) of corn flour	*1 tbs of oil*
2 egg whites	*1 tbs of sesame seeds*

Method:

Peel, core and quarter the apples, sprinkle them with plain flour. Pass the remaining flour with the cornflour through into a sieve, add the egg whites and stir to a paste. Coat the fruit in the butter and deep fry until golden. Drain on absorbent kitchen paper.

In a saucepan heat the sugar with two tablespoons of water, stir constantly until the sugar dissolves, add the oil and continue heating slowly until a light golden brown caramel has been achieved. Stir in the apple and sesame seeds and serve immediately in individual dishes which have been very lightly oiled.

GREEK NIGHT

MENU FOR FOUR PERSONS

Grilled Haloumi

Moussaka
Tossed Green Salad
Tomato & Fetta Salad

Water Melon Wedges

GRILLED HALOUMI

❀ ☆☆☆
PREPARATION TIME: 10 MINUTES
COOKING TIME: 10 MINUTES

Ingredients:

1 slice of haloumi per person   *Endives*
about ½" (1 cm) thick   *1 large beef tomato*

Method:

Place the haloumi on tin foil under a very hot grill, and cook until golden brown. Serve garnished with tomato, endive and some tasaki.

MOUSSAKA

❀ ☆☆☆
PREPARATION TIME: 25 MINUTES
COOKING TIME: 20 MINUTES
OVEN TEMPERATURE: 190C 375F M5

Ingredients:

3 tbs oil   *1 large aubergine, sliced*
1 small onion, finely chopped   *1 clove garlic, crushed*
1 lb cooked minced lamb   *½ lb tomatoes, peeled & sliced*
2 tbs tomato purée   *½ pt cheese sauce, (see page 307)*
Salt & pepper   *1 egg yolk*
½ lb sliced cooked potato   *Parsley*

Method:

Heat two tablespoons of oil and fry the onion until browned, add the meat and cook for a few minutes. Add the tomato purée and heat through, season. Put in an ovenproof dish and keep warm.

197

Arrange the potato slices on top of the meat in the dish.

Fry the aubergine slices for approximately 7 minutes until browned, add the garlic and sliced tomatoes. Heat the ingredients and arrange them over the potatoes and meat.

Make the cheese sauce, stir in the egg yolk and pour it over the ingredients in the dish.

Sprinkle grated cheese over the sauce and cook in the oven until browned on the top. Garnish with parsley and serve.

Serve with a tossed green salad, or a tomato and fetta cheese salad: Slice ripe tomatoes and onion rings, crumble fetta cheese over these. Dress with finely chopped parsley and oil and vinegar.

WATER MELON WEDGES

Chill the melon and serve a large wedge per person.

INDIAN NIGHT

MENU FOR FOUR PERSONS

Samosas

Tandoori Chicken
Cucumber Riata

Almond Ice Cream (Kulfi)

SAMOSAS

Buy the samosas and heat in the oven. There is ample choice, for example, spinach and cheese, vegetable or meat. Make your own mint sauce to serve with the samosas, natural yoghurt, lemon juice and finely chopped mint with a hint of cayenne pepper.

TANDOORI CHICKEN

❀ ☆☆☆
PREPARATION TIME: Overnight marinating plus one hour
COOKING TIME: 40 MINUTES
OVEN TEMPERATURE: 200C 400F M6

Ingredients:

2 cloves	*1½ tsp chilli powder*
6 small dried red chillies	*4-6 small chicken joints, skinned*
½ pt (300 ml) of natural yoghurt	*1 oz (25 g) of butter*
1½ tsp salt	*Lemon wedges*
1 tsp powdered red food colouring	*A few green chillies, finely sliced*
1 tsp ground ginger	*Salad*
2 cloves garlic, crushed	

Method:
Bruise and roast the cloves of garlic and red chillies until the aroma is released. Grind all these ingredients together as finely as possible.
Mix the yoghurt, salt, food colouring, ground ginger, garlic and chilli powder with the ground ingredients. Place the chicken joints in a dish and pour the yoghurt mixture over them and marinate overnight.
Grease a large piece of tinfoil with the butter and arrange the chicken on it with the marinade. Fold the foil around the chicken, sealing the edges well and bake for approximately 40 minutes. At the end of the cooking time, open the foil and cook under a hot grill until the juices have dried up. Garnish with lemon wedges, a few green chilli slices and salad. Serve immediately.

CUCUMBER RIATA

Cut cucumber into matchsticks and mix with natural yoghurt. Serve with the Tandoori chicken.

ALMOND ICE CREAM (KULFI)

❀ ☆☆☆
PREPARATION TIME: 1 HOUR
CHILLING TIME: 2-3 HOURS

Ingredients:

8 oz (225 g) of almonds, blanched   *½ pt (300 ml) of double cream*
3 pt (1.75 ltr) of milk   *2 tbs of rose water*
8 oz (225 g) of caster sugar

Method:

Place the almonds in a bowl with cold water and set aside. Boil 2½ pints (1.45 litres) of the milk in a saucepan and simmer until it has reduced by half, stirring from time to time. Drain the almonds and place ¾ of them in a liquidiser with the remaining milk. Blend the mixture until the almonds are roughly ground. Add the almond mixture and sugar to the hot milk and simmer for a further 10 to 20 minutes, stirring constantly. Remove from the heat and allow to cool to room temperature, then chill in the refrigerator. Chop the remaining almonds and add them to the double cream, rose water and chilled milk. Mix well. Pour into a suitable freezer container and freeze until solid. About 20 minutes before serving, place the ice cream in the refrigerator to soften slightly.

ITALIAN NIGHT

MENU FOR FOUR PERSONS

Tagliatelle with Asparagus & Cream

Canelloni with Chicken & Ham

Iced Zabaglione

TAGLIATELLE WITH ASPARAGUS & CREAM

❀ ☆☆☆☆
COOKING TIME: 10 MINUTES

Ingredients:

Can (14.5 oz/411 g) of asparagus tips	*2 tbs of freshly grated Parmesan cheese*
1 oz (25 g) of butter	*Grated nutmeg*
2 tbs of plain flour	*14 oz (425 g) of fresh tagliatelle*
6 fl oz (175 ml) of single cream	*Salt & pepper*

Method:
Drain the asparagus and reserve a few small tips for garnishing. Purée the remaining asparagus and set aside. Melt the butter in a heavy saucepan, add the flour and cook for 1 minute, gradually add the milk and bring to the boil, simmer for 3 minutes. Add the asparagus purée, cream and Parmesan. Season with nutmeg, salt and pepper. Remove from the heat. Cook the tagliatelle, reheat the asparagus sauce, drain the tagliatelle and mix with the sauce. Garnish with the asparagus tips.

CANNELLONI WITH CHICKEN & HAM

❀ ☆☆☆
PREPARATION TIME: 10 MINUTES
COOKING TIME: 45 MINUTES
OVEN TEMPERATURE: 190C 375F M5

Ingredients:

10 oz (275 g) of boneless chicken breasts, skinned	*8 oz (225 g) of button mushrooms, sliced*
	8 oz (225 g) of chopped spinach
¼ pt (450 ml) of water, 1 bouquet garni	*1 oz (25 g) of butter*
1 bay leaf	*1 oz (25 g) of plain flour*
1 slice of onion	*¼ pt (150 ml) of dry white wine*
1 oz (25 g) of butter with herbs & garlic	*¼ pt (150 ml) of double cream*
8 oz (225 g) boiled ham	

1 packet (8 oz/225 g) of 'no pre-cook'   *Salt & pepper*
cannelloni tubes   *Basil sprigs*
6 oz (175 g) of Gruyère cheese, grated

Method:

Put the chicken in a pan with the water, bouquet garni, bay leaf and onion, bring to the boil. Reduce the heat, cover and simmer for 15 minutes. Drain the chicken and keep the stock. Mince the chicken and ham.

Melt the garlic and herb butter, add the mushrooms and cook for 5 minutes. Add the spinach, cover and cook until tender. Season.

Melt one ounce of butter in a pan, add the flour and make a roux. Gradually add ½ pint (300 ml) of the stock, then the wine and the cream. Bring to the boil, turn down the heat, stirring continuously and simmer for 3 minutes. Add four fluid ounces (125 ml) of the sauce to the chicken and ham, seasoning with pepper and stir well.

Fill the tubes with the mixture, arrange them in a baking dish side by side in a single layer. Add ¾ of the Gruyère to the remaining sauce and heat gently until the cheese has melted. Pour the sauce over the tubes, sprinkle the remaining Gruyère over the top and bake in a preheated oven for 35 minutes. Garnish with basil sprigs and serve.

ICED ZABAGLIONE

❋ ☆☆☆
PREPARATION TIME: 15 MINUTES
CHILLING TIME: 4-6 HOURS

Ingredients:

4 egg yolks   *2 oz (50 g) of caster sugar*
4 tbs of Marsala wine or sweet sherry   *¼ pt (150 ml) of double cream*

Method:

Mix in a bowl the egg yolks, sugar, wine or sherry. Place over a saucepan half filled with simmering water and whisk the mixture until thick and light. Remove from the heat and whisk until cold. Chill. When the mixture is chilled lightly whip the cream and fold in. Pour into serving glasses. Serve.

MEXICAN NIGHT

MENU FOR FOUR PERSONS

Guacamole & Tortillas

Chilli Con Carne

Almendrado
(Almond Jelly)

GUACAMOLE

❀ ☆☆☆
PREPARATION TIME: 10 MINUTES

Ingredients:

2 large ripe avocados
4 oz (100 g) of peeled, finely chopped, tomatoes
1 small onion, finely chopped
2 fresh hot green chillies, seeded & finely chopped

2 tbs (300 ml) of chopped fresh coriander leaves
Salt
Lime juice

Method:

Cut the avocados in halves, remove and discard the stones. Scoop the flesh into a bowl and chop finely. Add all the remaining ingredients and mix well. Serve immediately with tortilla chips.

CHILLI CON CARNE

❀ ☆☆☆
PREPARATION TIME: 10 MINUTES
COOKING TIME: 1½ HOURS

Ingredients:

2 tbs olive oil, 1 bay leaf
2 medium-size onions, finely sliced
2 garlic cloves, chopped
2 green chillies, finely sliced
1½ lbs (700 g) of lean minced beef
1½ lbs (700 g) cubed stewing steak
15 oz (450 g) canned tomatoes
5 oz (150 g) tomato purée

2 tsp ground cumin
1 tsp dried oregano
1 tsp cayenne pepper
1 tsp chilli powder
2 tsp salt
12 fl oz (300 ml) of beef stock
14 oz (400 g) canned red kidney beans, drained

Method:

In a large frying-pan heat the oil. Fry the onions, chili and garlic for 5-6 minutes stirring constantly. Add the meat and brown.

Put all the ingredients except the kidney beans into a large heavy saucepan and stir well. Cover the pan and bring to the boil over a moderate heat. Reduce the heat and simmer for 1 hour, stir occasionally. Add the kidney beans, cover the pan, and simmer for 30 minutes. Remove the bay leaf and serve.

ALMENDRADO (Almond Jelly)

✿ ☆☆☆
PREPARATION TIME: 30 MINUTES

Ingredients:

1 tbs of gelatine	*6 medium-sized egg whites*
8 fl oz (220 ml) of boiling water	*Pinch of salt*
8 oz (225 g) of sugar	*5 oz (150 g) slivered almonds, toasted*
½ tsp almond essence	

Custard:

1¾ pt (1 ltr) of milk	*½ tsp of vanilla essence*
6 medium-sized egg yolks	*3½ fl oz (100 ml) thick cream*
2 oz (50 g) of sugar	

Method:

Sprinkle the gelatine on the cold water and leave for 5 minutes. Add the boiling water and stir until the gelatine is dissolved. Add the sugar and the almond essence and stir well. Chill the mixture until it begins to thicken, then whisk until frothy.

In a large bowl beat the egg whites and a pinch of salt until stiff. Fold into the gelatine mixture.

Rinse the mould under cold water. Pour half of the mixture into the mould and sprinkle with a layer of toasted almonds, add the remaining mixture. Chill for approximately 4 hours.

Prepare the custard about 45 minutes before serving. Heat the milk in the top of a double boiler until bubbles form around the edge, then remove from heat. Beat the egg yolks with the sugar until they are light. Add the hot milk to the yolks then return to the pan. Cook the mixture over the hot water, stirring constantly until it thickens slightly. Add the vanilla, remove from the heat and cool. Whisk the cream until stiff and fold into the cooled custard and chill for approximately 30 minutes.

Turn out the pudding from the mould, garnish with the remaining almonds and serve with the custard.

TURKISH NIGHT

MENU FOR FOUR PERSONS

Iman Bayudi

Levrec En Papillote

Figs Pistachio

IMAN BAYUDI (Stuffed aubergines)

❀ ☆☆☆
PREPARATION TIME: 20 MINUTES
COOKING TIME: 30 MINUTES
OVEN TEMPERATURE: 200C 425F M5

Ingredients:

4 aubergines	*8 peeled & chopped tomatoes*
2 oz (50 g) of parsley	*1 green pepper, finely sliced*
1 onion, finely sliced	*1 tbs of tomato paste*
2 cloves of garlic, finely sliced	*1 pt (570 ml) of tomato juice*
Salt	*Olive oil*

Method:
Prepare the aubergines by flattening the bottoms and peeling with a knife leaving rings of skin at the top and bottom (this holds the aubergine together during the cooking).
Gently fry the onion, garlic and green pepper in the òlive oil and season with a pinch of salt and sugar. Cook until soft but not brown. Add the chopped tomatoes and a little tomato paste. Cook over a gentle heat until very soft.
Deep fry the aubergines for a few minutes in very hot olive oil. Slit open the aubergines and stuff with the filling. Put into a baking dish and garnish with a tomato wedge and pour the tomato juice and some olive oil over them. Bake in a hot oven for 20 minutes, serve.

LEVREK EN PAPILLOTE (Sea bass in parcels)

❀ ☆☆☆ **A speciality served in Izmir.**
PREPARATION TIME: 15 MINUTES
COOK TIME: 20 MINUTES
OVEN TEMPERATURE: 180C 375F M4

Ingredients:

4 sea bass steaks or a whole sea bass	*1 onion, finely sliced*
3 oz (75 g) of parsley, roughly chopped	*Salt*

Olive oil

8 tomatoes, peeled & chopped

½ green pepper sliced

Sheets of greaseproof paper or tin foil

Method:

Mix the parsley, onion and a little salt together. Brush a sheet of greaseproof paper with oil and put some of the onion mixture in the centre. Lay a sea bass steak on top of the mixture and place more on top. Add some tomato and green pepper. Fold the paper up and seal. Place on an oiled tray, brush the tops with water to prevent burning, bake in a moderate oven for 20 minutes. Serve. The same method applies for a whole fish but bake for approximately 30 minutes.

FIGS PISTACHIO

✱ ☆☆☆☆
PREPARATION TIME: 15 MINUTES
CHILLING TIME: 2 HOURS

Ingredients:

16 fresh figs

3 oz (75 g) of pistachio, chopped

16 fl oz (440 ml) thick Greek yoghurt

4 oz (110 g) of brown sugar

Method:

Pour boiling water over the figs, peel and slice. In individual ramekins divide the ingredients in layers, finishing off with a layer of sugar. Place in the refrigerator and chill.

BASIC EQUIPMENT LIST

Saucepans	Choose saucepans with lids which have perforations to let the steam escape. You will need two large saucepans, one medium, and a couple of small pans. Milk pans are very useful, as they have a pouring lip which is ideal for sauce-making.
Frying Pan	Buy a pan with a lid. The bottom of a frying pan should always cover the ring, so that the heat is evenly distributed and the bottom should be flat to prevent uneven frying.
Omelette Pan	Used for omelette and pancakes. You should never wash an omelette pan, only burnish it with oil after each use.
Meat Roasting Tin	Heavy, good quality metal tins are strongly recommended. Two sizes will be useful, one large for the Christmas turkey or larger joints, and a smaller one for roast potatoes and smaller joints.
Gratin Dish	Gratin dishes are versatile, they can be used for cooking in the oven, or as a serving dish. Purchase 'oven to table' ones.
Casseroles	Cast-iron enamelled casseroles can be used on a hob and in the oven. An average casserole is 5 pints (2.5 litres). Earthenware casseroles are only suitable for use in the oven. All casseroles must have a close fitting lid.
Ramekins	Ramekins look like small soufflé dishes. They are inexpensive, extremely useful and versatile. Buy ovenproof ramekins.
Terrine	A terrine is used to cook pâté.
Tartlet Tin	Used for Yorkshire puddings.
Flan Case	China cases are versatile. Used for both sweet and savoury flans.
Baking Sheet	Buy one with a lip around the edge. The lip has got two advantages, it will prevent the food from slipping off the side when you take it out of the oven and will hold greaseproof paper so you can use the tin to cook Swiss rolls and soufflés.
Pie Dish	Buy one with a lip around the edge, so when you are making a pie the pastry will adhere to it easily.
Pudding Basin	A set of various sizes, preferably glass.
Mixing Basins	China or stainless steel, two or three sizes will be useful.
Soufflé Dish	Choose according to your need.
Measuring Jug	Pyrex or plastic. A two pint one is recommended.
Steamer	This can be a separate attachment which fits onto the top of your saucepan.

Deep fat fryer, kettle, electric mixer, or food processor, toaster or grill.

SMALLER ARTICLES

Knives

Stainless steel are easy to sharpen and clean. Plastic handles last longer than wooden ones, and resist hot temperatures when washed.
- Bread knife
- Carving set
- Filleting knife
- Chef's knives: two to three sizes
- Serrated knife
- Vegetable knife

Apple corer	Ladle	Scales
Ball scoop	Perforated spoon	Measuring spoons
Cheese grater	Wooden spoons of	Kitchen timer (most
Garlic press/cherry	various sizes	cookers have these)
stoner	Wooden fork	Storage jars and flour bin
Kitchen scissors	Strainers	Balloon whisk
Poultry shears	Sieves	Wooden cocktail sticks
Vegetable peeler	Colanders	Rolling pin
Skewers	Fish slice	Pastry cutters (plain and
Pepper mill	Spatulas	fluted)
Tin opener	Pastry brush	Hand rotary whisk
Corkscrew	Tongs	Electric hand held whisk
Large cook's fork	Chopping boards	Lemon juice extractor
Large tablespoon	Bread board	

The following items you will not need every day, but may choose to collect gradually.

Larding needle	Ring mould	Jelly moulds
Aspic cutters	Savarin mould	Meat tenderiser
Mouli food mill	Dariole moulds	Selection of piping
Pestle and mortar	Double saucepan	nozzles and bag
Fish kettle	Charlotte mould	Sugar dredger

Sundries

Aluminium foil	Plastic food bags	Cling film
Greaseproof paper	Absorbent kitchen paper	String

These lists do not include cutlery, tableware or glassware.

CONVERSION TABLES

Weights

Imperial ounces	Recommended conversion
½ oz	10 g
1 oz	25 g
1½ oz	40 g
2 oz	50 g
3 oz	75 g
4 oz	110 g
4½ oz	125 g
5 oz	150 g
6 oz	175 g
7 oz	200 g
8 oz	225 g
9 oz	250 g
10 oz	275 g
12 oz	350 g
1 lb	450 g
1½ lb	700 g
2 lb	900 g
3 lb	1 kg 350 g

American Measure - Dry Measures

½ oz	15 g	1 Tablespoon
4 oz	100 g	½ Cup
8 oz	225 g	1 Cup

Note: All tablespoon and teaspoon measure are level, unless otherwise stated.

Liquid Measurements

Imperial fluid ounces

2 fl oz	55 ml
3 fl oz	75 ml
5 fl oz (¼ pt)	150 ml
10 fl oz (½ pt)	275 ml
15 fl oz (¾ pt)	425 ml
20 fl oz (1 pt)	570 ml
35 fl oz (1¾ pt)	1 litre

American liquid measurement

ml	American	floz
½ fl oz	15 ml	1 Tablespoon
2 fl oz	50 ml	¼ Cup
4 fl oz	100 ml	½ Cup
8 fl oz	225 ml	1 Cup
½ Pint	300 ml	1 Cup
1 Pint	600 ml	2½ Cups

Oven Temperatures

Electric	Electric	Gasmark
C	F	
70	150	
80	175	
100	200	Low
110	225	¼ Very Cool
130	250	½
140	275	1
150	300	2 Cool
170	325	3
180	350	4 Medium
190	375	5
200	400	6 Medium Hot
220	425	7
230	450	8
240	475	9 Very Hot
250	500	
270	525	
290	550	Exceedingly Hot

ROASTING TIMES
FOR MEAT, POULTRY & GAME

Allow all joints that have been roasted to stand for approximately 10 minutes before carving.

BEEF
Oven temperature:	Electric oven 375F, 190C, Mark 5.
Rare:	15 minutes per lb (450 g) + 15 minutes
Well done:	20 minutes per lb (450 g) + 30 minutes

Cooking times vary upon the thickness of the joint and not always according to the weight. Allow:

- 45 minutes for joints under 1½ lbs (675 g),
- 1¼ hours for joints under 13 lbs.

Heat the lard in the pan and when it is hot roll the joint in the fat to seal the juices in. Lightly salt if you wish before roasting.

STEAK
No two steaks are the same, however a few basic guide lines will help achieve your aim.

We shall use an 8 oz (225 g) steak as an example. Cooking time depends on the thickness, increase or decrease the time by 1 minute per centimetre (½"/1cm).

A fillet steak, 1½/2" (4/5 cm) thick.

Raw: (bleu)	The steak has a thin brown crust, but is still very pink inside: 1 minute per side.
Rare: (saignant)	The steak has a brown crust, the inside is pink and the very centre still red and bloody: 2 minutes per side.
Medium: (à point)	The steak has a brown crust and is pink right through: 3/4 minutes per side.
Well done: (bien cuit)	The steak is completely cooked throughout (many people regard this method of cooking a sacrilege, it is of course only a matter of choice): 5 minutes per side.

If you are cooking several steaks at the same time, to various preferences, start with the well done ones first, then add the medium ones ½ minute later, and so on. These rules apply to pan-fried steaks, but grilling them under a hot pre-heated grill is roughly the same.

LAMB
Oven temperature:

Sear the meat in hot fat before roasting.
Electric oven 375F, 190C, Mark 5.
20 minutes per lb (450 g) + 20 minutes.
For rare, cut the cooking time by 5 minutes per lb (450 g).

MUTTON
Oven temperature:

Electric oven 375F, 190C, Mark 6 for the first 15 minutes,
then reduce to 5.
20 minutes per lb (450 g) + 20 minutes.

PORK
Oven temperature:

Sear the joint in hot fat before roasting.
Electric oven 375F, 190C, Mark 7 for the first 15 minutes
then reduce to 6.
25 minutes per lb + 25 minutes.

VEAL
Oven temperature:

425F, 220C, Mark 7.
On the bone: 25 minutes per lb (450 g) + 25 minutes.
Boned and rolled: 30 minutes per lb (450 g) + 30 minutes.

Bird	Weight	Cooking Time	Oven Temperature For Roasting
Chicken	4 lbs (1.8 kg)	20 mins per lb + 20 mins	375F, 190C, mark 5
Capon	5-7 lbs (2.2-3.1 kg)	20 mins per lb + 20 mins	375F, 190C, mark 5
Fresh turkey plucked	13-14 lbs (5.8-6.3 kg)	10 mins per lb + 10 mins	375F, 190C, mark 5
Frozen turkey oven ready	10 lbs (4.5 kg)	15 mins per lb + 15 mins	375F, 190C, mark 5
Goose	8-10 lbs (3.6-4.5 kg)	15 mins per lb	400F, 200C, mark 6
Duck	5-6 lbs (2.2-2.7 kg)	approx 2 hours	400F, 200C, mark 6
Wild duck		approx 45 mins	400F, 200C, mark 6
Pheasant		approx 1½ hours	400F, 200C, mark 6
Grouse		20-30 mins	400F, 200C, mark 6
Partridge		20-30 mins	400F, 200C, mark 6

The weight of the birds are oven ready, before being stuffed. Ensure all poultry and game are kept moist during roasting, by barding, or covering whilst cooking, remove the cover before the end of cooking so that the bird can brown.

TURKEY

Cover the bird in a layer of tin foil. Cover legs and wings with extra layers of foil to prevent them burning whilst cooking as they cook more quickly than the breast.

PHEASANT

Lay bacon slices over the breast. If you are aware that the bird is older, put water in the bottom of the roasting pan, put the bacon on the breast and then cover with foil to keep it moist whilst cooking.

PARTRIDGE

Cook as for pheasant.

GROUSE

Grouse can be eaten rare or well done. Cook as you prefer.

GLOSSARIES:
ENGLISH, FRENCH, AMERICAN

"Kissing don't last: cookery do!"
GEORGE MEREDITH

ENGLISH

Acidulated water	Lemon juice or vinegar is added to cold water to prevent discoloration of fruits and vegetables.
'Al dente'	Cooked pasta or vegetables firm to the bite.
Aspic	Clear jelly flavoured with meat or fish juices.
Barding	To cover lean meat or poultry with fat bacon to keep the moisture in during cooking.
Basting	To pour liquid over the food whilst cooking, i.e. hot fat during roasting.
Blanching	To cover food with cold water, bring to boil and strain.
Brine	A salt water solution.
Browning	Searing the outer surface of meat to seal in the juices in hot fat.
Clarifying	Clearing fat by heating and filtering to remove any impurities.
Curdle	To cause fresh milk or sauces to separate.
Deep-frying	To submerge food completely in hot fat or oil.
Dice	To cut small cubes of meat or vegetable.
Dredging	Sprinkling lightly with a powder using a perforated dredger.
Dress	To pluck, draw and truss poultry or game. To arrange or garnish a cooked dish. To prepare cooked shellfish, lobster or crab in their shells.
Dripping	The fat collected from a roasted joint.
Fillet	Lean meat with no bone. Flat fish off the bone.
Flan	Open pastry case, filled with sweet or savoury filling.
Folding in	Using a metal spoon to carefully combine two ingredients together incorporating air.
Forcemeat	Prepared stuffing.
Garnish	To decorate a finished dish.
Gill	A liquid measure equal to ¼ pt or 5 fl oz.
Glaze	To brush food with beaten egg, milk, or syrup.
Hanging	To suspend meat or game in a cool dry place until it is tender.
Hulling	To remove the green calyx from soft fruits.
Infusing	To steep herbs, tea leaves or coffee in water or other liquid to extract the flavour.
Kneading	To work together ingredients by hand.
Lard	Refined pork fat.
Larding	To thread strips of fat through lean meat using a larding needle.
Marinade	A blend of oil, wine, vinegar, herbs and spices.
Melba toast	Very thin slices of toasted bread.
Marinate	To steep in marinade.
Offal	Edible internal organs of meat, poultry and game.

Par-boiling	To boil food for a short time to partially cook.
Poaching	To cook food in a simmering liquid just below boiling point.
Raspings	Dried sieved breadcrumbs.
Reducing	To concentrate liquid by boiling and evaporation.
Rendering	To slowly cook meat tissues and trimmings to produce liquid fats.
Roux	To combine fat and flour, which is then cooked and used as a base for sauces.
Scald	To heat milk or cream to just below boiling point. To plunge fruit or vegetable into boiling water to remove the skin.
Searing	To brown meat rapidly in hot fat to seal in the juices.
Seasoned flour	Flour with salt and pepper added.
Seasoning	Salt, pepper, spices or herbs, which are added to food to improve flavour.
Score	To make incisions in the surface of fish, meat, poultry, vegetables or pastry before cooking.
Shred	To slice thinly.
Simmering	Liquid which is heated to just below boiling point, tiny bubbles should surface irregularly.
Steaming	To cook food in the steam rising from boiling water.
Stock	Is the liquid resulting from simmering ingredients together in water. White stock: pork, veal, chicken, vegetable or fish. Brown stock: beef.
Straining	To separate liquids from solids.
Stuffing	Meat, poultry, vegetables or fruits. A mixture of ingredients used to fill fish.
Suet	The fat around lamb or beef kidneys.
Syrup	A reduced liquid of sugar and water.
Terrine	Earthenware pot used for cooking and serving pâté. Food cooked in a terrine.
Trussing	To tie a bird or a joint in to a neat shape using string and skewers.
Vinaigrette	A mixture of oil, vinegar, and seasonings.
Whipping	To beat cream until thick.
Whisk	To incorporate air very rapidly.
Zest	The outer skin of citrus fruits.

FRENCH

Agneau	Lamb.
A la carte	Bill of fare from which the diner selects individual dishes.
A la crème	With cream or a cream sauce.
A la Jardinière	A garnish of fresh cooked vegetables arranged in separate groups.
A la Normande	Cooked with cider and cream.
Amandine	Cooked or coated with almonds.
A point	Medium cooked.
Au gratin	Finishing off food with grated cheese or breadcrumbs, then put under the grill or in the oven to brown.
Au poivre	With pepper.

Bain Marie	A process of cooking food slowly by putting the dish to be cooked into a pan which is then placed into a larger pan of hot water and heated gently.
Blanquette	Veal, poultry or rabbit stew in a creamy sauce.
Boeuf	Beef.
Bouchée	Small puff pastry case - savoury or sweet filling.
Bouquet Garni	A bouquet of herbs tied together: parsley, thyme, marjoram, bay.
Bourguignonne	Cooked in red wine.
Brochette	Skewer used for grilling chunks of meat, fish and vegetable over charcoal, or under grill.
Brioche	Soft bread made of rich yeast dough - slightly sweet.
Brûlée	A dish finished with a caramelised sugar glaze.
Cailles	Quails.
Canapé	A small appetiser of bread with a savoury topping.
Canard	Duck.
Canetons	Duckling.
Carbonnade	Beef stew made with beer.
Carré d'agneau	Best end of lamb.
Cervelles	Brains.
Champignon	Mushroom.
Chantilly	Sweet whipped cream.
Charlotte	Hot moulded sweet bread with fruit filling. Cold moulded sweet sponge finger with fruit and cream, or custard, set with gelatine.
Chasseur	Cooked with mushrooms, shallots and white wine.
Chaud-froid	Elaborate dish of meat, poultry, game, or fish masked with creamy sauce, decorated and glazed in aspic. Served cold.
Citron	Lemon.
Civet	Brown game stew.
Compote	Dessert of fresh or dried fruits, cooked in syrup and served cold.
Condé	Dessert made with rice.
Coquille	Scallop. Shell shaped ovenproof dish used to serve fish or poultry dishes in.
Cordon Bleu	Highly qualified cook. According to legend King Louis XV of France once awarded a blue ribbon to a female chef who had prepared an outstanding meal.
Côtelettes	Cutlets.
Crème	Applied to fresh cream, butter and custard. Also thick creamy soups.
Crêpe	Thin pancake.
Croûte	Fingers, rounds or squares of fried or toasted bread, used as a base for serving soft mixtures, little birds, meat or fish.
Croûtons	Small diced or neatly cut pieces of fried or toasted bread, used as an accompaniment to soups, or as a garnish.
Darne	Thick slice, cut from a round fish.
Daube	Stew of braised meat and vegetables.
Dindonneau	Young turkey.
En croûte	Pastry encasing meat, fish or vegetables.
Entrée	Third course in a formal meal following the fish course.
Entremet	Course before the main course.
Epaule	Shoulder.

Escalope	Thin slice of meat which is beaten flat and shallow fried.
Faisan	Pheasant.
Farce	Stuffing.
Filet suprêmes	The breast of chicken.
Fines herbes	Mixture of finely chopped herbs.
Flambé	Food tossed in a pan to which burning alcohol has been added.
Florentine	Fish or eggs, served on a bed of spinach then coated in a cheese sauce.
Foie de porc	Pig's liver.
Foie gras	Goose liver pâté.
Fraise	Strawberry.
Fraise des bois	Wild strawberries.
Frappé	Iced.
Fricassée	White stew of chicken, or rabbit or veal and vegetables which are pan-fried, cooked in stock, and finished with cream and egg yolks.
Fumet	A reduced stock of game, fish or meat.
Galantine	Dish of boned and stuffed poultry, game or meat, glazed with aspic and served cold.
Galette	Flat pastry cake, traditionally baked for the 12th night. Flat cake of mashed potato.
Genoise	A rich sponge cake.
Gigot	Leg.
Glacé	Glazed, frozen or iced.
Granité	Sorbet.
Gratiné	Any dish covered with grated cheese which is melted under the grill or in the oven.
Haricot vert	Green bean.
Hors d'Oeuvre	Hot or cold appetisers served at the start of a meal.
Jambon	Ham.
Langouste	Crawfish or king prawn.
Langue de chat	Flat finger shaped crisp biscuits, served with desserts.
Langues de mouton	Sheep tongues.
Lapin	Rabbit.
Légumes	Vegetables.
Levraut	Baby hare.
Lièvre	Hare.
Lyonnaise	Dish served with onions.
Macédoine	Mixture of fruit or vegetables.
Maître d'Hôtel	Grilled meat or fish served with lemon and parsley butter.
Marinière	Fish or mussels cooked in white wine and herbs.
Matelote	Fish stew with wine and cider.
Médallions	Small circular cuts of meat, fish or pate.
Mélangé	Mixed.
Meringue	Whisked egg whites, with sugar added.
Meunière	Fish cooked in butter, seasoned and sprinkled with parsley and lemon juice.
Moules	Mussels.
Mouton	Mutton.
Navarin	Lamb stew with vegetables.

Niçoise	Nice style - cooked with tomato, onion garlic and black olives.
Nouilles	Noodles.
Oeufs	Eggs.
Parfait	Frozen dessert made from whipped cream and fruit purée.
Parmentier	Containing potato.
Pâte à choux	Choux pastry.
Paupiette	Thin slices of meat rolled around a savoury filling.
Pavé	Cold savoury mousse set in a square mould. Coated in aspic jelly. Square sponge cake.
Perdrix	Partridge.
Perdreaux	Young partridge.
Petits fours	Bite size cake, fruit or marzipan served at the end of a meal. Sweetmeats.
Petits Pois	Peas.
Pigeonneau	Young pigeon.
Pintade	Guinea fowl.
Piquante	Pleasant sharp, appetising sauce.
Plat du jour	Dish of the day.
Poitrine	Breast.
Pomme de terre	Potato.
Porc	Pork.
Potage	Thick soup.
Poulet	Chicken.
Poussins	Baby chickens, spring chickens.
Printanier	Garnish of spring vegetables.
Provençale	Cooked with garlic and tomatoes.
Purée	Sieved raw or cooked food.
Quenelles	Light savoury dumplings, served as garnish, or with a delicate sauce.
Ragoût	Stew of meat and vegetables.
Ratatouille	Stew of aubergines, onion, pepper and tomato, cooked in olive oil.
Rognons	Kidney.
Roulade	Roll of meat, vegetable, chocolate cake etc.
Saignant	Of meat underdone.
Salade	Salad.
Salmi	Stew made by first roasting game, then cooking in a wine sauce.
Saucisses	Sausages.
Sauté	To cook in shallow hot fat, tossing and turning the food until it is evenly browned.
Savarine	Rich yeast cake.
Selle	Saddle.
Sorbet	Water ice.
Truffle	A rare fungus, black or white with a firm texture and delicate taste.
Veau	Veal.
Velouté	Basic white sauce made with fish, veal or chicken stock.

AMERICAN

Ham	Gammon.
Minced beef	Ground beef.
Broiled/fryer	Oven-ready chicken.
Prosciutto	Parma ham.
Squab	Pigeon.
Rock Cornish hen	Poussin.
Jumbo prawns	Scampi.
Shrimp	Prawns.
Lobster tails	Langoustine.
Heavy cream	Double cream.
Light cream	Single cream.
Shortening	Lard.
Eggplant	Aubergine.
Beet	Beetroot.
Belgium endive	Chicory.
Zucchini	Courgettes.
Chicory	Curly endive.
Snow peas	Mangetout.
Scallions	Spring onion.
All purpose flour	Plain flour.
Pie dough	Shortcrust pastry.
Extract	Essence.
Skillet	Frying pan.
To broil	To grill.

BEEF&LAMB

BEEF

The butcher divides a side of beef into what is known as primal cuts, he then sub-divides the meat to his customers' requirements. Beef is hung for approximately 12-14 days. On a well hung piece of beef the lean meat is plum red and slightly moist; it should always be well flecked with fat (marbling), marbling prevents the meat from drying out during cooking and enhances the flavour. When meat has not been hung for a sufficient period it will be bright red and not so tender. Meat from an animal not of prime quality will be dark red, lean, sinewy and likely to be tough. These cuts are only suitable for stewing, or longer periods of cooking.

The names given to cuts of meat vary with different parts of the country. Always avoid those you are unable to recognise. Avoid rolled joints which are likely to disintegrate whilst cooking. A good butcher will always advise you on the best buy. If you are unsure of your cuts, avoid pre-packed supermarket joints. By law the meat will always be labelled with the name of the country of origin. In anything you buy, remember that price is not an indication of nutritional content.

Blade
Sold as braising steak, in slices, or cubed with kidneys for pie fillings. This cut is lean and excellent for stewing and casseroles.

Brisket
Sold on the bone or rolled (boned). A good piece on the bone should have a fair proportion of meat to fat, it is best pot-roasted or braised. It can also be salted, e.g. salted beef. Boned and rolled, it is suitable for slow cooking, pressed between weights and served cold. An economical buy when cooking for large numbers.

Chuck
The best stewing steak. The meat is slightly coarse and gristly.

Neck
A muscular cut, used for braising or stewing. It is inexpensive, with a high proportion of gristle.

Fillet
Lean and boneless, the cut lies below the ribs of the sirloin. It can be sold as a whole piece or cut into steaks. These will grill well, with minimum cooking time. Fillet is expensive.

Flank
Inexpensive, fatty joint. Excellent for pot-roasting, braising and casseroling.

Leg
One of the hind legs. The meat is lean and has a good flavour, but it needs long and slow cooking. It is used to make consommé and beef tea.

Rib (fore)
A roasting joint which can be cooked on the bone or boned and rolled.

Rib (top and back)
Known as middle rib and comes from the ribs between the fore ribs and the shoulder. The joint is partially boned and rolled for easier carving. A good slow roaster.

Rib (wing and prime)

A large joint between the fore ribs and the sirloin. It is one of the more expensive joints and excellent for roasting. It should have a good eye muscle of meat and a good outer layer of firm yellow creamy fat.

Rump top

A large joint from the hind legs. Suitable for slow roasting at a low temperature. Fat is often tied around it for added flavour during cooking. It can also be cubed for casseroling.

Shin

From the foreleg, and quite gristly. Sold for stewing, casseroles and pies, and used for brawn. Inexpensive, but there is a lot of waste.

Silverside

A boned joint commonly used for salting or spicing. Suitable for slow cooking methods.

Sirloin

A traditional and national joint for roast beef. It is said to have been knighted by a King of England after he had feasted well on a roast loin of beef. For flavour and tenderness it is the best. If it is bought on the bone the fillet is present, but if sold rolled the butcher has usually removed the fillet.

Skirt

There are several skirts, the best being rump skirt. It is thick and heavy with membrane and gristle. The meat should be trimmed and then cubed or minced.

S T E A K S

Châteaubriand

Cut from the centre of the fillet. Weighing about 1-1½ lbs (450-675 g). Generally enough for two people. Usually grilled or fried.

Entrecôte

Lean tender eye muscle from the boneless sirloin.

Mignon

Also known as 'Tournedos'. The small cut from the centre of the fillet. Best grilled or sauté.

Porterhouse

A thick steak cut from the chump end of the sirloin, sometimes containing part of the fillet. Suitable grilled or fried.

Rump

Considered the best flavoured steak, excellent grilled or fried. It should have about ¼ inch fat on the outer edge, but no gristle.

T-Bone

A thick steak cut on the bone from between the chump end and the wing rib. Suitable grilled or fried.

Topside

A lean boneless joint with a fine grain to the flesh. Best slow, or pot roasted. If it is used for roasting, fat should be tied around the meat to prevent it from drying out.

V E A L

Veal is slaughtered at a very young age. There is a strong lobby against this practice. The method used to rear the calves greatly affect the quality and colour of the flesh. Milk-fed calves have a pale flesh, and are highly valued, they are slaughtered at approximately two to three months. Young calves called 'bobby calves', are slaughtered at three weeks old and provide most of the home veal market. This veal is more suitable for roasting, stewing and casseroling. Veal is tender because a calf has not had time to develop muscles, but it requires careful cooking to preserve its tenderness. As a rule carve beef and veal across the grain of the meat.

Best end neck
Sold on the bone for roasting. It can be boned, stuffed and rolled. Often sold as neck cutlets.

Best end neck cutlets
Should have the tip of the chine bone removed. They are cut 1 inch thick. Each cutlet should have a good round eye of meat. Suitable for grilling or frying.

Breast
An economical cut of veal. It can be roasted on or off the bone. Cubed it is ideal for stewing or braising.

Escalopes
From the prime muscle of the leg, such as topside. Escalopes are cut with the grain, no more than ¼" (¾ cm) thick then beaten into thin slices.

Fillet
The most expensive of the veal cuts. It is tender and delicately flavoured. It may be larded and roasted whole or cut into steaks.

Knuckle
It can be slow roasted whole or cut into cubes for the traditional dish 'Osso Bucco'.

Leg
A large joint with plenty of meat in proportion to bone.

Loin
A prime cut of meat. Sold on the bone, or boned and rolled. Suitable for roasting, or cut into portions and served as chops.

Loin chops
Single bone portions cut 1 inch thick, sometimes including the kidney. Suitable for grilling or frying.

Middle neck
A high proportion of bone to flesh. Best used for stewing.

Scrag
Sold for boiling or stewing. Inexpensive, more bone than flesh.

Shoulder
Known as the oyster of the veal. It is a roasting joint.

O F F A L

Offal means the 'off falls', the parts of the various carcasses which are left after the flesh has been removed. Offal is under-rated, it is delicious and nutritious. The American call offal 'variety meats'. They must not be considered humble leftovers. Offal deteriorates quicker than meat, and should be bought fresh. There is both meat and poultry offal. Size, texture and flavour varies with the species and age of the animal.

Liver
Calf's liver is sought for its delicate flavour and smooth texture. Lamb's liver is slightly darker in colour. Both calf's and lamb's liver can be rapidly grilled or sautéed. Larger

pieces of calf's liver roasted or braised. Ox and pig's liver is darker red and has a strong flavour which mellows with longer braising. Ox liver is suitable for stewing in pies, it can be grilled or sautéed but needs soaking in milk to mellow the strong flavour. Pig's liver is used in patés and terrines.

Kidneys

Ox kidney is the largest and coarsest, and has numerous lobes attached to a fatty core. Calf's kidneys are in short supply. The calf's kidney is paler in colour and surrounded by a creamy white suet. All kidneys are surrounded by suet and are suitable for braising, stewing, or stuffing. Pig's kidneys may be grilled or fried, or chopped for casseroling. Cut out the core of a kidney and remove the skin and suet before grilling or frying. Kidneys should be light brown and firm, and should not have an odour.

Tongues

The ox and lamb's tongue are edible. Calf's tongue is hard to find, it is a delicacy. The lamb's tongue is small and weighs about 8 oz (200 g). It should be soaked in slightly salted water before braising or boiling, then skinned before pressing and serving. Ox tongue weighs 4-6 lbs (1 kg 750 g-2 kg 700 g) , and is either bought salted or fresh. It is slowly boiled for several hours, and then skinned, served hot or pressed cold.

Brains

Calves' brains have the most delicate flavour, and a fragile structure. They require only brief cooking, and are commonly poached or sautéed, or puréed for sauces. Brains must be soaked in cold water for a couple of hours to remove any blood.

Heads

Calves', pigs' and sheeps' heads are sold whole or in halves. Calves' are sold fresh or salted, the fresh head may be boiled and served hot with a sauce, or used salted for brawn. The best brawn is made from boiled pig's head. The lamb's head is better boiled or stewed for pie fillings and broths.

Hearts

Hearts are nutritious, but require slow cooking. Calf's heart is not easily available, and needs the coarse fibres cut out. The smallest and most tender heart is the lamb's which should be bright red and firm. The ox heart is muscular and coarse, weighing up to 4 lbs (110 g), and better stewed. Pig's heart is less tender than lamb, larger and less expensive, and better stuffed and slowly braised.

Sweetbreads

Sweetbreads are the two portions of the thymus gland. Calf's sweetbreads are considered a delicacy, and highly prized. They are mainly sautéed, fried or braised. Lamb's sweetbreads are cooked in the same way.

Feet

Pig's trotters are the most commonly sold. Calves' trotters are used mainly for their high gelatine content for stocks as are pigs'.

Tripe

The collective term for the four stomachs of curd-chewing animals. The ox's stomach, of which the first stomach is the smoothest, known as the blanket, and the second which is the honeycomb. Tripe should be firm, thick and white, not slimy. It can be stewed, boiled or deep fried.

Ox cheek

An economical cut used for stews and brawns.

Oxtail

Sold skinned and usually jointed. The fat should be creamy white and the meat lean and deep red. Good for braising, casseroling, and a basis for soups.

Bone marrow

The thigh and shoulder bones from beef contain delicately flavoured marrow. Poached marrow can be spread on toast for an hors d'oeuvre. Excellent for broths and adding flavour to stews and casseroles.

Poultry offal

Chicken livers are superb grilled or sautéed and for pâté making. Chicken hearts can be included in a mixed grill, or poached along with the gizzard for use in stuffings and stews along with the neck. The heart, gizzard and neck should never be disregarded as they are invaluable when making gravy and sauces.

L A M B

The majority of lambs are slaughtered between three and twelve months old. The term 'mutton' is applied to the flesh of sheep at least eighteen months to two years old. Lamb is delicately flavoured and a rich source of vitamin B, iron and minerals.

The British eat more lamb than most nations, except perhaps, the Australians and New Zealanders. About 40 % of lamb eaten in Britain is home produced, the rest being imported from Australia and New Zealand. By law, the butcher must label all his meat from the country of origin.

Meat from a young animal is usually pale pink, the older the lamb is, the darker the meat. The fat should be creamy white and not oily or yellow. The flavour of the lamb does vary considerably, it depends on the quality of the grazing fields. Welsh lamb can often taste strongly of heather.

A prime joint of lamb should have a good depth of lean meat, covered with a moderate layer of fat. The skin should be pliable to the touch and not hard and wrinkled. A blue tinge in the knuckle and rib bones indicate that the animal is young.

Best end of neck

Excellent roasted on the bone. Two best ends of neck are used to shape a crown roast and guard of honour.

Breast

Sold boned, stuffed and rolled for roasting. A fairly fatty joint.

Chops

Come from either the leg or loin of the animal. Suitable for grilling, frying or braising.

Chump chops

Cut from the leg and the loin. Oval shape with a small bone in the centre.

Loin

Cut from the loin, they have a T-shaped bone. Fairly lean with a thin layer of fat on the outside edge.

Cutlets

Taken from the best end neck, they have a long bone with a thin layer of fat and a small round eye of sweet lean meat. Suitable grilled or fried.

Middle neck cutlets

Fattier and more gristly than best end neck cutlets and are better stewed or braised.

Fillet

The upper part of the leg, sold as a separate joint. The meat is lean with a little fat and no gristle. Suitable roasted whole on the bone.

Knuckle

The lower part of the hind leg, sold as a separate joint which is quite expensive. Commonly roasted whole or boned, rolled and stuffed.

Leg

This is the most popular roasting joint of the lamb. It is sold on the bone but can be boned and rolled. The leg is often divided into two and sold as the knuckle and fillet. In Scotland the leg is known as gigot.

Loin

This is a prime joint usually sold on the bone for roasting.

Middle neck

This joint comes from between the best end neck and the scrag. It has a large proportion of fat and bone to meat. It is better used for braising.

Noisettes

These are cut from the loin and best end. They are small round thick slices, boned, trimmed of fat, shaped and tied into round fillets, each weighing about 6 oz (175 g). They are suitable for frying and grilling.

Rib

The complete rib is seldom sold whole but divided into three sections, best end of neck, middle neck and scrag.

Saddle

A large prime joint comprising both the loins, cut from the best end and the legs with the tail left on. The meat is skinned, the cleaned kidneys are skewered and tied to the end of the loins. A saddle weighs about 8 lbs (4 kgs), a large expensive roast.

Scrag end of neck

This cut comes from nearest the head, it contains much bone and gristle. Used for stews, soups and broths.

Shoulder

This is a roasting joint from the fore-quarter. It is the least expensive of the roasting joints, fattier than the leg, but with a sweeter flavour.

PORK GAMMON

BACON & HAM

Most pigs are slaughtered at about eight months old or less. The prime loin joint is pale in colour, tinged with pink, and the fat pure white. Neck and shoulder joints are darker and coarser grained. The flesh and fat must be firm to touch. The bones of the young pig are tinged with red, in older pigs they are white and hard.

For ham and bacon the fat should be clean and white, whilst the flesh is pink and firm. Uncooked hams may have a bluish tinge on the surface of the meat known as a bloom, this is not decay.

Store pork in the coolest part of the refrigerator, unwrapped. Fresh pork will keep for three to four days, bacon and ham five to seven days. Fresh pork can be frozen for three to six months, hams and bacon are less suitable for lengthy freezing as the fat turns rancid. Never freeze cooked ham or bacon.

Although inspected for evidence of contamination, it is still necessary to cook pork and gammon thoroughly to protect against any infection. This does not mean that you must cook it beyond recognition, it only needs to reach the internal temperature of 59 degrees C (137 degrees F), about the temperature of rare beef. The rule is never serve pork underdone.

PORK JOINTS

Belly of pork
Streaky pork, fairly fatty with a good proportion of lean meat. It is a cheap joint, sold fresh or salted. Good roasted or stewed.

Blade
About 2 lbs (900 g) in size. This joint can be sold boned, rolled and stuffed, or on the bone. It is best roasted. Reasonably priced.

Chump chops
These have a round central bone. They lie between the loin and the leg, and are cut about three quarters of an inch thick.

Loin chops
They have a 'T' bone and often the kidney is left in. They should be bought with the rind on. Best grilled or roasted.

Spare rib chops
A smaller eye of meat than the loin or chump chops, but a sweeter taste. Grill or fry. They are not the same as the spare ribs which come from the belly but are cut from the spare rib joint.

Fillet or Tenderloin
The lean and very tender muscle which lies under the backbone in the hind loin. Fillet comes from the bacon pigs. It is covered in a near transparent skin which should be removed before cooking. A lean joint of meat best grilled or fried. When roasted it needs larding. Flattened, it can be a substitute veal escalopes, or be stuffed and rolled.

Fillet half leg
Top end of the hind leg, which can be roasted whole or cut into steaks and fried or grilled.

Hand

The lower part of the shoulder. It has a large area of rind for crisp crackling and so ideal for roasting, it can also be boned and rolled.

Hand and Spring

Also known as the shoulder. Quite inexpensive, sold fresh or salted. It should be well fleshed with fat.

Knuckle

Cut from the lower part of the leg. The knuckle joint is best roasted whole or boned and stuffed. Excellent for boiling and stewing. On a prime joint the knuckle bone should be tinged with blue.

Leg

A prime roasting joint. A whole leg weighs approximately 10/15 lbs (4.5/6.75 kgs). This is cut in half because of its size, and both joints are excellent for roasting on the bone.

Loin

This joint is considered the prime joint of the pig; it is also the most expensive. The whole loin weighs about 9/10 lbs (4.05/4.5 kgs). It is usually sold jointed as it is often too big for one meal, the choicest part being the hind loin which has both the kidney and the fillet attached. When buying a joint of loin look for a good proportion of pale pink meat to fat.

Neck end

An inexpensive joint which should have an even distribution of fat to a large amount of lean meat. It can be boned and rolled, or sold separately as spare ribs or blade. If cubed it can be used for kebabs.

Spare ribs

Cut from the rib part of the belly. All the rind and excess fat is removed to produce single bone strips. Much used in Chinese cookery and for barbecuing.

Spare rib

Suitable for roasting, braising or stewing.

Sucking (suckling) pig

This is a young pig from three weeks to two months old when it is slaughtered. Excellent spit roasted for outdoor parties. A whole apple is traditionally stuffed in its mouth.

BACON & GAMMON

Collar

An inexpensive bacon joint, best boiled, then roasted. It can be bought whole, but it is often cut into joints as follows:
- **end collar** good for boiling and as a base for soups.
- **middle collar** cooked in the same manner.
- **prime collar** which is excellent boiled then roasted, eaten hot or cold.
It can also be cut into rashers.

Back

A lean joint, weighing 8 lbs (3.6 kgs). Best boiled, braised or baked, or cut into rashers known as top back rashers, which are lean with a sweeter flavour and a more distinctive taste than other bacon rashers.

- The middle or cut through

Cuts are cheaper and are a combination of the streaky and the back bacon rashers. This joint is ideal roasted whole.

- The short back

The prime cut of the back, nearly always sold cut into rashers.

- The oyster cut

Comes from the rear part of the back, sold as a small joint suitable for boiling or cut into small rashers.

- Long back

Is another choice cut. The rashers are cut thinly and used for grilling and frying or cut into thin steaks.

Gammon

The whole gammon is the hind leg of the bacon pig, it is cut square at the top unlike the ham. The gammon is more expensive than the other bacon joints and is best part boiled and then baked whole. Because it is a large joint it is often sold cut into smaller joints which are as follows:

- corner gammon

From the top of the leg, about 4 lbs (1.8 kg) in weight and very lean, best boiled and baked.

- middle gammon

A lean joint from the middle of the leg, this has an even shape and an excellent flavour, ideally boiled and baked. It can be cut into gammon rashers and steaks for grilling or frying.

- hock and gammon knuckle

Has a high proportion of bone. This is suitable for boiling.

- gammon slipper

A small lean triangular joint from inside the hind leg, traditionally boiled.

Streaky or flank

A belly joint with alternative layers of fat and lean and a little gristle. Sold as bacon rashers. The flank is the end of the streaky joint and invariably fatty and so used for larding only.

Forehock

The whole leg of the bacon pig, often sold as three smaller joints:

- The butt suitable for boiling and baking.

- The fore slipper fattier and best boiled or baked and served cold.

- The small hock is the knuckle end and a tough and bony joint. In this case the meat is best cut from the bone and used in casseroles.

Ham

The hind leg of the pig, similar to the gammon but with a rounded end. It is removed from the carcass before salting and is then cured. A whole ham can weigh between 10/16 lbs (4.5/7.2 kgs). Usually sold cut into slices or whole.

Well known English hams are:

York

Lightly smoked, a delicate pink colour with a firm flesh.

Suffolk

Soaked in molasses, it has a delicate flavour.

Wiltshire

Cured before being removed from the side of the pig. Green gammon rather than ham. Mild cured, delicate taste.

Bradenham

Smaller than other hams, soaked in molasses rather than salt which turns its skin black. The flesh is more red than pink. The hams are hung for months to develop their distinctive, slightly sweet flavour. This ham is not easily available and very expensive.

POULTRY & GAME

"A wonderful bird is the pelican,
His bill will hold more than his belly can
He can take in his beak
Food enough for a week,
But I'm damned if I see how the hell he can."
(The Pelican)
DIXON LANIER MERRITT 1879-1954

POULTRY

Poultry are domestic birds bred specially for the table. These include: chicken, duck, goose, guinea fowl and turkey. When possible it is much better to buy free-range, as free-range birds have more flavour than battery reared ones. The age of the bird is key to its flavour and texture. As a rule the younger the bird the more subtle the flavour. In a young bird the backbone is soft and flexible, the feet are smooth with fine scales; they are more tender and therefore suitable for grilling, roasting and sautéing. In an older bird the meat becomes tougher, the flesh develops a depth of flavour, the breastbone is rigid, the skin is darker and the scales on the feet coarser. Older birds will stand longer cooking times. The length of time the bird is left before drawing will also affect its flavour. The skin and flesh colour varie according to the breed, and the diet of the bird.

Chicken
Most chickens' flavours are enhanced by stuffing them before roasting.
Poussin a small six week old chicken.
Spring Chicken traditionally should be a young cockerel, or a two to three month old chicken of either sex, most suited to roasting or grilling.
Boiling Fowl or Rooster a year old fowl.
Capon a cock bird castrated to make it grow fatter and retain the succulence of a young bird.
Duck
There is a delightful old saying "A duck for four, thank heavens there are no more". There are many ducks reared specially for eating, amongst the most sought after are the Nantais and Rouennais of France, the Aylesbury duck of England, and the Long Island duck of the United States. A good duck should weigh approximately 4/6 lbs (1.8/2.7 kgs). The breast should be plump, the bird's underbill soft enough to bend and the feet pliable. The fresh bird is best from August to December, but they are usually available all year round. The term duck applies to a bird two months old and over, anything younger is called a duckling, weighing approximately 3½/4 lbs (1.75/1.8 kg) and at its best eaten between April and July.
Goose
This bird was traditionally served at festive occasions, but the introduction of the turkey to Europe curtailed this tradition. Goose is considered by many gourmets to be the best of all poultry, with a slightly gamey flavour. The average weight is 6/12 lbs (2.7/5.4 kgs). Choose a young bird with soft yellow feet and legs which still have a little down left on them. Fresh birds are eaten from October to February. The French force feed geese to

enlarge their livers thus producing 'foie gras', animal lovers regard this method cruel, but the pâté is quite delicious and used frequently in gourmet cookery.

Wild Goose

Commonly known as the 'Canada goose'. The flesh of the wild goose is dark and lean. They hang for 4/5 days. Wild goose weighs approximately 7 lbs (3.15 kgs) and will serve six persons. The season is October to the end of December.

Green Goose or Gosling

A young goose not more than six months old.

Guinea Fowl

The guinea fowl was originally a game bird but it is now farmed. It is similar in taste to the pheasant, and should be hung for several days, as the meat can be on the dry side. The flesh is creamy-white and firm, benefiting from barding before roasting. At its best eaten between February and April.

Turkey

Turkey can weigh anything from 6/40 lbs (2.7/18 kgs). The flesh should be pale white with a blue tinge. To retain moisture during cooking it is advisable to stuff the bird before roasting.

G A M E

Game refers to wild birds and animals which are hunted for sport and eaten. In England there is a close season when hunting is forbidden. The quail, rabbit and pigeon are not protected by law and are available throughout the year.

For roasting and grilling, game should be young, it must be hung to tenderise the flesh and produce the flavour. Hanging should take place in a cool, dry, well ventilated room away from insects or flies. Birds are usually hung by the neck, rabbits and deer by the hind legs. Birds are hung unplucked and undrawn and are ready for cooking when the feathers can be pulled out easily. Furred game is usually hung for approximately two weeks.

Grouse (Red or Scottish)

One grouse is served per person. The young bird is better roasted, and older ones casseroled. The season is August 12th to mid-October, but they can be eaten up until December 10th. The first day of grouse shooting is called 'The Glorious 12th'. The diet of the grouse will affect the flavour of the flesh. A grouse needs to hang for about three days.

Mallard (Wild Duck)

This is the largest of the wild ducks and the flesh is lean and dry. Allow one bird for two persons. Wild duck is only hung for one day. The season is September 1st to 28th February, it is at its best between November and December.

Teal

The most common wild duck, which requires no hanging. One teal is served per person, it is excellent grilled or roasted. The season is September 1st to February 28th.

Partridge

The English and grey partridge have a better flavour than the French partridge. The flesh is light-coloured. Hang for 3/4 days before roasting or grilling. One is served per person. The season is September 1st to January 31st.

Pheasant

Sold as a brace, one cock and one hen. The hen pheasant is considered the tastiest and will serve up to three people, and the cock pheasant four people. The season is October 1st to January 31st, but pheasants are best in November and December.

Pigeon

The wood pigeon is inexpensive and best casseroled as it is often tough. The very young birds are excellent roasted, grilled or casseroled. Hang for one day, serving one per person. Pigeons are available all year round, but best eaten between August and October.

Quail

Quail has a less gamey flavour than other game birds, and is now more common because it is farm reared. It is not hung, and should be served the day of killing. Serve three birds per person as they are very small. Available all year round, as are quail eggs.

Snipe

This small bird is rarely on sale in the shops. Some gourmets maintain that it should not be drawn before being cooked. The long bill, after twisting the neck around is pushed like a skewer between the legs and into the body. One snipe is served per person. They are hung for 3/4 days and then roasted. The season is August 12th to January 31st.

Woodcock

The bird weighs on average 12 oz (350 g) and closely resembles the snipe. It is hung for three days and roasted undrawn, trussed with its long bill. The season is October 1st to January 31st.

There are other small game birds which are not so popular in Britain, but are eaten widely in France, they are a great delicacy. For example: Buntings (ortolans), Larks (alouettes or mauviettes), Thrushes (grives) and Blackbirds (merles). They are all best braised or roasted with plenty of fat or liquid, and are served on small croûtes.

Note: When buying game birds, choose plump firm specimens, with supple skin and smooth firmly-attached feathers. Avoid damaged shot birds. The odour should never be disagreably pungent, but should smell gamey.

FURRED GAME

Hare

A good hare has soft ears, white teeth and smooth fur. There are two different types, the English or brown hare and the Scottish or blue hare. A young hare weighs approximately 6/7 lbs (2.7/3.15 kgs) and should hang for about one week. The young hare can be roasted, but older hares are better casseroled. The season is August 1st to the end of March.

Rabbit

The flesh of the wild rabbit often has a gamey flavour, it should not be hung, and skinned at once after killing. The rabbits sold in shops are domesticated rabbits and resemble chicken in flavour. They are prepared and cooked in a similar fashion to that of the hare.

Venison

Deer flesh should be dark red with a fine grain and firm white fat. The best meat comes from the male deer known as the 'buck' when it is 1½/2 years old. It should be hung for at least one week. Venison is usually sold in joints, the choicest cut being the saddle. It is roasted or braised. The season is June to January.

FISH & SHELLFISH

There are so many varieties of fish that it would take a whole book to name them. The range of both fresh fish and shellfish available in Europe is extensive and rarely used to its full potential, we hope to help you select for economy, variety and quality.

Buying fresh fish, and shellfish.

There is no connection between price and quality, for the simple reason that fish and shellfish are caught in their natural environment. Supply is more erratic than that of vegetables or meat, and subject to considerable price variations. Fish in season is caught in greater quantity and becomes cheaper.

Try not to be conservative, seafood which we consider to be inferior in England, might be highly prized in another country. The Venetians regard the tail of the angler fish as one of the finest marine delicacies, while in North America the same is virtually unknown.

Fish is highly perishable, so great care must be taken to ensure that it is absolutely fresh when purchased. Ideally it should be kept alive until cooked, but this is quite impractical, as the fish is often caught hundreds of miles away. The appearance and odour of fish provide the necessary clues to its freshness and condition. The whole fish should have a shiny skin, pink gills and full bright eyes with black pupils and transparent corneas. To the touch it should be soft and springy. Fish should have a clean pleasant odour, and not smell fishy.

However skate, shark and ray are the exception to this rule. Fresh, they contain a chemical called urea which smells of ammonia, this smell breaks down. The fish should not be eaten for a couple of days, until the smell subsides.

Fish should have a translucent look to it and not appear milky. Fillets which show discoloration around the edges and appear dry are not fresh.

Shellfish deteriorate more rapidly, and so are usually sold alive or in the case of lobsters, crabs and other crustaceans pre-cooked. The general rule is, fresh shellfish does not have an odour. Seafood will keep fresh for no longer than a day stored in a refridgerator loosely wrapped. Neither fish or shellfish respond well to freezing. Fish lends itself to drying, salting, smoking and combinations of these curing techniques.

COOKING TECHNIQUES

Fresh fish and shellfish can be fried, grilled, stewed, braised and steamed. Cooking time for fish varies with size, heat and method.

To find out whether fish is cooked, without harming the presentation, cut into the flesh with the point of a knife at its thickest part, just behind the gills. When the flesh no longer clings to the bone it is cooked, it will have changed from translucent to opaque. At this point the fish should be removed from the heat as rapid deterioration takes place after this, the flesh will shrink, toughen and flake apart.

Fish is classified into: **white fish, oily fish and shellfish.**

WHITE FISH

Small white fish are either sold whole or filleted, whether flat or round. Larger white fish may be sold whole, filleted, in cutlets or steaks. A steak is cut from a round fish in the thickest part. A cutlet is cut from in between the head and the middle part of the fish.

Bass (White Salmon, Sea Perch, Bar)
A round, silvery fish, greyish blue back with a white underside. The flesh should be pink and sweet smelling. Bake, poach, or grill small whole fish. The season is May to August.

Bream (Sea Bream)
A round bony fish with coarse scales and a black spot behind the head. The flesh is pink and delicate. The fish needs careful scaling. It is best grilled or fried. The season is June to December.

Brill
A flat fish similar to turbot, but smaller. The skin is slightly slimy when the fish is fresh, grey yellow in colour with small scales, and a yellow white delicate flesh. Best baked or grilled, in season from January to April.

Catfish (Rockfish)
A round blue-grey fish. Firm flesh tinged with pink. Best use is in stews and soups. The season is September to February.

Cod
The cod is a large round fish with an elongated body which can weigh up to 80 lbs (36 kgs). Its back is olive brown with yellow and brown spots and small soft grey scales, the underside is white. The flesh is firm, sold either in fillets (fresh or wood-smoked), or in steaks. Avoid cod with pink or grey discoloration. Best for poaching, baking or grilling. It is best during October to April.

Cod Roe
The female roe is pinkish and hard, and the male roe soft known as chitterlings. Sold boiled or uncooked. The hard roe is often sold smoked.

Coley (Coal Fish)
A round fish with a near black skin and pinky grey flesh which goes white when cooked. Sold filleted for grilling, frying or baking. Available most of the year.

Dab
A flat fish related to the plaice but smaller and with rough scales. The fish should have a slimy skin. It is sold whole, weighing about 6/8 oz (175/225 g). Best grilled or fried. Season April to January.

Dogfish
Related to the shark. It is always sold skinned, on the bone and split through. The flesh is firm, creamy flavoured and white in colour. It is one of the least expensive white fish, and best used in soups and stews. The season is all year but it is best between September to May.

Flounder (Fluke)
A flat fish of the same family as plaice and brill. It has a light brown upper side with orange red spots and a creamy white underside. The skin should have a little slime on it. Season September to February.

Haddock

A round fish of the cod family. It has a grey skin and a dark line runs along both flanks, with a dark smudge behind the gills. The flesh is white and firm. It is usually sold whole, filleted or in steaks. Suitable for poaching, baking, grilling and frying. Available all year round but best between November and February.

Smoked Haddock

A pale yellow colour. If on the bone it is called finnan haddock or it is sold as fillets. If the haddock is a strong yellow colour it has been artificially dyed.

Arbroath Smokies

Small whole haddock smoked to a brown colour.

Hake

A round long and slender fish with a scaly silver grey skin. The flesh is white and flaky and practically boneless. Sold as fillets or cutlets and best suited to baking. Season July to March.

Halibut

A flat fish which can weigh anything from 9 lbs/400 lbs (4 kg/18 kgs). It has a dark olive skin, marbled with lighter olive. The flesh should be quite firm, white and dry. It is sold both smoked and fresh, and best between August and April. Chicken halibut is a smaller fish 1/8 lbs (0.45/3.6 kgs). Greenland or mock halibut 2/5 lbs (0.9/2.25 kgs), and is always sold frozen, best between March and October.

Plaice

A flat fish, grey-brown with orange spots on the upper side, and a creamy white underside. Fresh, the fish spots should be quite bright and the flesh soft and white. The fish is more often sold whole or filleted. Excellent for grilling, frying or poaching. Available all year round, but best between January and April.

Skate

A flat ray-shaped fish, with a slightly moist, smelly skin, with pink flesh. Only the wings should have prominent bones. Poach, grill or fry. Best bought between October and April.

Sole (Common Dover or Black)

The oval body is almost completely surrounded by fins and covered with tiny hard scales. Olive brown colour with irregular black markings on the upperside, the underside is white. The flesh has a delicate flavour and is finely textured. Fresh sole is covered in slime, and the skin difficult to peel off. Available all year round, but best between May and February.

Lemon sole

A wider and more pointed fish than the Dover sole. The skin is a lighter brown with darker brown spots on the upper side. The flesh is more stringy, and some say with less flavour. Best, December to March.

Turbot

A flat fish with a black spot and raised growths on its back and a creamy white underside. It has a white firm flesh similar to halibut, but with a moister delicate flavour. This fish is sold whole, in steaks or fillets. Best for baking, poaching and grilling. Sold all year but better between April and July.

Whiting

A round fish from the cod family. Grey-olive-green on the back, with pale yellow spots and a silvery underside. When the fish is fresh the flesh is soft and flaky, but it deteriorates rapidly. It is best poached, baked or fried. Available all year round.

OILY FISH

Oil is found throughout the flesh, whereas in white fish it is only found in the liver. Oily fish are caught from the sea, freshwater lakes, rivers and streams or produced in fish farms. Oily fish are eaten fresh, smoked or salted.

Carp
A round freshwater fish with a small mouth. There are many varieties. They are best baked, stuffed or braised, the season is mid-June to March.

Conger Eel
The most common sea eel, it is pale grey to jet black in colour. The flesh is hard and tough when fresh and better boiled or steamed. The season is March to October.

Common Eel
A richly flavoured freshwater fish. Its skin is shiny black and flesh firm and white. It is always sold alive and should be cooked as soon as possible after killing It is usually steamed, braised or fried and skinned. It is also available smoked or jellied. Fresh eel is best between autumn and early winter.

Herring
A small saltwater fish, delicately flavoured, with numerous bones. It has silvery scales on the back, silvery flanks and underside, and firm brown flesh. The skin should be shiny and bright and firm to touch. Sold whole it is suitable for frying and grilling. Herrings are also sold smoked or pickled. The season is all year but best between June and March.

Bismarch Herrings
Flat fillets, marinated in spiced vinegar and onion rings.

Bloater
Lightly smoked, salted whole herring. Best on day of purchase as they do not keep well.

Buckling
Whole smoked herring, requires no cooking.

Herring roe
Both hard and soft roes, in short supply.

Kipper
The most common smoked herring. It is split and put in brine before being smoked. The un-dyed kipper keeps a lot longer than the dyed varieties. All kippers should have a sheen to the flesh and be soft to the touch. Kippers are sold whole, usually in pairs, or as fillets.

Red Herring
A dried and smoked whole fish dyed red. Strong salty flavour mainly used in mousses and pâtés.

Rollmop
Herring fillets marinated in spiced vinegar and rolled round chopped onions, gherkins and peppercorns.

Salt Herring
Whole or gutted herring preserved in a heavy salt brine.

Mackerel
A long slender saltwater fish with a striped blue and green back, silvery underside and firm flesh. It is sold whole, best grilled, baked, fried or barbecued. The skin should be shiny and the flesh quite stiff. The season is all year, but best between winter and spring.

Smoked Mackerel
Smoked whole or in fillets ready for eating.

Mullet Grey

A large estuary fish, of 12/15 " (30/38 cm) long. It has a grey scaly back, striped on the sides with darker lines, and silvery white underside. The flesh is coarse, firm and fatty. Avoid over large fish. Bake, poach or grill. The season is July to February.

Mullet Red

A red skinned saltwater fish with a firm white flesh and a delicate flavour. It is unrelated to the grey mullet. Best grilled or baked. The fish is in short supply and mainly imported frozen. Best between May to September.

Perch

A brightly coloured, round freshwater fish with hard scales. Seldom available in the fishmongers'. Grilled whole. The season is June 16th to March 14th.

Pike

A large lean freshwater fish with a long body. The flesh is coarse and needs soaking before being baked or boiled. The season is June 16th to March 14th.

Pilchard

A small saltwater fish similar to the herring. Sold tinned because they deteriorate quickly. Caught off the Devon and Cornwall coasts.

Salmon

This is considered the king of fish. It is caught in cool fast-running rivers. It is a saltwater fish which travels up-river to spawn. The perfect fresh salmon has bright silvery scales, red gills and pink red close-textured flesh. It can weigh between 8/20 lbs (3.6/9 kgs) and is sold whole or in steaks. Fresh Scottish salmon is at its best between May and July. Imported salmon is also readily available on the market. A small salmon is known as a Grilse and weighs 4/8 lbs (1.8/3.6 kgs).

Salmon Trout

A freshwater fish, similar to salmon. The scales are silvery when fresh. The flesh is firm, pale pink, with a delicate flavour. The average weight is 2/6 lbs (0.9/2.7 kgs). It is sold whole, cooked in the same ways as salmon. Best eaten between March and July.

Smoked Salmon

Scotch smoked salmon has strips of fat between the meat and is considered the finest. Other smoked salmons are available.

Sardine

A small herring-like saltwater fish usually sold tinned in oil or tomatoes. Imported fresh sardines from France are becoming increasingly popular. The season is March to September.

Sprat

A small silvery-skinned saltwater fish of the herring family.

Trout Rainbow

The most common trout is reared on trout farms, it is green-gold in colour with a whitish flesh. Available all year round.

Trout River or Brown

This fish has a darker skin than the rainbow and is spotted. The flesh is superior and it is best grilled or fried. In scant supply. Eaten between March and September.

Trout Smoked

Rainbow trout are smoked to a rich brown colour and require no further cooking.

Whitebait

Whitebait are the young of the herring or sprat, about 1½ " (3½ cm) long. The flesh is firm and grey-white, with a silvery skin. Sold deep frozen all year, but fresh whitebait are in season February to July.

Tuna fish

A huge fish. The flesh is deep red brown and close textured. Excellent grilled, baked or stewed. Sold fresh, tinned in oil or brine.

Shark

An unpopular fish in Britain, but eaten regularly in warmer climates. It is a good stewing fish.

SHELLFISH

"Oysters are more beautiful than any religion. There's nothing in Christianity or Buddhism that quite matches the sympathetic unselfishness of an oyster."
'SAKI' (H H MUNRO) 1870-1916

Shellfish are divided into two groups: molluscs, such as oysters, scallops and mussels which all have hinged shells, and crustaceans which have jointed shells such as lobsters, shrimps and crabs. Much confusion about the naming of shellfish arises, as many British shellfish do not have a foreign equivalent and vice versa. In Britain we refer to the Dublin Bay Prawn as Scampi, but in the true sense the scampi is only caught in the Bay of Naples. Molluscs are ignored by most cooks which is a pity as there is an abundant variety available.

Squid and Octopus

These are members of the cephalopod family. The flesh is eaten mainly in the Mediterranean countries and the Far East. They are delicious deep-fried, stewed or marinated for salads.

Clam

This is an American mollusc which is now farmed in Britain. It should always be sold alive in its shell and it is usually served raw like an oyster. They can also be cooked like a mussel, or smoked. Their season is all year but they are best eaten in the autumn.

Cockles

A tiny mollusc with a white fluted shell. They are usually sold cooked and shelled and often used in fish dishes to replace oysters or mussels. The season is between September and April, but they are available all year round.

Crab

There are numerous varieties of crabs. The spider crabs are usually poached and served in their shells. The small swimming and shore crabs have very little meat on them, and are usually used for flavouring stews or soups. The crab we commonly see on the slab of the fishmongers is the larger crustacean which is grey-brown when alive, and red-brown when it has been cooked. It is sometimes sold alive, but usually the fishmonger cooks and dresses the crab before he sells it. The claws provide the white meat and the shell the brown meat. Male cock crabs have the larger claws and the female hen crabs contain the edible roes or red coral. Fresh crabs should weigh between 2/2½ lbs (0.9/1.15 kg), and the claws should be intact and not damaged. When shaken it should feel heavy and have no sound of water inside. They are available all year round, but best between May and October.

Crawfish (Spiny Lobster, Rock Lobster)

Similar to the lobster but heavier, weighing 5/6 lbs (2.25/2.7 kgs). This crustacean does not have large claws, all the meat is contained in the tail. The flesh is coarser than lobster. It is sold alive or cooked, but is in scant supply. The season is between April and September.

Lobster

This crustacean is dark blue, it turns a deep red orange when cooked. The male lobster is brighter than the female and smaller, but it has larger claws. They should weigh about 1/2 lbs (450/900 g). The female's tail is broader and the flesh more tender, it also contains the coral spawn or eggs which are used for lobster butter. When buying a lobster make sure it feels heavy for its size and the tail springs back when straightened out. Avoid any lobster with white shells on its back as this indicates it is older. They are available all year, but best between April and August. Season and availability affect the market price considerably.

Mussels

A blue black shelled mollusc which is cooked alive in its shell in many traditional dishes. Discard mussels with broken shells before cooking and any which do not close when tapped. Mussels are sold by the pint allowing one pint per person. They are also available smoked in tins. The season is September to March.

Oysters

These molluscs are highly priced and usually eaten raw, but can also be cooked. The shells should be closed or shut when tapped. It is maintained that a raw oyster should be swallowed whole from the shell, but others prefer to chew the oyster to obtain the full flavour. You should only open an oyster just before eating and they must be very fresh. Serve on ice, with lemon. Allow about six oysters per person. It is said that an oyster should only be eaten when there is a 'R' in the month. The season is September to April.

Portuguese Oyster

Imported from various countries. It is larger than the native oyster and the shell more irregular. It also has less flavour but is available all year round.

Prawns

A grey, soft-shelled small crustacean. The shell turns bright red and the flesh pink when cooked. They are usually sold already boiled, shelled or unshelled. Available all year round.

Dublin Bay Prawns (Scampi, Norway Lobster)

The largest of the British prawns, approximately 4" (10 cm) long. Alive they have a pale pink hard shell and become bright pink when boiled. Available all year round.

Scallops

This mollusc has white flesh and an orange roe. It is native to Britain. They have a pinkish brown shell and usually sold opened. Delicious poached, baked or grilled and in stews. The season is September to March, but available all year round.

Shrimps Common or Brown

These crustaceans have small grey-brown soft shells which turn pink when boiled.

Pink Shrimps

These are less tasty than the brown shrimps and are usually sold cooked and unpeeled. They are bright pink when cooked.

Whelks

A mollusc which is always sold cooked and shelled. They are eaten with vinegar and brown bread. Available all year round but best between September and February.

Winkles

Similar to whelks but smaller, sold cooked and shelled. All year availability, but best between October and May.

Sea urchin (Oursin)

A spherical spiky sea creature. The soft orange inside is eaten. It can have a slight iodine flavour.

VEGETABLES

ARTICHOKES, GLOBE

The base of the flower, scales and heart are eaten. A thick cluster of silky hairs covers the choke which is embedded in the fond. The edible parts of a globe artichoke are the fleshy half-moon shape at the base of each scale and the fond, once the silky hairs have been removed.

❀ ☆☆☆
PREPARATION TIME: 10 MINUTES
COOKING TIME: 40 MINUTES

Ingredients:

Globe artichokes   *Lemon juice*

Preparation:

Trim the stalk level with the base of the head. Trim the leaves with a pair of scissors, wash well and leave upside down to drain. Lemon juice prevents any discoloration of cut areas. Cook in boiling water with lemon juice added until the scales can easily be pulled away, approximately 40 minutes. Drain thoroughly upside down.

Serving:

Artichokes make an excellent starter. Serve hot or cold with melted butter, hollandaise sauce, French dressing, mayonnaise or tartar sauce.

GARLIC DRESSED ARTICHOKES

❀ ☆☆☆ **Serves 2 Persons**
PREPARATION TIME: 10 MINUTES
CHILLING TIME: 1 HOUR

Ingredients:

l tin of globe artichokes or six fresh small   *6 tbs olive oil*
ones   *6 tbs of lemon juice*
1 lemon   *1 tsp of fresh chopped marjoram*
2 garlic gloves crushed   *Seasoning*

Advance Preparation:

Drain the artichokes and submerge in a bowl of acidulated water. Gently wash them and drain. Blend the lemon juice, garlic, and oil together, season with salt and black pepper and the chopped marjoram. Marinade the artichokes in the dressing and chill in the refrigerator for at least 1 hour. Serve chilled on a bed of endive leaves.

ARTICHOKES VINAIGRETTE

✿ ☆☆☆ **Serves 4 Persons**
PREPARATION TIME: 15 MINUTES
COOKING TIME: 40 MINUTES

Ingredients:

4 fresh globe artichokes,   *French dressing (see page 315)*
1 lemon

Preparation:
Trim the leaves and the stalk. Cut a slice of lemon and secure with string at the base of the stalk. Lightly salt a large pan of water and bring to the boil. Add the artichokes, cover and cook for 40 minutes or until the outer leaves can be easily pulled from the artichokes. Drain. Serve one artichoke per person, providing a small bowl with French dressing to dip the leaves in, one for the discarded leaves and a finger bowl.

JERUSALEM ARTICHOKES

Jerusalem artichokes are potato-like tubers, with a sweet delicate flavour. Brought to Europe from Massachusetts in the early seventeenth century. They are a member of the sunflower family.

✿ ☆☆☆
COOKING TIME: 30 MINUTES
PREPARATION: Same as potatoes, add lemon juice to prevent discoloration.

Method:
This vegetable can be served in a number of ways. The simplest method is to boil them in salted acidulated water until tender. The skins need to be scrubbed and it is definitely easier to cook them in the skins and remove the flesh afterwards. The flesh can then be blended with butter and seasoning. Tender young skins need not be removed after cooking. If you par-boil artichokes they can then be sliced and sautéed in butter, seasoned with chopped parsley, Tabasco sauce, salt and pepper. Artichokes can be roasted as potatoes or used as a root vegetable in casseroles.

A S P A R A G U S

They are expensive because the plant only shoots for six weeks each year. It is best eaten a few hours after harvesting, when the spears are tightly compressed, the stems green or white and moist. Any traces of brown on the cut edges indicates that the grass is past its best.
Serve: Hot or cold as a first course or vegetable.

BOILED ASPARAGUS

✿ ☆☆☆☆☆
PREPARATION TIME: 10 MINUTES
COOKING TIME: 10-15 MINUTES

Method:
Wash carefully and trim any woody parts from the base of the stem.   White-stemmed asparagus skin needs peeling from the top downwards as it has a bitter taste.   Tie the grass in bundles with fine string and stand upright in a pan of boiling salted water for 10 to 15 minutes until tender.   The tips must be kept above the water level as these cook in the steam. Served with melted butter or mayonnaise.

ASPARAGUS SOUP

❀ ☆☆☆
PREPARATION TIME: 5 MINUTES
COOKING TIME: 10 MINUTES

Ingredients:

Two tins of asparagus soup   *10 fl oz (275 ml) of single cream*
One tin of asparagus spears   *Ground black pepper*

Method:
Drain the asparagus spears, chop roughly into the soup.   Season with black pepper, add the cream, heat very gently not allowing the soup to boil.   Serve with fried croûtons and a whirl of cream.

ASPARAGUS QUICHE

❀ ❀ ☆☆☆
PREPARATION TIME: 20 MINUTES
COOKING TIME: 40 MINUTES
OVEN TEMPERATURE: 375F 190C M5
Special Equipment:1" x 8" Flan Case

Ingredients:

6 oz (175g) of ready made short crust   *10 fl oz (300 ml) single cream*
pastry   *4 eggs*
1 tin of asparagus spears   *Seasoning*
2 oz (50 g) grated parmesan cheese

Method:
Roll out the pastry and line the flan ring. Leave to rest for 1 hour. Beat together the eggs, seasoning and single cream. Arrange the asparagus in the flan dish, sprinkle the cheese and strain the egg mixture over the ingredients. Decorate with tomato slices and finely chopped parsley. Bake in the oven. Serve hot or cold as a main meal or at buffets. For drinks parties use the same recipe but line individual Yorkshire bun tin moulds, making individual tartlets.

A U B E R G I N E

This vegetable is usually served fried in oil or stuffed and baked. It keeps a long time if stored in a salad basket in the refrigerator. Trim both ends and wipe clean, peeling is not necessary.

To fry: Slice crossways, sprinkle with salt and leave for 30 minutes. Rinse in cold water and dry on kitchen towel, fry in butter or oil until golden brown. Drain, season and serve with chopped marjoram, basil, black pepper, ginger or paprika

AUBERGINES A L'AIL

❀ ☆☆☆
PREPARATION TIME: 30 MINUTES
COOKING TIME: 10 MINUTES

Ingredients:

Aubergines	*Oil for frying*
Garlic	*Seasoned flour*

Method:
Dice the aubergines and sprinkle with salt and leave for 20 minutes, wash, drain and dry. Toss the aubergines in the flour. Heat the oil in a large frying pan, add the crushed garlic and aubergines and fry until golden brown, serve immediately garnished with finely chopped parsley.

RATATOUILLE

❀ ☆☆☆ **Served as a supper dish with crusty bread, or with grilled meat.**
PREPARATION TIME: 20 MINUTES
COOKING TIME: 30 MINUTES

Ingredients:

1 large aubergine	*Green & red peppers*
1 lb (450 g) of tomatoes	*2 tbs oil*
1½ lb (700 g) of onions	*Fresh parsley, thyme, marjoram*
2 cloves of garlic	*Salt & freshly ground black pepper*
1 lb (450 g) of courgettes	

Method:
Dice the aubergines and sprinkle with salt and leave for 20 minutes. Peel and slice the onions. Skin the tomatoes, dice the red and green peppers. Cut the courgettes into mouth-sized pieces. Heat the oil in a heavy based pan, add the crushed garlic and onion, fry for about 5 minutes. Wash and drain the aubergines and add all the ingredients together. Simmer gently for about 30 minutes. Garnish with finely chopped parsley.

B R O A D   B E A N S

"There was an old person from Dean,
Who dined on one pea and a bean;
For he said, 'More than that,
Would make me too fat,'
That cautious old person of Dean."
LEAR

The bean was bought to Britain by the Romans and became an important crop during the Middle Ages. Young beans are delicious cooked in their pods, whilst older beans are shelled and only the bean cooked. Cook broad bean tops as you would spinach leaves.

BROAD BEANS IN PARSLEY SAUCE

❀ ☆☆☆
COOKING TIME: 10/15 MINUTES

Ingredients:

Broad beans   *White sauce (see page 304).*
Parsley

Method:

Cook the broad beans in salted boiling water until tender. Drain well, meanwhile make the white sauce and add the finely chopped parsley and seasoning. Pour the sauce over the broad beans and serve.

F R E N C H   B E A N S

French beans originated in Peru and they were brought over to Mexico and Central America. The name derives from their long-standing popularity in France.
For speed a good tip for topping and tailing beans is to take a small bunch of about ten beans and shuffle them on a work surface so all the ends are even and slice them off. Turn them round the other way and repeat the process.

JULIENNE OF FRENCH BEANS & CARROTS

Cut the carrots into thin julienne strips. Top and tail the French beans and cut to the same length as the carrots. Tie the vegetables in individual small bundles and boil in salted water until cooked.

SALADE NIÇOISE

❀ ❀ ☆☆☆ **Serves 4 Persons**
PREPARATION TIME: 30 MINUTES

Ingredients:

4 hard boiled eggs   *4 tomatoes*
8 oz (225 g) of cooked French beans   *One finely sliced onion*
One head of lettuce   *8 oz (225 g) tin of tuna fish*
One glove of garlic   *Black olives*

Method:

Peel the garlic and slice, rub this around the bowls to give a slight flavour of garlic. Quarter the hard-boiled eggs and tomatoes, divide the lettuce between the bowls, arrange the egg, tomato, French beans, onions, tuna fish and olives in the bowls, dress with French dressing just before serving.

FRENCH BEANS WITH GARLIC BUTTER

❋ ☆☆☆
PREPARATION TIME: 10 MINUTES
COOKING TIME: 10 MINUTES

Ingredients:

French beans	*Butter*
Garlic	

Method:
Top and tail the French beans and cook in boiling salted water until cooked but crisp to the bite. Drain well. Heat the butter in a pan and add the crushed garlic, toss the beans in the butter and serve garnished with finely chopped parsley.

FRENCH BEANS WITH HAZELNUTS

Top and tail the French beans, cook in slightly salted water, drain, toss in melted butter with finely chopped hazelnuts.

R U N N E R   B E A N S

❋ ☆☆☆
PREPARATION TIME: 15 MINUTES PER POUND
COOKING TIME: 5 TO 7 MINUTES

Method:
Top and tail the beans, removing any stringy side membrane. Slice diagonally at 45° angle. Cook in boiling salted water until tender.

B E E T R O O T

Trim the leafy stalks 1"- 2" (2.5-5 cm) above the bulb and leave the roots on. Do not cut or bruise the skin as this will cause bleeding. Boil the beetroot in salted water for 1-2 hours. Refresh in cold water and rub off skins.

BEETROOT & SOURED CREAM SALAD

❋ ☆☆☆
PREPARATION TIME: 20 MINUTES
COOKING TIME: 2 HOURS

Ingredients:

4 medium-sized beetroots	*5 fl oz (150 ml) soured cream*
1 small grated onion	*1 tin of corn on the cob kernels*

Method:
Cube the beetroot and mix in a bowl with the corn, onion and soured cream. Chill in the refrigerator for 1 hour.

BEETROOT BÉCHAMEL

Cook the beetroot, peel and coat with béchamel sauce, serve as a vegetable. Use small young beetroot.

B R O C C O L I   (C A L A B R E S E)

There are white, green and purple varieties of calabrese. The flavour is reminiscent of asparagus. Wash and trim the spears, cook in salted boiling water for no more than 12 minutes, drain.

BROCCOLI WITH ALMONDS

❀ ☆☆☆
PREPARATION TIME: 12 MINUTES
COOKING TIME: 12 MINUTES

Ingredients:
1 lb (450 g) broccoli spears   *2 oz (50 g) almonds*
2 oz (50 g) butter   *Juice of half a lemon*

Method:
Cook the broccoli in salted boiling water until tender, drain well. Heat the butter in a pan and fry the almonds until golden brown, stir in the lemon juice. Arrange the broccoli in a dish and garnish with the almonds.

B R U S S E L S   S P R O U T S

Brussels are a descendant of the wild cabbage first grown in Belgium. They are rich in vitamin C and should be no larger than a walnut, with tight firm leaves. Discard the outer ragged leaves and cut a cross (X) on the base before cooking in boiling salted water for 8-10 minutes, they should be slightly chewy, not watery.

BRUSSELS WITH BACON

Trim the Brussels and cook in slightly salted water. Meanwhile, fry some bacon until crisp and break into small pieces. Drain the Brussels and serve with the bacon pieces.

BRUSSELS SPROUTS WITH CHESTNUTS

❀ ☆☆☆
PREPARATION TIME: 10 MINUTES
COOKING TIME: 10 MINUTES

Ingredients:
8 oz (225 g) of peeled fresh or tinned   *1 lb (450 g) of Brussels*
chestnuts

Method:

Peeling fresh chestnuts is a laborious task, it is quicker to use the tinned variety. Cook the Brussels in boiling salted water until they are tender, add the chestnuts to the pan and heat for about 1 minute. Drain well and serve.

BRUSSELS SPROUTS TOSSED IN BUTTER & NUTMEG

❀ ☆☆☆
PREPARATION TIME: 10 MINUTES
COOKING TIME: 10 MINUTES

Ingredients:
1 lb (450 g) of Brussels
2 oz (50 g) melted butter

1 dsp of soft brown sugar
1 tsp of grated nutmeg

Method:
Prepare the Brussels and cook in salted boiling water until tender. Drain thoroughly and pour over the melted butter and coat evenly. Put in the serving dish and sprinkle with nutmeg and the sugar.

C A B B A G E S

All cabbage should only be cooked for a short time and in the minimum of boiling salted water. Dutch cabbage is eaten raw used in salads, as are Chinese cabbage leaves.

CABBAGE WITH BACON

Cook the cabbage in slightly salted water. Meanwhile, fry the bacon until crisp. Drain the cabbage and serve with the bacon broken into small pieces.

RED CABBAGE & APPLE

❀ ☆☆☆
PREPARATION TIME: 15 MINUTES
COOKING TIME: 25 MINUTES

Ingredients:
1 red cabbage
2 cooking apples
2/3 of a cup of malt vinegar

2 tbs of soft brown sugar
2 oz (50 g) butter

Method:
Peel and core the apples, slice the red cabbage. Cook gently. Add the vinegar, brown sugar and butter, cover and cook until the cabbage is soft. This is an excellent vegetable served with fatty meat.

COLESLAW

❀ ☆☆☆
PREPARATION TIME: 20 MINUTES

SAUCE PREPARATION TIME: 20 MINUTES
Note: When you slice a white cabbage you will be amazed at the quantity it produces.

Ingredients:

1 white cabbage
2 carrots

½ an onion
Coleslaw dressing (see page 316)

Method:
Finely grate the carrots and onion and slice the cabbage. Mix together and dress.

C A R R O T S

In the sixteenth century, the British learned to cultivate and cook carrots. They are highly nutritious, and have many uses, as a vegetable, for flavouring stocks, casseroles and stews, used raw in salads and with cocktail dips, or as a garnish.
New young baby carrots only need to be scrubbed, and if you leave the young tender stalk on, about ½" (1.25 cm), this adds good colour and is edible. Older carrots need to be peeled. Boil in slightly salted boiling water or white stock for approximately 10-30 minutes according to size.

LEMON CARROTS

❀ ☆☆☆
PREPARATION TIME: 15 MINUTES
COOKING TIME: 20 MINUTES

Ingredients:

1 lb (450 g) of carrots
Zest of one lemon
Juice of one lemon

Ground black pepper
Salt to taste
3 oz (75 g) of butter

Method:
Cut the carrots into thin strips of the same width and length. Grate the zest from the lemon and squeeze the juice. Add the ingredients to a pan and cover with a lid. Cook the carrots over a gentle heat until they are tender. Serve garnished with finely chopped parsley.

CARROTS A LA FORCALQUIER

❀ ☆☆☆
PREPARATION TIME: 5 MINUTES
COOKING TIME: 10 MINUTES

Ingredients:

1 lb (450 g) scrubbed new baby carrots
Fresh thyme leaves
Finely chopped chives

Finely chopped parsley
Butter

Method:

Boil the carrots until tender in slightly salted water. Melt the butter adding the fresh herbs. Season with salt and freshly ground black pepper. Toss the carrots in the butter and serve.

CAULIFLOWER

Cauliflower should never be over cooked, it should be tender and remain crispy. Eaten cooked and raw. Remove any coarse outer leaves, trim the base flush and make a cone-shaped incision to enable the stem to cook evenly with the florets. Cauliflowers can be cooked whole or broken up into florets in boiling salted water.

CAULIFLOWER POLONAISE

❀ ☆☆☆
PREPARATION TIME: 10 MINUTES
COOKING TIME: 10-15 MINUTES

Ingredients:
1 egg hard boiled   *A few breadcrumbs*
1 cauliflower

Advance preparation:
Hard boil the egg and when cold separate the yolk from the white and sieve each individually. Brown the breadcrumbs.

Method:
Cook the cauliflower whole in salted boiling water. Drain well. Sprinkle the egg white and yolk and the crumbs over the top. The cauliflower should look like a flower.

CAULIFLOWER SALAD VINAIGRETTE

❀ ☆☆☆
PREPARATION TIME: 25 MINUTES
COOKING TIME: 10 MINUTES

Ingredients:
1 cauliflower broken into florettes   *Crushed garlic*
French mustard dressing

Advance preparation:
Cook the cauliflower so it is crisp to the bite. Leave submerged in cold water. Drain well and put into the serving dish.

Method:
Marinate the cauliflower in the dressing for a couple of hours in the refrigerator.

CELERIAC

Celeriac has a similar flavour to celery, but with a turnip shaped root. It is used in soups, stews and salads. A root should only weigh approximately 1 lb (500 g), as larger roots become woody. Trim the upper leafy parts, peel and use in soups, sauces, bouquet garni, or salads. It can be sliced, cubed, grated or cut into narrow strips.

Cook in boiling salted water for approximately 10-20 minutes, according to size of the pieces. Serve as an accompanying vegetable, in a white sauce or mashed and creamed as potatoes.

C E L E R Y

The Greeks cultivated celery for the medicinal value of the seeds. Nowadays it is widely used as a vegetable, eaten both cooked and raw. It is excellent for flavouring soups and stews or braised as a vegetable.

Trim away the base and any damaged stems. Wash in cold water.

BRAISED CELERY

❀ ☆☆☆
PREPARATION TIME: 5 MINUTES
COOKING TIME: 1 HOUR
OVEN TEMPERATURE: 190C, 375F, MK5

Ingredients:

2 heads of celery   *1 oz (50 g) butter*
Seasonings   *¼ pt (150 ml) of milk*
½ pt (275 ml) of white stock

Method:
Wash and scrub the celery and trim any damaged parts. Cook in salted boiling water for approximately 10 minutes. Drain the celery well and put into a buttered fireproof dish. Cover with the stock and milk and a knob or two of butter. Cover with a tightly fitting lid and cook in the oven for 45 minutes until tender. Serve sprinkled with finely chopped parsley.

C H I C O R Y

Chicory is in its prime when the leaves begin to turn yellow. The spears should be young and firm, older spears become green and bitter. Store chicory in the dark in waxed or brown paper bags. Chicory is eaten raw in salads or braised and served as a vegetable.

CHICORY & HAM CASES

❀ ☆☆☆☆ **Serves 4 Persons**
PREPARATION TIME: 20 MINUTES
COOKING TIME: 30 MINUTES
OVEN TEMPERATURE: 220C, 425F, GAS MARK 7

Ingredients:

4 heads of chicory   *4 oz (110 g) grated Cheddar cheese*
4 large slices of ham   *Seasoning*
½ pt (275 ml) of white sauce

Method:

Trim the base of the chicory, and remove any discoloured leaves. Put in a pan of slightly salted boiling water and cook for 12 minutes until tender. Drain thoroughly. Wrap the ham slices around the chicory spears. Place in an ovenproof dish. Make a white sauce to coating consistency and add the cheese. Pour the sauce over the chicory and sprinkle some grated cheese over the top. Put in the oven for about 15 minutes until browned on top. Serve garnished with chopped parsley.

BRAISED CHICORY

❀ ☆☆☆☆
PREPARATION TIME: 5 MINUTES
COOKING TIME: 30 MINUTES
OVEN TEMPERATURE: 200C, 400F, GAS MARK 6

Ingredients:

4 heads of chicory
½ pt (275 ml) of white stock

¼ pt (150 ml) of milk
Seasoning

Method:

Grease an oven proof dish and place the trimmed chicory spears into the dish. Season and cover with the milk and stock. Seal with a lid and cook in the oven for 30 minutes until tender.

CORN SALAD

Corn salad leaves are available when most other salad greens are not. They were introduced from the Low Countries to Britain about 400 years ago. They are commonly called lamb's lettuce because the leaves are at their greenest and crispest at the end of winter when lambing starts. Use as you would lettuce.

CUCUMBERS

Cucumbers originated from Africa. There are three different sorts:
- Ridge cucumbers.
- Frame cucumbers
- Apple-shaped cucumbers.
Cucumbers are commonly used in salads, but can also be cooked. Small cucumbers known as gherkins are usually pickled whole.

CUCUMBER & CHEESE MOULD

❀ ❀❀ ☆☆☆☆
PREPARATION TIME: 45 MINUTES
Special Equipment: 1½-2 Pint Ring Mould

Ingredients:

1 large cucumber
6 oz (175 ml) cream cheese
1 tsp onion juice

Seasoning
¼ pt (150 ml) of vegetable or chicken stock

½ oz (10 g) of gelatine soaked in 3 tbs of
water
2 tbs of white wine vinegar
1 tbs caster sugar

Pinch of ground mace
¼ pt (150 ml) of lightly whipped double
cream

Method:
Oil the ring mould. Dice the cucumber and sprinkle with salt and leave pressed between two plates for 30 minutes. Meanwhile work the cheese, onion juice and seasoning together. Pour the boiling stock over the soaked gelatine and stir until it has dissolved. Add to the cheese mixture, drain the cucumber thoroughly and mix the vinegar, mace and sugar together. When the cheese mixture is cold, fold in the cucumber and the double cream. Pour into the oiled ring mould and leave to set in a cool place. To serve, dip the mould into hot water and loosen the edges and turn onto a damp plate (the wet plate enables you to manoeuvre the mould around and to centre it.)

Serving Suggestions:
Trim a bunch of watercress and place in the centre of the mould. Serve with fresh bread rolls or Melba toast.

CUCUMBER SALAD

❀ ☆☆☆
PREPARATION TIME: 15 MINUTES
CHILLING TIME: 30 MINUTES

Ingredients:

½ cucumber	*Caster sugar*
Malt vinegar	*Boiling water*

Method:
Peel the cucumber and slice very thinly. Arrange on a plate or in a bowl. Sprinkle a small amount of sugar over the cucumber, pour equal parts water to vinegar to cover the cucumber. Chill. An excellent accompaniment to cold poached salmon.

E N D I V E

Endive has been a winter salad vegetable since the sixteenth century. It has a slightly bitter taste, and can be eaten raw in salads, or cooked.

K A L E & R A P E K A L E

Kale and rape are descendants from the cabbage, the leaves can be curly or plain. It is a popular vegetable in Northern England and Scotland. Kale is rich in vitamin C, and can be cooked as a vegetable or served raw in salads. When cooking remove any tough stems, wash then shred. Boil in salted water for 5 minutes, drain, chop, and add a little butter and seasoning.

K O H L R A B I

Kohlrabi has a nutty turnip flavour. This root vegetable can be either white or purple.

Preparation:
Remove the leafy top and trim away any fibrous roots, scrub thoroughly and peel rather thickly. Blanch the prepared vegetable in acidulated water for 5 minutes, refresh in cold water before cooking. Cook for 10-15 minutes in a very small amount of boiling water, slightly salted. Serve with some of the cooking water or in a white sauce. Alternatively mash with butter, milk or cream. Kohlrabi can be eaten raw in salads.

LAND CRESS

Land cress is similar to watercress, the leaves are smaller and have a less delicate flavour.

LEEKS

The leek has been the national emblem of Wales since AD 640, when Welsh forces under King Cadwallader, wearing the vegetable as a badge of recognition, defeated a Saxon Army. Along with potatoes and onion, it is a most versatile and popular vegetable. Used to flavour soups and stews, an addition to bouquet garni, as an accompanying vegetable, boiled, steamed, braised or fried. The young leeks, finely chopped, can be used in salads.

Preparation:
Trim the root base, and remove any damaged outer leaves. Score the upper leaves and rinse in cold water to remove any grit inside the leaves. Boil the leeks in a minimum of lightly salted water for 10-20 minutes depending on the size until tender.

LEEKS WITH BACON

❀ ☆☆☆
PREPARATION TIME: 10 MINUTES
COOKING TIME: 10 MINUTES

Ingredients:
4 leaks   *4 rashers streaky bacon*

Method:
Wash and trim the leeks and cook in boiling salted water for 7 minutes until tender. Drain thoroughly. Meanwhile, fry the bacon in small pieces until crispy. Sprinkle over the leaks and serve.

CRISPY FRIED LEEKS

Wash the leeks thoroughly in cold water, drain well and dry on kitchen paper. Season the flour, whisk one egg white, cut the leeks into finger shaped lengths and dip the leek into the egg white then the flour. Heat the oil to 190° and deep fry the leeks until crispy and golden. Serve immediately.

LEAKS WITH GRATED CHEESE

❀ ☆☆☆
PREPARATION TIME: 10 MINUTES

COOKING TIME: 10 MINUTES

Ingredients:
4 leaks   *Grated cheddar*

Method:
Trim the leeks and cook until tender in slightly salted boiling water. Drain thoroughly.
Sprinkle the cheese on the hot leeks and put under a hot grill until the cheese has melted.
Serve.

CHEESY LEAKS

❀ ☆☆☆
COOKING TIME: 20 MINUTES
OVEN TEMPERATURE: 375F, 190C, MARK 5

Ingredients:
Leeks   *White sauce*
Slices of ham   *Grated cheese*

Method:
Trim and cook the leeks whole until tender. Drain thoroughly. Wrap a slice of ham around
each leek and place in an ovenproof dish. Make the white sauce and add the grated cheese
reserving some to sprinkle on the top. Pour the sauce over the leeks and sprinkle the
remaining cheese on top. Put into a pre-heated oven for 10 minutes until brown on top.

LEEKS BÉCHAMEL

❀ ☆☆☆
PREPARATION TIME: 10 MINUTES
COOKING TIME: 15 MINUTES

Ingredients:
½ pt (275 ml) of béchamel sauce (see   *4 young tender leeks*
page 304)

Method:
Trim the leeks and leave whole, ensuring any grit and damaged leaves are removed. Cook
in slightly salted boiling water until tender. Meanwhile make the béchamel sauce and pour
it over the cooked well-drained leeks.

L E T T U C E S

Lettuces were believed to have been grown thousands of years ago in the Far East. In
England the lettuce appeared in the sixteenth century, and today is the most popular salad
vegetable. There are a wide variety of lettuces, the most common being the Cabbage, Cos,
Iceberg and Little Gems. Outer damaged leaves should be removed. Wash in cold water,
tear the leaves, (never use a knife as this bruises the leaves) and serve.

MARROWS, COURGETTES, SQUASHES

Marrows have a high water content, and so should be cooked in the minimum of water or steam. Older marrows need peeling and the seeds scooped out. Cooked marrow should be firm to touch and not watery. Marrow can be stuffed and baked, either whole or sliced. Courgettes should be 4-6" (10-15 cm) long.

BUTTERED MARROW

❀ ☆☆☆
PREPARATION TIME: 10 MINUTES
COOKING TIME: 10 MINUTES

Ingredients:

1 marrow   *Seasoning*
Butter

Method:
Peel and slice the marrow into 2" (5 cm) pieces, removing the seeds. Heat 2 oz (50 g) of butter in a heavy-based pan and sauté the marrow. Season with salt and black pepper, turn the heat down and cover and cook until tender.

COURGETTES A LA GRECQUE

❀ ☆☆☆
PREPARATION TIME: 15 MINUTES
CHILLING TIME: 2 HOURS

Ingredients:

8 tender young courgettes   *8 whole black pepper corns*
1 clove of garlic freshly crushed   *Oil*
1 bay leaf   *Malt vinegar*

Method:
Boil the sliced courgettes in salted boiling water until tender. Drain well. Boil the vinegar, oil, garlic, bay leaf and peppercorns and pour over the courgettes. Leave to marinate in the refrigerator.

DEEP FRIED COURGETTES

❀ ☆☆☆
PREPARATION TIME: 10 MINUTES
COOKING TIME: 7 MINUTES

Ingredients:

8 courgettes   *Oil for deep frying*
Seasoned flour

Method:

Cut the courgettes into 2" (5 cm) fingers. Toss in the seasoned flour. Heat the fat and deep fry the courgettes until golden brown and tender. Drain onto kitchen paper.

M U S H R O O M S

Cultivated and field mushrooms should be eaten very fresh. Flat mushrooms need peeling, and button mushrooms only need wiping with a cloth or gently washing.

MUSHROOMS WITH PINE KERNELS

✽ ☆☆☆☆ **Can be prepared in advance and heated through at the last minute.**
PREPARATION TIME: 10 MINUTES
COOKING TIME: 20 MINUTES

Ingredients:

1 lb (450 g) of button or flat mushrooms	*Black pepper*
2 oz (50 g) butter	*Salt*
1 clove of crushed garlic	*2 oz (50 g) pine kernels*
10 fl oz (300 ml) of single cream	

Method:
Wash the mushrooms and peel if they are the flat variety. Melt the butter in a frying pan and add the garlic and pine kernels and fry until brown. Add the mushrooms and sauté gently until they are cooked. At this stage you can leave the mushrooms to stand until needed. The next stage is to drain any liquid off the mushrooms if there is any excess. This is optional but you must remember that the juices from the mushrooms will turn the cream a brown colour (if this happens, leave it, as the taste is delicious). Just before serving, season and heat the mushrooms until very hot, add the cream and turn down the heat. Gently heat through. Serve in a ramekin or on a small plate with finely chopped parsley.

STUFFED FLAT MUSHROOMS

✽✽ ☆☆☆ **Serves 4 Persons**
PREPARATION TIME: 20 MINUTES
COOKING TIME: 20 MINUTES
OVEN TEMPERATURE: 375F, 190C, GAS MARK 5
Special Equipment: Round Pastry Cutters

Ingredients:

16 medium-sized flat mushrooms	*1 clove of fresh crushed garlic*
1 slice of ham	*1 tbs of chopped parsley*
4 oz (110 g) fresh breadcrumbs	*Seasoning, cayenne & lemon juice*
2 oz (50 g) of butter	

Method:
Peel the mushrooms and with a round cutter trim the edges of the mushrooms so that they are a neat shape. Mince the ham or chop finely. Heat the butter in a pan and add the garlic, ham, breadcrumbs, parsley, seasoning, lemon juice and mix well. Press the mixture into the mushrooms and put into an ovenproof dish. This can be prepared well in advance and

cooked when required. Put in a pre-heated oven for 20 minutes until cooked and moisture has come out of the mushrooms. These are excellent served as a starter, or as a garnish with roasted or grilled meats.

MUSHROOMS A LA GRECQUE

❀ ☆☆☆ **Serves 6 Persons**
PREPARATION TIME: 5 MINUTES
COOKING TIME: 15 MINUTES
CHILLING TIME: 2 HOURS
An ideal salad to serve at a buffet, or in individual portions as a starter, on a bed of endive leaves.

Ingredients:

1 lb (450 g) of small button mushrooms	*Thyme*
Juice of 1 lemon	*Seasoning*
1 cup of vinegar	*2 shallots sliced finely*
½ clove of crushed garlic	*4 tbs of olive oil*
1 bay leaf	*1 tbs of tomato ketchup (optional)*

Method:

Wash the mushrooms and simmer for 5 minutes in salted water with the lemon juice. Boil together the vinegar, garlic, bay-leaf, thyme, seasonings and shallots for 5 minutes. Cool and then add the olive oil and tomato ketchup. Drain the mushrooms and marinade in the above mixture in the refrigerator for several hours. Serve with the marinade.

O K R A

Okras are called 'ladies fingers', they originate from the Caribbean and Kenya. They should only measure about 3-5" (5-12cm) long and be green in colour.

MEDITERRANEAN OKRA

❀ ☆☆☆☆ **Serves 4 Persons**
PREPARATION TIME: 10 MINUTES
COOKING TIME: 45 MINUTES

Ingredients:

1 lb (450 g) of okra	*1 lb (450 g) of tomatoes, blanched*
1 oz (25 g) of butter	*skinned, seeded and chopped*
2 tbs of olive oil	*1 tsp of dried oregano*
2 shallots finely chopped	*Salt*
2 cloves of garlic finely chopped	*Freshly ground black pepper*
1 tbs lemon juice	*1 tbs finely chopped parsley*

Method:

Heat the butter and oil in a saucepan and add the finely chopped shallots and garlic. Cook for 5 minutes until the shallots are soft. Meanwhile, remove the hard stems from the okras and add to the pan and cook for 5 minutes until they are lightly golden. Add the tomato, lemon juice, oregano and seasonings to your taste. Cook for 20 minutes until the okras are tender. Transfer to a warmed serving dish and sprinkle with the parsley. Serve immediately.

O N I O N S

Onions are very versatile and essential to many recipes. They can be eaten fried, raw, boiled, baked, casseroled, pickled or used in chutneys. Spring onions are used in salads, and the green leaves are eaten as well, they also make an excellent garnish.
Shallots are used for pickling and to flavour sauces.

P A R S N I P S

Parsnips are a sweet root vegetable; they were more popular before the introduction of the potato. Prepare the roots by cutting off the tops and tapering the end. Peel and cut lengthways into thick slices. Parsnips can be boiled or roasted, served mashed or puréed with butter and nutmeg.

PARSNIP BAKE

❀ ☆☆☆ **Serves 6 Persons**
PREPARATION TIME: 20 MINUTES
COOKING TIME: 30 MINUTES
OVEN TEMPERATURE: 400F, 200C, MARK 6

Ingredients:

2 lbs (900 g) of parsnips	*Salt*
10 fl oz (300 ml) single cream	*Parsley*
1 pt (570 ml) chicken stock	*Fresh breadcrumbs*
Black pepper	

Method:
Peel the parsnips and slice crossways. Arrange in an ovenproof dish which has been well greased with butter. Mix the cream with the stock and season, pour this over the parsnips. Bake in the pre-heated oven for 15 minutes. Mix the breadcrumbs with the chopped parsley, season and sprinkle over the dish, put back in the oven for approximately 15 minutes or until the parsnips are tender and the crumbs have browned. Serve.

ROAST PARSNIPS

❀ ☆☆☆
PREPARATION TIME: 10 MINUTES
COOKING TIME: 10 MINUTES
ROASTING TIME: 20 MINUTES

Ingredients:

4 medium sized parsnips	*Roasting fat*

Method:

Peel the parsnips and par-boil in slightly salted water until tender. Drain. Place the parsnips around the joint and baste, roast for about 20 minutes until they are golden and crispy.

P E A S

"I eat my peas with honey,
I have done it all my life,
I know it might sound funny,
But it keeps them on my knife."
JOHNSON

PETIT POIS WITH GARDEN FRESH CHIVES

❀ ☆☆☆☆ **Serves 4 Persons**
PREPARATION TIME: 10 MINUTES
COOKING TIME: 7 MINUTES

Ingredients:

1 lb (450 g) of mange tout peas   *Freshly chopped chives, butter*

Method:
Top and tail the peas and remove any stringy outer sides. Cook in slightly salted boiling water until tender (about 3-4 minutes). Drain thoroughly. Melt the butter in the pan and toss the peas in the butter, adding the fresh chives. Serve.

PEAS SERVED WITH CRISPY FRIED BACON

❀ ☆☆☆
PREPARATION TIME: 5 MINUTES
COOKING TIME: 10 MINUTES

Ingredients:

1 lb (450 g) of fresh or frozen garden   *4 rashers of streaky bacon*
peas

Method:
Cook the peas in slightly salted boiling water until tender. Drain well. Fry the bacon until crisp and break up into small pieces. Mix with the peas and serve.

TOMATO CUPS WITH PEAS

❀ ☆☆☆
PREPARATION TIME: 15 MINUTES
COOKING TIME: 10 MINUTES
OVEN TEMPERATURE: 375F, 190C, GAS MARK 5
Used as a garnish with grilled meats or fish.

Ingredients:

6 large tomatoes   *8 oz (225 g) of peas*

Seasoning

Method:
Cut the tops off the tomatoes near the core so you are able to take out the pulp easily without splitting the skins. Cook the peas in slightly salted water and drain well. Season and fill the tomatoes with the peas. Cook in a pre-heated oven for 10 minutes.

PEPPERS & CHILLIES

Commonly known as sweet peppers or capsicums. Chillies are a form of capsicum, they are hot and used in curries, pickles and sauces. The sweet pepper can be green, red, yellow or dark purple. Remove the seeds before using. Peppers are eaten raw in salads, and used cooked in many dishes such as ratatouille and goulash.

CHILLI VINEGAR

❀ ☆☆☆
STEEPING TIME: 2 WEEKS

Ingredients:

One bottle of white vinegar   *8 white whole peppercorns*
3 dried red chillies

Method:
Put the chillies and the peppercorns into the vinegar and leave for two weeks.

STUFFED PEPPERS

❀ ☆☆☆ **Serves 4 Persons**
PREPARATION TIME: 20 MINUTES
COOKING TIME: 1½ HOUR
OVEN TEMPERATURE: 375F 190C M5
This dish can be prepared in advance and frozen.

Ingredients:

4 medium size green or red peppers   *Glove of crushed garlic*
12 oz (350 g) ground beef   *Butter*
Half a cup of long grain rice   *Freshly ground black pepper*
l medium onion   *Salt*
7 oz (200 g) tin of tomatoes   *Finely chopped fresh parsley*

Method:
Boil the rice until cooked, drain. Sauté the finely chopped onion and crushed garlic in the butter until the onion is translucent, add the ground beef and fry. Add the rest of the ingredients and seasoning.
Cut the top off the peppers and take the seeds out. Put into a pan of cold water and bring to the boil (blanching), strain, stuff the peppers with the above mixture and put into an ovenproof casserole, pour some stock in the bottom of the dish and cover. At this stage this

dish can be left until you are ready to cook it or, cook in the oven for approximately 1½ hours until the peppers are tender.

P O T A T O E S

Potatoes were brought to Britain by Sir Francis Drake in the hull of his ships from South America where they originated. Potatoes started as cattle food. In the eighteenth century, they became the second most important crop in Ireland and Scotland. There are many varieties of potatoes.

ROAST POTATOES

Peel the potatoes and cut in half. Parboil in slightly salted water until soft but not mushy. Drain well. Heat lard in a hot oven. Add the potatoes and baste, roast in a hot oven for approximately 1 hour or until golden and crispy. Alternatively, roast potatoes around a joint, using the juices from the pan to baste.

POTATO DUCHESS

❀ ☆☆☆
PREPARATION TIME: 30 MINUTES
COOKING TIME: 25 MINUTES
OVEN TEMPERATURE: 400F 200C M6
Special Equipment: Piping Bag & Large Star Shaped Nozzle

Ingredients:

2 lbs (900 g) of potatoes	*A little milk & seasoning*
1 oz (25 g) butter	*1 egg yolk*

Method:
Boil the potatoes until cooked. Drain well. Add the butter, milk and seasoning, egg yolk and cream, mix well using a potato masher or fork. Add the egg yolk and mix, put the potato into the piping bag and pipe moulds of about 2" (5 cm) high on a lighted greased baking sheet. Bake in the oven until golden brown.

GRATIN DAUPHINOIS

❀ ☆☆☆
PREPARATION TIME: 20 MINUTES
COOKING TIME: 2 HOURS
OVEN TEMPERATURE: 400F 200C M6
Special Equipment : Mandoline

Ingredients:

1 lb (450 g) of peeled potatoes	*10 fl oz (300 ml) of single cream*
1 large onion	*Freshly ground black pepper*
1 pt (570 ml) of vegetable stock	*Salt*

Method:
Slice the potatoes and onion thinly. Grease an ovenproof gratin dish and layer alternately the onion and potato dispersing small knobs of butter and seasoning as you go along, pour the stock and cream over them. Bake in the oven for 2 hours or until tender.

POMMES DAUPHINE

❀ ❀ ☆☆☆
PREPARATION TIME: 30 MINUTES
DEEP FRYING TIME: 7 MINUTES

Ingredients:

2 oz (50 g) of butter	4 medium size potatoes
¼ pt (150 ml) of water	½ oz (10 g) of butter
2½ oz (60 g) of flour	Pinch of nutmeg
2 eggs	Deep fat for frying

Method:
Choux pastry:
2 oz (50 g) of butter, water, flour and eggs. Make a choux pastry by melting the butter in the water and bring to a rapid boil, quickly adding the flour in one swoop and beating with a wooden spoon, quickly, until a smooth paste has been achieved. At this stage it is important to beat the mixture until it leaves the side of the pan clean. Leave the mixture to cool until you are able to touch the sides of the pan. Lightly beat the eggs and very gradually beat them into the mixture until a soft and shiny consistency has been achieved (this mixture is not runny). Meanwhile cook the potatoes and then sieve them, adding ½ oz (10 g) of butter, and the nutmeg. Mix with the choux pastry bearing in mind that the choux should be of equal proportion to the potato. Heat the fat to a high temperature and add one teaspoon of the mixture (the size of a walnut) to the hot fat and cook until fluffy and brown. Whilst the mixture cooks it will expand so be sure not to overfill the fryer. Keep warm in the oven on kitchen paper to absorb the fat while proceeding with the others. Garnish with chopped parsley. Grated Parmesan, or Gruyère may be added to the choux pastry, and served as a starter with a horseradish sauce.

POTATO LYONNAISE

❀ ☆☆☆
COOKING TIME: 20 MINUTES

Ingredients:

1 lb (450 g) potatoes	¾ tbs olive oil
2 medium sized onions	Seasoning & chopped parsley

Method:
Boil the potatoes in their skins then peel and cut them in thin slices. Chop the onions in thin slices and fry until brown, drain and keep warm. Add the potatoes to the pan and sauté until golden brown, season, add the onions and serve. Alternatively, cut the potatoes into cubes and sauté in the same way but add lightly fried green and red peppers.

DEEP FRIED POTATO BALLS

Peel large potatoes and with a melon baler scoop out potato balls. Heat the oil and deep fry until golden brown. Drain on kitchen paper and serve immediately.

PUREE POTATOES

❋ ☆☆☆
COOKING TIME: 30 MINUTES

Ingredients:

1 lb (450 g) potatoes   *Seasoning, a little milk*
1 oz (10 g) of butter   *Vegetable purée of your choice*

Method:

Cook the potatoes, drain well, season, add the butter and milk and cream with a potato masher or a fork. Add an equal quantity of your chosen vegetable purée and mix well.

BAKED HORSERADISH POTATO

Make the above creamed potato but add two large tablespoons of horseradish and some cayenne, mix well and spread onto a lightly greased baking sheet. Bake in the oven at 200C, 400F, M6 for 20 minutes until golden brown on top.

NEW POTATOES

❋ ☆☆☆
COOKING TIME: 20 MINUTES

Ingredients:

2 lb (900 g) of new potatoes   *Grated nutmeg*
4 fl oz (110 ml) single cream

Method:

New potatoes can be cooked in their jackets or scraped. Simmer until cooked, drain well, toss in the single cream and grated nutmeg, serve garnished with chopped parsley.

NEW POTATOES VINAIGRETTE

❋ ☆☆☆
COOKING TIME: 20 MINUTES
MARINADING TIME: 2 HOUR

Ingredients:

2 lb (900 g) new potatoes
Dressing:
¼ pt (150 ml) of olive oil or salad oil   *¼ pt (150 ml) of vinegar*
½ tsp dry mustard   *Freshly ground black pepper, salt*

Roughly chopped spring onion leaves or   *onion.*
Fresh chives, or finely chopped raw

Method:
Cook the potatoes. Mix the rest of the ingredients together and pour over the potatoes and chill in the refrigerator. If the new potatoes are large cut them into mouth sized pieces.

POTATO SALAD

❀ ☆☆☆
COOKING TIME: 20 MINUTES

Ingredients:
2 lb (900 g) new potatoes   *Chopped spring onion tops or fresh*
Mayonnaise   *chives, cayenne*

Method:
Cook the potatoes, leave to cool. Make the mayonnaise (see page 312). When the potatoes are cold gently coat with the mayonnaise and onion tops. Sprinkle cayenne over the top just before serving. Decorate with watercress.

P U M P K I N S   &   S Q U A S H E S

Pumpkins and squashes are related to the marrow, the smaller varieties are cooked like courgettes after the skin has been removed. Young ripe squashes are also suitable for steaming or baking whole with a savoury filling. Pumpkins are large squashes, which are very popular in America, and associated with Hallowe'en. Pumpkins can be roasted for about 1 hour, the pulp is scraped out, and purée with cream, butter and seasoning. Boiled pumpkin is served with a cheese sauce.

R A D I S H E S

Eaten in salads or used as a garnish.

S A L S I F Y   O R   S C O R Z O N E R A S

Salsify is known as the vegetable oyster, with its long fleshy roots. The difference between salsify and scozonera is the colour of the skin. Salsify has a light brown skin, scorzonera a black skin. Both have a soft white sweet flesh, salsify having a faint oyster flavour. Both are prepared in the same way and recipes are interchangeable. Wash the vegetable under cold water, cut off the base and roots and leafy tops. Peel or scrape, and cut in 1-2" (2.5-5 cm) lengths. Boil in acidulated water for 20-30 minutes until tender. This vegetable can be grated for winter salads, mixed with mayonnaise, soured cream or vinaigrette.

SALSIFY WITH MOUSSELINE SAUCE

❀ ☆☆☆
PREPARATION TIME: 5 MINUTES

COOKING TIME: 30 MINUTES

Ingredients:
1 lb (450 g) of salsify
Sauce Mousseline:
3 yolks of egg   *3 oz (75 g) of unsalted butter*
Juice of half a lemon   *¼ pt (150 ml) of double cream*
Seasoning

Method:
Prepare the salsify and cook until tender. Make the mousseline sauce. Break the yolks into a bowl and add half the lemon juice, seasoning and a nut of butter. Place the bowl in a bain-marie and work the sauce with a small whisk until thick. Remove the bowl from the heat and whisk in the softened butter. Add the rest of the lemon and lastly add the whipped cream. Serve the sauce as soon as possible poured over the salsify.

SHALLOTS

French cooks prefer shallots to onions. In England the bulbs are used mainly for pickling. The small bulbs are used for flavouring rather than as a vegetable. Their mild flavour enhances stocks, soups and marinades. Peel as for onions.

SPINACH

Spinach is highly nutritious, and should be used as soon as possible after harvesting. The leaves should be stripped from the stalks, immersed in cold water and washed thoroughly. Spinach has a high water content and needs no extra water for cooking. Put the leaves in a large pan, sprinkle with salt and cover with a lid, gently heat for 7-10 minutes until soft. Drain thoroughly squeezing out as much water as possible.

SPINACH MOULDS

❀ ❀ ☆☆☆
COOKING TIME: 45 MINUTES
OVEN TEMPERATURE: 180C 350F M4
Special Equipment: Ring Mould or Individual Dariole Moulds.

Ingredients:
2 lbs (900 g) of spinach   *4 eggs*
Salt, pepper & nutmeg   *½ pt (275 ml) of cream*

Method:
Strip the leaves from the stalks and wash. Cook until tender, drain thoroughly. Chop the leaves finely. Beat the eggs adding a pinch of salt, pepper and nutmeg. Gradually beat in the cream, until you have a smooth blended mixture. Fold in the chopped spinach and spoon into a buttered ring mould or individual dariole moulds.
Place the mould in a roasting tin with 1" (2.5 cm) of hot water and bake in the oven for 35 minutes until set and firm. Turn out the moulds onto a warm serving dish. Serve.

BEAN SPROUTS

Possibly the first crop harvested by man 5,000 years ago. Long before the Great Wall of China was built, a Chinese emperor made special mention of those 'health giving sprouts'. Only recent research has shown the remarkable quality of these food plants and their wealth of vitamins, minerals and protein. Bean sprouts can be eaten raw or cooked.

BEAN SPROUTS TOSSED IN GARLIC BUTTER

❀ ☆☆☆
COOKING TIME: 10 MINUTES

Ingredients:
1 lb (450 g) of bean sprouts   2 cloves of crushed garlic
2 oz (50 g) of butter

Method:
Heat the butter with the crushed garlic in a wok or pan and add the bean sprouts and cook until tender.

SWEDES

A round root winter vegetable.

PUREE SWEDES

❀ ☆☆☆
COOKING TIME: 30 MINUTES

Ingredients:
1 medium swede   Freshly ground black pepper
2 oz (50 g) of butter   Salt

Method:
Boil the swede until tender in slightly salted water. Drain well, purée incorporating the butter and seasoning. With this recipe it is absolutely delicious to cook and purée together a selection of root vegetables i.e. carrot, swede and turnip or celeriac and kohlrabi.

SWEETCORN

Sweetcorn was introduced to Europe from America by Christopher Columbus at the end of the fifteenth century. The kernels should be a pale milky yellow. The outer leaves are removed before cooking to reveal the corn. Cook for approximately 8 minutes in boiling water and add salt half way through cooking. Drain and serve with melted butter.

SWEETCORN & KIDNEY BEAN SALAD

❀ ☆☆☆

PREPARATION TIME: 10 MINUTES

Ingredients:

1 can of sweet corn kernels
1 can of red kidney beans drained
Mayonnaise

2 red dessert apples, cored, finely
chopped

Method:

Mix all the ingredients together and dress with mayonnaise.

T U R N I P S

Turnips have been a favourite since Roman times. They consist of 90% water, with some sugar and pectin, but have no nutritional value. The small turnips are the best, and do not need peeling before cooking. Older turnips are better used in stews, and need peeling. Cook young turnips whole in slightly salted boiling water, or braise in the oven. Old crop turnips are delicious mashed with butter, and seasonings, traditionally served with haggis.

BAKED BABY TURNIPS

❀ ☆☆☆
PREPARATION TIME: 5 MINUTES
COOKING TIME: 30 MINUTES
OVEN TEMP: 200 C 400 F M6

Ingredients:

1 lb (450 g) of baby turnips
1 chicken stock cube
¼ pt (150 ml) of water

Ground black pepper
1 oz (25 g) of butter

Method:

Grease a pie dish large enough to hold all the turnips. Wash and tail the turnips leaving a small amount of stalk on. Arrange in the pie dish with the chicken stock. Dot with butter, season, cover and bake until tender, approximately 30 minutes.

WATERCRESS

Watercress is used chiefly as a garnish for savoury dishes. It is also eaten in salads, chopped and blended with mayonnaise, added to cream cheeses and to chilled soups. Watercress must always be washed well. Small bunches are placed in the crop end of roast game birds, chicken and duck to garnish.

FRUIT

ruits are divided into four main categories:

Top fruit:	The term used by fruit growers for all tree fruits.
Soft fruits:	Raspberries etc.
Citrus fruits:	Oranges, lemons etc. In general all citrus fruits should be taut with slightly moist skins, which when pressed are aromatic. Citrus fruits are rich in vitamin C.
Exotic fruits:	Various fruits imported from around the world.

ALMOND

An almond is an oval flat nut, with a light brown pitted shell. To blanch an almond and remove the thin outer skin, pour boiling water over the nut, with thumb and forefinger twist the nut, and the skin should come off. Almonds can be fried in oil until brown, salted and served as a titbit, or used in many other dishes, chopped, flaked or otherwise.

APPLES

"Stolen sweets are always sweeter,
Stolen kisses much completer,
Stolen looks are nice in chapels,
Stolen, stolen be your apples."
(Song of Fairies Robbing an Orchard)
LEIGH HUNT

The apple is the oldest fruit known to man, originating in Europe and the Near East. There are numerous varieties grown abroad and in Britain, each variety having its own season. The skin of an apple should be firm and glossy, old waxy apples become furry inside.

FRESH APPLE SAUCE

✻ ☆☆☆
COOKING TIME: 10 MINUTES

Ingredients:

1 lb (450g) of cooking apples   *1 oz (25g) caster sugar*
4 tbs of water   *A little nutmeg if desired*

Method:
Peel and core the apples, add all the ingredients together in a saucepan and cook until tender. This can be left as a chunky sauce or sieved to make a purée.

APPLE FONDUE

❀ ☆☆☆☆
PREPARATION TIME: 10 MINUTES
COOKING TIME: 10 MINUTES

Ingredients:

1 bar of Toblerone chocolate

4 dessert apples

5 fl oz (150ml) of double cream or soured cream

Method:

Gently melt the chocolate in the top of a double boiling saucepan (if you do not have this take a small saucepan and find a bowl which sits in the top. Put water in the pan and bring to the boil. The heat from the water will warm the bowl sufficiently to melt the chocolate). Just before serving stir in the cream, arrange the fruit around the bowl with skewers or small forks to stab the fruit to dip into the chocolate.

WALDORF SALAD

❀ ☆☆☆
PREPARATION TIME: 20 MINUTES

Ingredients:

1 head of celery

4 red dessert apples

2 oz (50 g) of shelled walnuts

6 oz (175 g) of cooked long grain rice

2 tangerines

½ pt (275 ml) of mayonnaise

Method:

In a bowl mix the rice with the chopped cored dessert apples, the chopped celery, chopped walnuts, peeled and chopped tangerines, and mix thoroughly with the mayonnaise. Season to taste.

AVOCADO

This fruit is extremely versatile, it can be served as a starter, vegetable, main course or dessert. The avocado has a faintly nutty flavour and a reputation as 'the subtlest of all foods'. The avocado originated in the fifteenth century, in Mexico, it has been the staple diet of the Aztecs for many centuries. Avocados are almost sugarless, and rich in vitamins, minerals, protein and fat. Avocados are grown in many countries and exported to Britain, they are available all year round.

Avocados need gentle handling, and should not be bullet hard, or soft. Gently press the top and bottom of the pear to test for ripeness. Cut avocados go black very quickly, sprinkle any exposed avocado with lemon juice to prevent this.

AVOCADO WITH RASPBERRY VINAIGRETTE

❀ ☆☆☆ **Serves 4 Persons**
PREPARATION TIME: 20 MINUTES

Ingredients:
2 avocados
Vinaigrette:

¼ pt (150 ml) of oil
¼ pt (150 ml) of raspberry vinegar
Salt
Freshly ground black pepper

¼ tsp of dried mustard
1 small tin of raspberries
Endive to garnish

Method:
Make the vinaigrette by mixing all the ingredients together in a screw-top jar and shaking well until incorporated. Liquidise or sieve the tinned raspberries and add to the other ingredients. To serve, cut the pears in half, remove the stone and peel the outer hard skin away. Place the pears on a board and with a sharp knife starting from the thin end, cut slices lengthwise without cutting entirely through the top. Make about ¼" (.7 cm) incisions and then gently press down so each pear forms a fan. Lay half a pear on each plate, garnish with the endive and pour the raspberry vinaigrette over it.

GUACAMOLE

A Mexican hors-d'oeuvre.
❀ ☆☆☆ **Serves 6 Persons**
PREPARATION TIME: 15 MINUTES
CHILLING TIME: 30 MINUTES

Ingredients:
3 ripe avocado pears
½ a small grated onion
2 crushed cloves of garlic
1 tbs of lemon juice
1 tbs of olive oil

Salt & black pepper
Cayenne pepper
¼ tsp of Worcester sauce
Tabasco sauce

Method:
Cut the avocado pears in half and remove the stone. Scoop the flesh from the skins and put into a bowl. Mash the avocado along with the onion and garlic until smooth. Blend in the lemon juice, oil and seasonings. Chill for 30 minutes. Serve garnished with lettuce, endive or watercress on individual plates, with crudités or Mexican chips to dip into the guacamole.

AVOCADO & FETTA CHEESE SALAD

❀ ☆☆☆ **Serves 4 Persons**
PREPARATION TIME: 20 MINUTES

Ingredients:
2 ripe avocado pears
6 oz (175 g) of fetta cheese
Vinaigrette:
²⁄₃ of oil
¹⁄₃ of Champagne vinegar

6 slices of streaky bacon
Endive

Black pepper, Salt
Finely chopped fresh parsley

Method:

Shake the vinaigrette ingredients in a screw-top jar until well mixed. Cut the fetta cheese into cubes. Fry the streaky bacon until crisp and then crumble. Arrange the endive on the plates and cut the pears in half, remove the stone, and slice thinly. Arrange the avocado on a plate, sprinkle the bacon, and divide the fetta cheese between the plates. Pour the dressing over it and serve.

AVOCADO WITH CRAB

❀ ☆☆☆
PREPARATION TIME: 15 MINUTES

Ingredients:

2 ripe avocados	*½ a red pepper, seeded & finely chopped*
Juice of ½ a lemon	*Salt, ground black pepper*
2 oz (50 g) of canned or fresh crab meat	*Lettuce leaves to garnish*
per person	

Dressing:

1 tbs of lemon juice	*2 tbs of tomato chutney*
3 tbs of olive oil	*1 tbs of finely chopped parley*
½ tsp of French mustard	*Salt, freshly ground black pepper*
½ clove of crushed garlic	

Method:

Cut the pears in half and remove the stone, sprinkle with lemon juice. Arrange on individual serving plates and garnish with the lettuce leaves. Flake the crab meat with a fork and add the red pepper. Mix gently. Pile into the centre of the avocados. Mix together all the ingredients for the dressing and shake well. Dress the avocados with the dressing and serve immediately.

B A N A N A

When harvested bananas are green, the flesh becomes sweeter as the fruit matures; avoid blackened squashy fruit. For cooking buy slightly under-ripe bananas.

BRANDY BAKED BANANAS

❀ ☆☆☆ **Serves 4 Persons**
PREPARATION TIME: 10 MINUTES
COOKING TIME: 15 MINUTES
OVEN TEMP: 180C 350F M4
This dessert is ideally suited for barbecuing.

Ingredients:

4 bananas	*Zest & juice of one lemon*
4 tbs of honey	*2 tbs of brown sugar*
4 tbs of brandy	

Method:

270

Peel the bananas and lay on a piece of tin foil (enough to make a parcel). Divide the rest of the ingredients between the four bananas and wrap. Cook in a pre-heated oven for 15 minutes or barbecue for the same time. Serve individual parcels to your guests with fresh cream.

BANANE CHARTREUSE

✿✿✿ ☆☆☆☆ Serve 6 Persons
PREPARATION TIME: 1 HOUR
SETTING TIME: 2 HOUR
Special Equipment: 1½ Pint Soufflé Dish

Ingredients:

4 bananas	½ lime jelly
½ pt (275 ml) of double cream	2 oz (50 g) of caster sugar
Juice of one lemon	

Method:
Make the lime jelly with ¼ of a pint (150 ml) of water. Pour enough jelly to just cover the base of the soufflé dish and put in the refrigerator to set. Meanwhile slice one of the bananas into thin slivers and soak in the lemon juice. When the jelly has set in the soufflé dish arrange the bananas, overlapping around the outer rim. Very carefully spoon some more of the jelly over the pattern in the dish until it is covered. Put back into the refrigerator to set. Mash the remaining bananas in a bowl and add the lemon juice and caster sugar. Lightly wisp the double cream until it stands in soft peaks, fold the cream into the bananas along the remaining lime jelly until evenly mixed. Place the banana mixture into the soufflé dish and leave to set. When the soufflé has set run a blunt-edged knife around the inside of the mould. Fill a bowl with boiling water and quickly put the base of the soufflé dish into it to loosen the jelly for turning out.
Wet a plate and put this over the soufflé dish. Holding the soufflé dish in position turn upside down. (If you wet the plate you will find it much easier to manoeuvre the Chartreuse to obtain the correct position). Serve.

BILBERRIES

Bilberries are similar to blackcurrants, but firmer, smaller and dark blue. They have a sharp taste and are suitable for pie fillings. The season is July to August.

BLACKBERRIES

Blackberries are used mainly for pie fillings, jams and wines. The fruit is soft and dark black when ripe. The season is from July to October.

BLACKBERRIES & YOGHURT FOOL

✿ ☆☆☆ Serves 4 Persons
PREPARATION TIME: 15 MINUTES
CHILLING TIME: ½ HOUR

Ingredients:

½ lb (250 g) of blackberries

Caster sugar

1 pt (575 ml) of natural yoghurt

Method:

Hull and wash the blackberries and drain thoroughly, blend the blackberries until smooth and strain through a sieve to remove all the pips. Sweeten the blackberry mixture to your taste, gradually incorporating the yoghurt. Pour into individual glasses and chill in the refrigerator.

BLACK, RED, & WHITE CURRANTS

Currants are high in vitamin C, and should be the size of a good pea and their colour vivid. The berries are used in compotes, summer pudding, toppings on cheesecakes, jams and making redcurrant jelly.

COMPOTE OF SOFT FRUITS

❀ ☆☆☆☆ **Serves 4 Persons**
PREPARATION TIME: 30 MINUTES
COOKING TIME: 10 MINUTES
CHILLING TIME: 2 HOURS

Ingredients:

2 lb (900 g) of soft summer fruits:

Red, black and white currants

Gooseberries, blueberries, raspberries

Loganberries, strawberries, stoned fresh cherries

Sugar

Method:

Hull and wash all the various fruits you are using, put into a saucepan with the sugar. It is sensible at this stage to put in a small amount of sugar and decide at the end of cooking if you need to add more. Add water, about 1" (2.5 cm) from the bottom and cook over a gentle heat literally until it comes to the boil. Take off the heat, taste, and decide at this point how much sugar is needed. Many of the fruits above can be quite tart and need a lot of sugar. Put into a bowl and chill.

B L U E B E R R I E S

BERRY BRULÉE

❀ ☆☆☆
PREPARATION TIME: 10 MINUTES

Ingredients:

½ lb (225 g) of blueberries

3 oz (75 g) of caster sugar

1½ level tsp of arrowroot

5 fl oz (150 ml) of soured cream

Soft brown sugar

Method:

Clean and wash the berries. Put into a pan with 6 tablespoons of water and simmer until tender. Sweeten to taste with the sugar, stirring until it has dissolved. Blend the arrowroot with some water and add to the berries and bring gently to the boil until it has thickened. Leave the berries to cool before dividing them between 4 ramekins. Cover with a layer of soured cream and then the sugar. Put under a hot grill for a few minutes until the brown sugar caramelises. Serve.

BRAZIL NUTS

Brazil nuts have a hard dark brown three-edged shell. The nut is oily and firm with a hazelnut flavour. Avoid buying brazils which rattle in their shells. The season is November to February.

CAPE GOOSEBERRIES

The berries are covered by a shrivelled papery orange-yellow husk, looking similar to a Chinese lantern (physalis). The plump golden round berries are best served as a dessert fruit, but can be stewed or made into preserves. The berries can be dipped into fondant icing and served as petit fours. The season is October to February.

CHERIMOYAS

The cherimoyas are a member of a large family of fruits known as custard apples, because of their creamy soft flesh. The fruit is heart-shaped with smooth, bumpy or scaly skin, and their flavour is reminiscent of pineapple. In spite of its appearance the skin is fragile and should be handled with care. The sweet white flesh can be eaten spooned from the skin or sieved for a natural custard.

CHERRIES

Both sweet and acid cherries are available. Cherries should be firm and dry when bought, and avoid boxes with a high proportion of leaves to cherries. Dessert cherries are either white, pink or black. The acid cherry is the morello, used for jam making.

COMPOTE OF CHERRIES

✹ ☆☆☆
PREPARATION TIME: 15 MINUTES
COOKING TIME: 5 MINUTES

Ingredients:
1 lb (450 g) of cherries
2 tbs of caster sugar
Pinch of powdered cinnamon

1 wine glass of port
Grated rind & juice of 1 orange
4 tbs of redcurrant jelly

Method:
Stone the cherries and place in a pan with the sugar and cinnamon. Cover and cook slowly for 5 minutes, remove from the heat and leave to cool. Reduce the wine by half, adding the

orange zest, orange and cherry juice. Add the redcurrant jelly, and when this has melted add to the cherries. Serve.

CHERRY FLAMBÉ WITH KIRSCH

❀ ☆☆☆
PREPARATION TIME: 20 MINUTES

Ingredients:

4 oz (100 g) canned stoned black cherries   *Lemon juice*
Pinch of ground cinnamon   *2-3 tbs of Kirsch*
2 tbs of caster sugar   *1 pt (425 ml) of vanilla ice-cream*
5 oz (125 g) of redcurrant jelly

Method:
Drain the cherries and reserve 5 fl oz (130 ml) of the syrup. In a heavy-based saucepan combine the reserved fruit syrup, cinnamon, sugar and redcurrant jelly. Over a low heat bring the liquid slowly to the boil, simmer gently for about 5 minutes. Add the cherries and simmer for a further 2 minutes. Remove the cherries with a slotted spoon and keep warm. Sharpen the syrup with some lemon juice if required. Warm the Kirsch and set alight, when flaming pour over the cherries, along with syrup. Serve whilst still flaming with the ice-cream.

CHESTNUTS

The shiny brown fruits of the sweet chestnut are enclosed in a hard leathery skin. The large French chestnuts 'marrons' are sold tinned or preserved. To shell chestnuts, make an incision in the husk, and pour boiling water over them.

CHINESE GOOSEBERRIES - KIWI FRUIT

The kiwi fruit is brown and hairy, and the size of an egg. The skin is inedible and should be peeled very thinly and discarded. The flesh is apple-green in colour pitted with tiny black seeds. The fruit should be firm to the touch not rock hard or soft. The fruits are available almost all the year round as they are imported.
Kiwi fruits are versatile and delicious, as well as being a complete food. They brighten up fruit salads and make an eye-catching garnish, served with all manner of sweet and meat dishes. Exceptionally good with fatty meat.

CLEMENTINE

Clementines are a cross between oranges and tangerines, with a stiff orange-like skin. They are practically seedless and the pink tinged flesh is slightly acid. The fruits are imported from Cyprus, Israel, Morocco and Spain, the season being November to February.

COCONUTS

The coconut is a large oblong-shaped fruit, with a dark brown hairy hard shell which is very fibrous. On the top of the nut are three eye indentations, and these are punctured to allow the milk to be poured out. Both the milk and the flesh are used. When the nut is opened the white milky flesh can be prised from the husk using a blunt knife. A ripe coconut contains milk.

C R A N B E R R I E S

The cranberry has a pink to dark red lustrous skin. Its sharp bitter flavour is used for sauces or preserves. Usually sold in punnets. The season is October to February.

CRANBERRY SAUCE

Is traditionally served with roast turkey but will be excellent with pork and all manner of cold meats.
❀ ☆☆☆
COOKING TIME: 5 MINUTES

Ingredients:
1 punnet of cranberries   *2 fl oz (100 ml) of water*
3 oz (75 g) of white sugar

Method:
Put all the ingredients in a saucepan and bring to the boil and cook for approximately five minutes. Whilst the cranberries are cooking you will hear them pop. Packets of cranberries are sold with cooking instructions.

D A T E S

Dates are sold fresh or dried. Fresh dates are plump, shiny, and a yellow red to golden brown colour with a smooth skin. They are approximately 1-2" (2.5-5 cm) long, sweet and sugary. Dried dates are less plump and should appear sticky and not shrivelled or crystallised.

F I G S

Fresh figs are imported from Mediterranean countries. Ever since Henry VIII, gardeners have tried to produce figs in Britain, but our harsh winters and unpredictable summers cause crops to fail. The squat, pear-shaped fruits are soft to touch when ripe, the skins can be white, red or purple. The pulp is sweet, deep red and heavily seeded. Figs are mainly served as a dessert fruit with cream. The whole fig is edible. Figs are sold dried, crystallised, or bottled in port or brandy syrups.

FIGS IN NATURAL YOGHURT

❀ ☆☆☆☆☆ **Serves 4 Persons**
PREPARATION TIME: 15 MINUTES
CHILLING TIME: 2 HOURS

Ingredients:
12 fl oz (400 ml) of thick   *(preferably Greek) natural yoghurt*

12 fresh figs   6 oz (150 g) demerara sugar

Method:
Peel the figs (pour boiling water over them, and drain after about 30 seconds). In either individual ramekins or glasses, arrange a layer of sliced figs and alternate with the yoghurt until you have filled each ramekin. Make sure that the final layer is yoghurt, and then coat with the demerara sugar and gently press down. Put in the refrigerator for 2 hours. During this time the sugar dissolves and penetrates through the yoghurt and figs. Serve.

FIGS CLEOPATRA

❀ ☆☆☆☆☆
PREPARATION TIME: 20 MINUTES

Ingredients:
Fresh ripe figs   Brown sugar
Slivered toasted almonds   Brandy
Single cream   Icing sugar

Method:
Arrange the figs on individual serving plates and slice in quarters without going right through the bottom and open out to resemble flowers. In a saucepan heat gently a carton of single cream with two tablespoons of sugar until dissolved. Add brandy to your taste. Pour the cream around the figs, sprinkle the almonds over the figs and cream and dust with icing sugar, serve immediately.

GOOSEBERRIES

Gooseberries have been popular in Britain since Tudor times. The sweet dessert gooseberry is red or yellow and usually served fresh. The smaller acid hard gooseberries are only suitable for cooking. To prepare gooseberries top and tail and wash. Gooseberry sauce is traditionally served with mackerel, goose and pork.

GOOSEBERRY FOOL

❀ ☆☆☆
PREPARATION TIME: 15 MINUTES
COOKING TIME: 45 MINUTES
CHILLING TIME: 30 MINUTES

Ingredients:
1 lb (450 g) of gooseberries   1 tbs of caster sugar
5 tbs of water   2 egg yolks
4 oz (100 g) of sugar   5 fl oz (150 ml) of double cream
2 tbs of ginger wine (optional)   Sponge fingers & whipped cream to
½ pt (275 ml) of milk   garnish
½ a vanilla pod

Method:

Top and tail the gooseberries, wash and drain. Put the berries in a pan with the water, cover and simmer for 20 minutes. Rub the gooseberries through a sieve and sweeten the purée with the sugar, and ginger wine at this stage. Set aside to cool. In a pan add the milk with the vanilla pod and heat gently, then cover with a lid and leave to infuse for 10 minutes. Remove the pod and add the sugar. Whisk the egg yolks until creamy, gradually beating in the milk. Strain the custard back into the pan or a double saucepan and heat very gently, stirring continuously until the custard has thickened. Pour into a bowl and leave to get cold. When the custard is cold, whip the cream lightly and fold carefully into the cooled custard, then fold this into the gooseberry purée, blending the mixture evenly. Spoon the mixture into serving glasses and chill for 30 minutes. Decorate with whipped cream and serve with sponge fingers.

G R A P E F R U I T

The grapefruit is the largest of the citrus fruits. The squat round fruit has a pale yellow skin which varies in thickness, and the juicy flesh is pale yellow. If the skin is spongy soft it often means there is more skin than flesh. Pink grapefruit have a slightly pink bloom to their skins and flesh.

HOT BAKED GRAPEFRUIT

❀ ☆☆☆ **Serves 4 Persons**
PREPARATION TIME: 15 MINUTES
COOKING TIME: 15 MINUTES
OVEN TEMP: 400F 200C M6 OR A HOT GRILL

Ingredients:

2 grapefruit, halved	*Butter*
Soft brown sugar	*Sherry*

Method:
Cut the grapefruit in half and cut down each segment to loosen the flesh. Place on a baking sheet, sprinkle with brown sugar, a knob of butter and pour a little sherry over the grapefruit if desired. Put into the hot oven or under the grill and cook until hot and brown on the top. Serve.

GRAPEFRUIT & PRAWN SALAD

❀ ☆☆☆☆ **Serves 4 Persons**
PREPARATION TIME: 20 MINUTES

Ingredients:

½ pt (275 ml) of cocktail sauce (see page 313)	*2 grapefruits*
	Endives leaves
6 oz (150 g) of cooked shelled prawns	

Method:
Segment the grapefruit, removing the skin. Mix with the prawns and coat with the cocktail sauce, arrange the endive leaves on a plate and divide the mixture between the four plates.

Decorate with a lemon wedge and a sprig of parsley. Serve with thinly sliced brown bread and butter.

G R A P E S

Vines have been grown successfully in Britain since the Romans, the first are believed to have been planted only 70 years after Julius Caesar's invasion in 55 BC.
Grapes are red, black or white, seedless or otherwise, and should be bought in bunches with no squashed or damaged grapes apparent.

GRAPES DELIGHT

❀ ☆☆☆ **Serves 4 Persons**
PREPARATION TIME: 20 MINUTES

Ingredients:

10 fl oz (300 ml) of thick natural yoghurt	*Medium bunch of black grapes*
2 oz (50 g) caster sugar	*2 egg whites*

Method:
Cut the grapes in half and remove the pips. Whisk the egg whites until they form stiff peaks. Fold in the natural yoghurt and caster sugar. In individual glasses rub a twist of lemon around the rim and frost with caster sugar, arrange layers of grapes and yoghurt to fill the glasses and decorate with a few grapes on top. Serve immediately.

STUFFED COCKTAIL GRAPES

❀ ☆☆☆ **These can be served as a starter or as a canapé.**
PREPARATION TIME: 8 MINUTES
CHILLING TIME: 8-12 HOURS

Ingredients:

2 oz (50 g) of Gorgonzola or Dolcelatte cheese	*½ tsp of grated onion*
	½ tsp of medium dry sherry
3 tbs of full fat soft cheese	*4 oz (100 g) of large firm dessert grapes*

Method:
Work the cheeses together with the onion juice and sherry. Sieve the mixture to make a creamy smooth paste. Chill in the refrigerator for up to 12 hours. Slit the grapes deeply lengthways and remove any pips. Stuff with the cheese and re-shape. Chill until needed.

G U A V A S

A highly aromatic fruit, with a soft grainy flesh and smooth or ridged skin that may be white, yellow, green, red or purple. The flesh can be eaten raw, stewed or puréed. Guavas can also be halved and stuffed with a sweet or savoury filling.

HAZEL / COB NUTS

The cob is a small grey-brown nut partly covered with leafy husks. Ripe husks should be firm and not shrivelled. The nuts' season is autumn.

CHOCOLATE HAZELNUT FONDUE

❀ ☆☆☆ **Serves 4 Persons**
PREPARATION TIME: 15 MINUTES

Ingredients:

10 oz (275 g) of milk chocolate
10 fl oz (300 ml) of whipping cream
For serving:
Apples, bananas, oranges & grapes, lemon juice

2 oz (50 g) of clear honey
2 oz (50 g) of ground hazelnuts

Method:
Peel the fresh fruits and coat with lemon juice to prevent discoloration. Cut into mouth-sized pieces. Grate the chocolate into the fondue pot and add the honey and cream. Heat the pot very gently stirring all the time until the chocolate has melted and the mixture is smooth. Stir in the hazelnuts. Each person skewers a piece of fruit and dips it into the fondue.
Note: If you do no have a fondue set, it is still quite possible to prepare this dish over a conventional stove or in the microwave oven.

KUMQUAT

A small, oval, orange-like fruit, with a bright yellow-orange skin and a bitter flesh. Originally a Japanese fruit, but now grown in Morocco. Kumquats are used for making marmalade, and in all manner of dishes.

LEMON

Lemons are highly valued in the kitchen. The juice and zest are used to flavour, and lemon wedges or slices are used as a garnish.

LEMON WATER ICE

❀ ☆☆☆
PREPARATION TIME: 10 MINUTES
COOKING TIME: 10 MINUTES

Ingredients:

1 pt (575 ml) of water
6 oz (150 g) of loaf sugar

Grated rind & juice of three lemons

Method:

Put the lemon zest, loaf sugar and water into a spotlessly clean saucepan. Dissolve the sugar and boil rapidly for 6 minutes. Cool, add the juice of the lemons, mix and strain. Freeze, stirring occasionally until frozen.

It is optional to gently fold in a stiffly whipped egg white before freezing.

SYLLABUB

❀ ☆☆☆

PREPARATION TIME: 15 MINUTES
CHILLING TIME: 1 TO 2 HOURS

Ingredients:

½ pt (275 ml) of double cream　　　*Juice & zest of one lemon*
4 tbs of sherry or brandy　　　*Champagne biscuits*
4 oz (100 g) of caster sugar　　　*Fresh fruit*

Method:
Whisk together the cream, sherry or brandy, caster sugar, and juice and zest of one lemon with an electric beater until it stands in soft peaks. Serve in frosted glasses, decorated with fresh fruit of your choice.

L I M E

A small fruit similar to the lemon, but rounder and light green in colour. The lime has a thin skin, and the flesh is tart and yellow. A lime can always replace lemon.

LIME POSSET

❀ ☆☆☆

PREPARATION TIME: 20 MINUTES PLUS CHILLING TIME

Ingredients:

1 pt (575 ml) of thick cream　　　*2-3 tbs of sugar*
Finely grated zest & juice of 2 limes　　　*3 large egg whites*
5 fl oz (150 ml) of dry white wine　　　*Candied violets & fresh lime slices*

Method:
Add the zest to the cream and whisk until stiff. Stir in the wine, then whisk in the lime juice little by little. Add the sugar to taste, the posset should not be too sweet. Whisk the egg whites until they form peaks. Fold into the cream mixture. Chill. Before serving whisk the posset once more and pile into the serving dishes. Garnish with the lime slices or candied violets.

L O G A N B E R R I E S

The loganberry is a cross between the blackberry and raspberry. It was first grown in 1881 in the garden of Judge Logan of Santa Cruz, California. The ripe fruit is a purple-black colour, and excellent as a desert fruit. Loganberries hold their shape when cooked. The season is July to August.

EXOTIC FRUIT SALAD

✤ ☆☆☆☆
PREPARATION TIME: 20 MINUTES
CHILLING TIME: 2 HOURS OR MORE

Ingredients:

4 passion fruits	*2 tbs of sugar*
2 mangoes, peeled & sliced	*Grated zest & juice of 1 lime*
8 oz (200 g) of blueberries	*1 tsp of Angostura bitters*
8 oz (200 g) of loganberries	*5-7 mint sprigs*
8 oz (200 g) of raspberries	

Method:
Cut the passion fruits in half and sieve through over a bowl, discarding the seeds. Combine the flesh with the mango and the berries, sprinkle with the sugar, lime juice, zest and bitters. Toss. Reserve a few of the mint leaves for garnishing and cut the remaining leaves into thin strips. Scatter the leaves over the fruit, toss and put into a serving bowl in the refrigerator for at least 2 hours. Just before serving garnish with the remaining whole mint leaves.

L O Q U A T S

Loquats are also known as Japanese medlars. They appear similar to plums, with a smooth golden yellow-orange or red-brown skin. The flesh is cream-coloured and juicy, but slightly tart. The fruit should be firm, and eaten raw or cooked.

L Y C H E E S   O R   L I T C H I S

Lychees are of Chinese origin. The fruit is the size of a small tomato, with a hard scaly pinky-brown skin. The flesh is white, pulpy, and very juicy. Lychees are at their best when the red skin is turning brown. Avoid any lychees with brittle, dry brown skins. The skin or stone are not eaten, only the flesh. Lychees are used a great deal in Chinese cookery for both sweet and savoury dishes.

M A N D A R I N E   O R   M A N D A R I N

The mandarin is a Christmas dessert fruit, similar to the orange, but flatter. The skin is oily bright and bright orange, and the flesh, pinkish-white with pips. The fruit is imported from Italy, Spain and Morocco. The season is October to March.

M A N G O E S

The mango is a large stoned fruit which comes in different shapes and sizes, weighing up to 3 lbs (1.35 kg). The skin is tough and hard, and ranges in colour from yellow to green, or orange and red flushed with pink. The pulp is yellowy orange and has a delicate fragrant and spicy taste; some taste of paraffin, and are called 'paraffin fruits' in some countries. A mango should be firm, and not very soft when ripe. It is eaten as a dessert fruit, used in Indian cookery, and for chutney.

MANGO FOOL

❀ ☆☆☆☆ **Serves 6 Persons**
PREPARATION TIME: 20 MINUTES PLUS COOLING

Ingredients:

4 large mangoes	6 oz (150 g) of sugar
1 tbs of lemon juice	Pinch of salt
2 large eggs lightly beaten	16 fl oz (430 ml) of thin cream

Method:
Peel the mangoes and chop coarsely. Purée in a blender with the lemon juice and half the sugar. Sieve the purée to remove any stringy bits and chill. In the top of a double boiler combine the eggs, sugar and salt. In a small saucepan heat the cream until it bubbles around the edge. Slowly pour the cream onto the egg mixture stirring constantly. Place the mixture over hot but not boiling water, stir constantly until the mixture coats the spoon, about 5 minutes. Pour the custard into a bowl and chill in the refrigerator. Fold the chilled mango mixture into the custard stirring it only lightly so that the mixture streaks. Serve chilled.

M E L O N S

Melons have been cultivated for thousands of years in Egypt and only reached northern Europe in the fifteenth century. Melons can be served as a dessert course or a starter. They are very refreshing. A melon's flesh is 95% water. Melons are served chilled, but bare in mind that prolonged refrigeration destroys the melon's delicate flavour.

There are three categories:
The musk or netted melons: musk melons are called Gallia, and are distinguished by the reddish net pattern on the skin.
Canteloupe: are grooved and knobbly, or smooth skinned. Two popular types of cantaloupe are Charentais or Ogden. These melons are small enough for one melon to one person, or if larger, half each. Both canteloupe and musk melons have scented green or orange flesh. Canteloupe and musk melons should be fragrant, and very slightly soft around the base.
Winter melons: ripen later in the season, and because of this they can be stored for much longer and are therefore usually cheaper to buy. The honeydew melon, is shaped like a rugby ball, and has yellow smooth ridged skin. The flesh is sweet and pale green to pink in colour.
No part of the melon need be wasted. The seeds toasted can be served as tit-bits, the flesh eaten, and the shell makes a receptacle for fruit salads or cocktails. The thick inner rinds of winter or watermelons can be crystallised.

MELON GINGER BASKETS

❀ ☆☆☆☆
PREPARATION TIME: 30 MINUTES
CHILLING TIME: 1 HOUR

Ingredients:

1 small melon per person

12 white seedless grapes per person

Caster sugar to taste

Very finely grated fresh ginger,

or powdered ginger

Method:

Place the melon on a board, with a sharp knife make a horizontal incision from the top, but not all the way round, leaving 1" (2.5 cm) in the centre. Then make a vertical incision and cut away 2 wedges which will leave you with a handle. Carefully cut away the flesh from the outer skin in the handle. Remove the seeds from the melon and with a melon bowler, scoop out the remaining flesh and put aside. You should now be left with a melon basket. Mix the grapes with the melon balls and add the ginger and sugar to taste. Put back into the baskets and chill. Serve.

MELON WITH PORT

❀ ☆☆☆
PREPARATION TIME: 5 MINUTES

Ingredients:

1 melon per person

White port

Method:

Take the tops off the melons making a zigzag incision. Remove the pips and fill the cavity with white port, put in the refrigerator to chill. Serve on a bed of crushed ice.

N E C T A R I N E S

Nectarines are similar to peaches, with a smooth skin, and a juicy sweet flesh. A ripe nectarine should be firm but soft to touch and the skin red.

O R A N G E S

There are bitter and sweet oranges, and numerous varieties. The most common bitter orange is the Seville, which is a thick-skinned orange, with an acid deep yellow flesh and many pips, exclusively used for marmalade. This orange is imported from Spain, and the season is January to February. The shape and flavour of dessert oranges varies according to the origin.

GRAND MARNIER ORANGES

❀ ☆☆☆☆ **Serves 4 Persons**
PREPARATION TIME: 30 MINUTES
CHILLING TIME: 2 HOURS

Ingredients:

8 oranges

1 pt (575 ml) of water

8 oz (200 g) of sugar

3 fl oz (75 ml) of Grand Marnier

Method:

With a sharp knife remove the outer skin of a couple of the oranges without taking the white pith with it. Cut into very fine long strips. Put into a pan of water and bring to the boil, drain, and repeat. Put aside. Boil together the water and sugar until a light syrup has formed. Put aside, adding the orange strips and Grand Marnier. Again with a very sharp knife remove the skin and pith and inner membrane from the oranges so that you are left with just the segments. Slice the oranges thinly crossways and arrange on a dish and pour the syrup over them. Serve chilled.

ORANGE SAUCE

❀❀ ☆☆☆
PREPARATION TIME: 20 MINUTES
COOKING TIME: 5 MINUTES

Ingredients:

4 oranges
10 fl oz (275 ml) giblet stock or a good
chicken stock
Juice of ½ lemon

1 level tbs arrow root
3 tbs Curacao (optional)
4 fl oz (100 ml) red wine vinegar
1 level tbs caster sugar

Method:

With a sharp knife remove the peel ensuring that no pith is on the peel. Bring to the boil in cold water, strain and repeat. Set aside. Remove the skin and pith from the 4 oranges and segment. Put aside (do this over a plate to keep the juices). In a pan boil the sugar and vinegar until it has reduced to a light caramel. Add the stock, orange and lemon juice, and boil for 5 minutes. Thicken the sauce with diluted arrowroot and stir until shiny. Strain the sauce, add the orange segments and Curacao. Serve hot with roast duck.

SUGARED ORANGE CUBES

❀ ☆☆☆
PREPARATION TIME: 10 MINUTES

Ingredients:

1 orange   *Six cubes of white sugar*

Method:

Gently rub the sugar cube over the outside of an orange skin until the cube has absorbed the oil from the orange. The end product should be a highly perfumed orange cube.

CRÈPES SUZETTE

❀ ☆☆☆☆ **Crêpes can be prepared in advance, stored either frozen or in a container.**
PREPARATION TIME: 30 MINUTES
COOKING TIME: 2 TO 3 MINUTES PER CRÈPE

Ingredients: *For 12 pancakes:*
Batter:

4 oz (100 g) of plain flour	*Pinch of salt*
1 egg	*½ pt (275 ml) of milk*

Flavourings:

Juice of ½ lemon	*1 oz (25 g) of unsalted butter*
Juice of 1 orange	*4 tbs of orange liqueur*
Six sugared orange cubes (see page 284)	

Method:
Make the crêpes (see page 216), melt the butter in a large frying pan and stir in the sugar and cook gently until a golden-brown caramel is formed. Add the lemon and orange juice, stir until a thickish sauce is formed, drop a flat pancake into the pan, fold in half and then in half again. Push to one side of the pan and do the next pancake (It is advisable only to attempt 4 pancakes in one pan at any one time) When the pancakes are in the hot sauce add the orange liqueur, heat and flambé. Transfer the pancakes onto a hot serving dish, pour the sauce over them and serve at once.

ORTANIQUE

An ortanique is a cross between an orange and a tangerine, similar in size to a navel orange. Their thin skin is orange-yellow, and their flesh sweet and juicy. It is a dessert fruit, but makes a good marmalade. The ortanique is imported from Spain, the season October to March.

PASSION FRUITS

A tropical fruit similar in size and shape to a large plum. The ripe fruit has a tough wrinkled skin, which is a deep purple-brown colour. The aromatic orange pulp is sweet and juicy, and deeply pitted with small black seeds, which are eaten with the flesh.

PASSION FRUIT POSSET

❀ ☆☆☆☆ **Serves 4 Persons**
PREPARATION TIME: 20 MINUTES
CHILLING TIME: OVERNIGHT

Ingredients:

10 fl oz (275 ml) of thick cream	*1½ large egg whites*
Juice of half a lemon	*2½ fl oz (60 ml) of dry white wine*
1½ fl oz (37 ml) of canned passion fruit concentrate	*Fresh passion fruit seeds to garnish*

Method:
In a large bowl whip the cream until stiff. Stir in the wine then fold in the lemon juice and passion fruit concentrate, be very careful not to overheat. Add the sugar to taste. Whisk the egg whites until stiff but not dry, using a metal spoon, fold the egg whites into the cream mixture and leave to chill overnight. About 1 hour before serving, whisk the posset once more, pile into serving glasses and garnish.
To make fresh passion fruit concentrate, squeeze the juice of four passion fruits and add sugar.

P A W P A W S   O R   P A P A Y A S

This tropical fruit resembles an elongated melon. Their smooth skins ripen from green to yellow or orange. The sweet juicy pulp is pink or orange with a texture resembling melon. The brown-black seeds lie in the centre, and should be removed. Pawpaws are prepared the same way as melons and served similarly. The season is June to December.

P E A C H E S

There are two varieties of peaches, free-stone and cling stone. The free-stone peach has a better flavour, but is seldom seen in the shops. Avoid purchasing bruised or split peaches, they should be soft but firm to touch. Imported peaches are available from March to December.

CINNAMON HOT BAKED PEACHES

✿ ☆☆☆
COOKING TIME: 15 MINUTES
PREPARATION TIME: 5 MINUTES
OVEN TEMP: 375F 180C M5

Ingredients:

1 tin of peach halves
Ground cinnamon

Brown sugar

Method:
Arrange the peach halves with the syrup in a oven-proof dish, sprinkle the cinnamon and brown sugar over the peaches. Bake in the oven for 15 minutes. Serve with single cream.
Note: It is optional to add a little brandy to the syrup.

STUFFED PEACH HALVES

✿ ☆☆☆ **Served with ham, boiled gammon or as a dessert.**
PREPARATION TIME: 15 MINUTES

Ingredients:

1 tin of peach halves, drained.
3 oz (75 g) of cream cheese

1 oz (25 g) of browned almond slivers

Method:
Brown the almond slithers under the grill. Mould the cream cheese into balls which will sit comfortably in the well of the peach half, roll the balls in the browned almonds and place in the peach. Serve. As a dessert serve with a slightly sweetened soured cream, or as a garnish decorate with a little sprig of parsley.

LEMON POACHED PEACHES

✿✿ ☆☆☆☆ **Serves 4 Persons**
PREPARATION TIME: 10 MINUTES

COOKING TIME: 20 MINUTES
CHILLING TIME: 2 HOURS

Ingredients:

4 peaches	*1 pt (575 ml) of water*
2 lemons	*Fresh mint leaves*
6 oz (150 g) of caster sugar	

Method:

Slice 1 lemon into eight round slices, put the water and the sugar into a pan, place 4 of the lemon slices on the bottom and place a peach on top of each one, bring slowly to the boil and simmer gently for approximately 15 minutes. Gently remove the peaches and peel. Remove the lemon slices and discard. Boil the remaining syrup until it reduces and thickens, and then add the 4 remaining lemon slices and allow the syrup to slightly caramelise (the syrup will turn a very pale brown colour, at this stage you must remove it from the heat). Place the 4 caramelised lemon slices on individual plates and place a peach on top, pour over the syrup and decorate with a sprig of fresh mint leaf. Chill and serve.

FRESH PEACHES ROMANOFF
Named in honour of Russia's Imperial family.

❀ ☆☆☆☆☆ **Serves 4-6 Persons**
PREPARATION TIME: 20 MINUTES
CHILLING TIME: 2½ HOURS

Ingredients:

6 ripe peaches	*3 tbs of Rum*
Juice of one lemon	*10 fl oz (275 ml) of thick cream*
6 tbs of icing sugar	*3 tbs of Kirsch*
3 tbs of Cointreau	*Zest of one orange*

Method:

Loosen the peaches's skins and peel. Cut in half and remove the stone. Slice the peaches lengthways. Put into a bowl with the lemon juice to prevent discoloration. Gently toss the peach slices with 4 tablespoons of icing sugar. Pour over them a mixture of Cointreau and rum. Cover the bowl and put into the refrigerator to chill. Whip the cream and incorporate all the ingredients together. Serve.

P E A R S

Pears are native to Europe and Western Asia. By the sixteenth century, 232 varieties were available in Italy, of these, 209 were served to the Grand Duke Cosmo III during a single year. Today there are probably three times that many varieties in existence, but no more than a dozen generally available. Dessert pears should always be just ripe. A pear when ripe should yield when gently pressed at the stalk end.

PEARS IN STILTON CREAM

✿ ☆☆☆ **Serves 4 Persons**
PREPARATION TIME: 20 MINUTES

Ingredients:

2 firm ripe dessert pears	*10 fl oz (275 ml) single cream*
Acidulated water	*Seasoning*
4 oz (100 g) of Stilton	*Watercress*

Method:
Peel, halve and core the pears and put into acidulated water, pound the Stilton, gradually incorporating the cream until you have a smooth coating consistency. Season to taste. Arrange a pear half on an individual plate either left whole or fanned out and coat with the Stilton mixture. Garnish with watercress.
Note: The single cream can be substituted by natural yoghurt.

PEARS WITH ALMONDS

✿ ☆☆☆ **Serves 4 Persons**
PREPARATION TIME: 20 MINUTES
COOKING TIME: 20 MINUTES
CHILLING TIME: 2 HOURS

Ingredients:

4 even-sized dessert pears	*¾ pt (425ml) water*
2 oz (50 g) of almond slithers	*Juice of half a lemon*
6 oz (150 g) of caster sugar	*1 slither of orange peel*

Method:
Peel the pears leaving them whole. In a heavy pan boil the water, lemon, orange, and sugar. Add the pears and simmer gently for 15 minutes or until the pears are tender. Remove the pears, and rapidly boil the syrup until it reduces and thickens slightly. Meanwhile brown the almond slithers under a hot grill, insert the slithers into the pears. Put each pear onto an individual plate and pour a little of the syrup over each one. Decorate with a crystallised violet or fresh mint leaves. Chill.

P E R S I M M O N S

The persimmon is also known as the Sharon fruit if it has been grown in Israel. This tropical fruit looks like a large tomato, with a leathery bright red-orange skin, and orange pulp. The Sharon fruit is the only persimmon which can be eaten when firm, all other varieties must be left until the orange-red skin turns translucent and the flesh becomes like jam. The persimmon's flesh can be spooned from its skin and served with cream, stewed, baked in tarts or puréed for sauces. Avoid fruits with pitted or cracked skins. The season is October to January.

PINEAPPLE

The pineapple is not one fruit but many, formed by the fusion of about 100 separate flowers. The fruit has a hard knobbly top skin, yellow to bright orange and green hard leaves at the top. The flesh is sweet, and becomes heavily scented as the fruit ripens. A simple test for ripeness is to tap its base, a dull solid sound indicates ripeness. Another indication is that the inner leaves pull out with ease. The sweet-and-sour flavour of the pineapple makes it a good companion to rich foods such as glazed ham.

Raw pineapples contain an enzyme that attacks gelatine, so if your recipe combines pineapple and gelatine, cook the fruit beforehand to destroy the enzyme.

PINEAPPLE & KIWI

❁ ☆☆☆☆
PREPARATION TIME: FOR EACH PINEAPPLE 15 MINUTES

Ingredients:
1 small pineapple per person *One kiwi per person*
Syrup:
1 pt (575 ml) of water *4 fl oz (100 ml) Grand Marnier*
6 oz (150 g) of sugar

Method:
Make the syrup by boiling together the water and sugar for 15 minutes. Put aside and add the Grand Marnier. Meanwhile remove the top of the pineapple about 1" (2.5 cm) down from the leaves. With a sharp knife and spoon cut and scoop out the flesh from the shell. Put the pineapple pulp in the syrup with the peeled and sliced kiwi. Pour the mixture back into the pineapple and replace the lid. Serve.
Note: The shell of a large pineapple makes an excellent receptacle for presenting fresh fruit salad. It makes a superb centre piece. A medium-size pineapple cut lengthways down the centre with the flesh scooped out, is an interesting way to serve fruit salad.

PINEAPPLE WITH MINT SYRUP

Trim the pineapple, cut into rings. Boil together ½ pint (300 ml) of water with 4 oz (110 g) of sugar and ten fresh mint leaves until a light syrup has formed. Remove the mint leaves and add fresh ones. Pour the liquid over the pineapple and chill in the refrigerator. Serve.

PINEAPPLE IN KIRSCH

❁ ☆☆☆☆ **Allow two slices of pineapple per person**
PREPARATION TIME: 20 MINUTES
CHILLING TIME: 2 HOUR

Ingredients:
Fresh pineapple slices
Syrup:
1 pt (575 ml) of water *8 oz (225 g) of caster sugar*

Kirsh to taste

Method:
Slice and trim the pineapple. Boil together the water and sugar until a light syrup has formed (approximately 15 minutes). Add the kirsch to your taste. Pour over the pineapple slices and chill in the refrigerator. Serve.

P L U M S   &   G A G E S

Plums and gages were introduced from France and Italy in the fifteenth century. They were considered a staple food in Britain until the second World War, when there came an unaccountable slump.
There are both dessert and culinary plums. Gages are round, and green-yellow in colour, and a dessert plum. The damson has a dark blue to black skin, and is oval in shape and smaller than gages and only used in cooking or for preserving. Dessert plums are firm with a bloom on the skin.

P O M E G R A N A T E S

The pomegranate is similar in size to an orange, with a tough thin rind. The rind should be brightly coloured, pink to red and firm. The juicy flesh is bright crimson, and the translucent seeds eaten. Grenadine is made from the pomegranate, and used in cocktail making, or in syrups for fruit salads. The season for the fruit is September to January.

P R I C K L Y   P E A R S

The prickly pear is known as the Indian fig. The pear's skin has ribs of hair like spikes, and it is the edible berry of the cactus. This fruit must be handled cautiously until its spiky skin has been removed. Peeled and sliced, the sweet juicy flesh is delicious served with a dash of lime or lemon juice. Prickly pears can also be stewed or puréed.

Q U I N C E S

The quince is available between October and November. The fruit has a tough golden skin when ripe, with an acid flesh which is highly aromatic. The quince is used in jelly and jam making, or to flavour pies.

R A S P B E R R I E S

Raspberries need eating as soon as possible after harvesting. The season is July to August.

RÖSCHEN IM SCHNEE
Also known as Watte-ums-Herz 'cottonwool round the heart'.
Translated into English the title is 'Roses in the snow'.

☆ ❀❀❀ **Serves 4 Persons**
PREPARATION TIME: 30 MINUTES PLUS CHILLING

Ingredients:

12 fl oz (325 ml) of sweetened raspberry	*2½ oz (65 g) of potato flour*
or cherry juice	*4 medium-sized egg whites*
To Serve:	
12 fl oz (325 ml) of thick cream	*Vanilla sugar*
2½ oz (65 g) of icing sugar	

Method:

Gently heat the fruit juice. Moisten the potato flour with 9 fl oz (250 ml) of water and add it to the fruit juice. Cook the mixture gently until thickened. Remove from the heat. Whisk the egg whites until stiff and fold them carefully into the thickened juice. Mould the mixture onto a serving dish and refrigerate. Thirty minutes before serving whisk the cream until stiff, whisk in the sugar and a little vanilla sugar. Take large dollops of the cream with a little spoon and arrange them like snowflakes or tufts of cotton wool around the fruit juice dome. Serve.

R H U B A R B

Rhubarb is acid and so only eaten stewed or poached. The leaves of the rhubarb are poisonous. Buy young tender rhubarb stems, trim off the leafy tops and pale pink root, and cut into pieces. Old rhubarb needs the stringy covering peeled off before poaching.

S A T S U M A

Satsumas are similar to tangerines with a smooth, fairly thick skin, and pale orange-yellow flesh without pips. The season is October to February.

S T R A W B E R R I E S

Strawberries need to be eaten soon after harvesting. Hull and wash them carefully. To cut strawberries use a stainless steel knife to prevent discoloration.

HOT STRAWBERRIES WITH GREEN PEPPERCORNS

☆☆ ❀❀❀❀ **Serves 4 Persons**
PREPARATION TIME: 40 MINUTES

Ingredients:

2 oranges	*1 tbs of green peppercorns, drained and*
1 lemon	*rinsed*
8 oz (200 g) of sugar	*1 lb (450 g) of hulled strawberries*
2 tbs of Brandy	

Method:

Grate the zest from the orange and put into a heavy based saucepan. Squeeze the juice from the 2 oranges and the lemon and add to the pan. Add the sugar to the orange and heat, letting it form a light caramel, then carefully add the brandy. Remove from the heat and strain the syrup into a clean saucepan. Add the green peppercorns and bring to the boil.

When the mixture has boiled add the strawberries, and heat through for only 1 minute. Serve.

WILD STRAWBERRIES

Also called European alpine strawberries, which are smaller and more scented than cultivated berries.

TANGERINE

A small sweet orange characterised by its loose, bright, orange to red skin and small juicy segments. The season is October to March.

UGLI - TANGELO

The ugli fruit is a cross between a tangerine and a grapefruit, and the size of a large grapefruit. The fruit has a thick knobbly greenish-yellow skin, with a juicy yellow flesh, which is sweeter than a grapefruit and, only has a few pips. The fruit is imported from Jamaica, and the season is October to February.

TOMATOES

The tomato is strictly a fruit, but classified as a vegetable because of its uses in savoury dishes. This fruit was also called 'Love Apples'. To skin tomatoes, pour boiling water over them and leave for 1 minute, then pierce the skin with a fork and peel, alternatively hold the tomato over a naked flame until the skin breaks.

STUFFED TOMATOES

Pick firm tomatoes, cut off the top and with a teaspoon remove the pips. Place in a shallow baking tin. Lightly fry in some butter a finely chopped onion, add this to some fresh bread crumbs along with seasonings of your choice. Stuff the tomatoes, add a knob of butter on top of each and bake for about 15 minutes in a hot oven. Serve as an accompaniment with grilled meat or fish.

WALNUTS

Avoid nuts which rattle. Green wet walnuts are available from September to October and are eaten fresh.

HERBS & SPICES

There is no substitute for the aroma of fresh herbs and spices. Both have medicinal and culinary properties, they are used to flavour and preserve food.

H E R B S

Never keep dried herbs longer than six months, as they go stale. Use twice the quantity of fresh herbs to dried. Herbs contain oils which have distinctive savour.

Angelica
Stem of a large leafy plant, green in colour. Used raw in salads, or crystallised to decorate desserts.

Balm
Strong lemon-scented leaves, used chopped in salad dressings, omelettes, stuffings, sauces to accompany fish, fruit drinks, or as a substitute for lemon peel in sweets.

Basil
Clove-like flavour. Traditionally used in preparation of tomato dishes. Young fresh leaves are shredded and added to salads, butters and white sauces served with fish or poultry.

Bay leaves
Delicately sweet and fragrant. The leaves are dried and sold whole or ground. Used to flavour fish, stews, sauces, milk pudding and custards. Ingredient for bouquet garni.

Borage
The young leaves are used in salads and wine cups. When the leaves are bruised and shredded they taste like cucumber. Tea is made from young chopped leaves. The flowers can be candied and used for cake and sweet decorations.

Chervil
Aromatic herb of the parsley family. The leaves are feathery with a slight aniseed flavour. Used in egg and cheese dishes, soups and omelettes. Added towards the end of cooking time.

Chives
Chives have a mild onion flavour. Chopped, they are added to cheese dishes, soups and omelettes. Can also be sprinkled on salads and vegetables.

Coriander
Feathery green leaves with a distinctive flavour. Used in Indian cuisine, added chopped to soups, stews and salads.

Dill
A feathery green herb added to green salads. The flavour is delicate and complements fish or vegetable dishes. Used to flavour vinegars and pickling ingredients. Commonly used in Scandinavian dishes.

Fennel
The leaves are blue-green and make a most attractive garnish. Sweetly aromatic with an aniseed flavour. Fennel is popular in Mediterranean cuisine.

Garlic

"Garlic, the smell of which is so dreaded by our little mistresses, is perhaps the most powerful remedy in existence against the vapours and nervous maladies to which they are subject."
BERNARDIN DE SAINT-PIERRE
Cultivated in Britain from the beginning of the sixteenth century. The juice of garlic is a powerful antiseptic and was used by the French army during the first world war. Used with discretion, garlic enhances the flavour of almost any savoury dish.

Ityssop
Mint-flavoured leaves. Ityssop is added to fruit salads and punches. Used in making the liqueur Chartreuse.

Lavage
An extremely popular medieval herb. The leaves look and taste like celery leaves. The leaves are used for flavouring vegetable soups and stews, chopped in omelettes, salad dressings and cream sauces. The stems are crystallised and used as decorations similar to angelica.

Marjoram
There are two types of marjoram. The leaves of sweet marjoram are similar to thyme, and can be used as a substitute. Used to flavour roast or grilled meats, stuffings, in omelettes, soups and stews. Used in bouquet garni. Pot marjoram is used in the same ways, but the leaves are slightly bitter.

Mint
Sweet fragrant herb, most commonly used with lamb and veal.

Parsley
Sweet mild leafy herb, an essential ingredient in bouquet garni. Parsley is used to enliven most savoury dishes and as a garnish.

Rosemary
Pungent fragrant herb. It is particularly good with grilled meat and barbecued food.

Sage
Only the leaves are used. Sage has a strong flavour and complements fatty meats and stuffings.

Tarragon
The leaves are sweet and aromatic. Used to flavour soups and stuffings. Added to béarnaise and tartare sauce and sprinkled on chicken, grilled fish and vegetable dishes.

Thyme
A strong aromatic herb, an essential ingredient in bouquet garni. Used chopped in fish, meat, poultry dishes and added to stuffings.

S P I C E S

Spices have played an enormous part in world economy for many centuries.
There are sweet spices and seed spices.

SWEET SPICES

Cloves
A pungent aromatic spice. Its tropical flower has been imported for over 2000 years. Cloves contain up to 18% oil. They are bought whole or powdered and used sparingly. Used in mulled wine, and many sweet and savoury dishes.

Cinnamon
Is the bark of a small evergreen tree, grown in Ceylon and South India. It has been traded for thousands of years. The paper-thin strips of bark are peeled off, rolled into thin sticks and left to dry. Cinnamon is bought in sticks or powdered. Used to flavour milk puddings, hot drinks and is an essential ingredient in curry powders.

Nutmeg
The nutmeg is the kernel of an evergreen tree, with a yellow plum-like fruit, from Indonesia and the West Indies. The process of extracting nutmeg is long and complicated. Whole nutmegs are dark brown, oval and about half the size of a walnut, they are easily grated and superior in flavour to powdered. Used in vegetable and cheese dishes.

Mace
Mace is the husk which comes from around the nutmeg kernel. It is scarlet when fresh, but orange-brown dried, sold either in blades or powdered. Mace was popular in the sixteenth to eighteenth centuries in Britain. The delicate flavour enhances chicken and fish. Powdered mace is traditionally added to potted shrimps, white sauces and egg dishes.

Allspice
Allspice is the dried unripe berry of the pimento or 'Jamaican pepper' tree, grown in abundance in Jamaica. It tastes similar to cinnamon, nutmeg and cloves mixed together. It is brought whole or ground, added to marinades, chutneys, fruit and vegetable mixtures.

Mixed spice
A combination of ground cloves, allspice, nutmeg and cinnamon.

Vanilla
The bean or pod of a climbing tropical orchid from Mexico or Madagascar. The long black bean is gathered before it is fully ripe and dried. The pod has a delicate flavour and is used to flavour sweet dishes. Vanilla is sold in liquid form, essence or dried pods.

SEED SPICES

Aniseed
Beige small seeds, with a slightly sweet liquorice flavour, sold whole or ground. Used to flavour Pernod, ouzo and arrak.

Caraway seeds
Small brown crescent-shaped seeds with a pungent sharp flavour. Sold whole or ground. The seeds become bitter if they are subject to prolonged cooking. Traditionally used in English seed cake, German and Austrian breads, cabbage and sausage dishes. In Hungary the traditional dish goulash is flavoured with caraway and paprika. The Dutch cheese Leyden is flavoured with the seeds.

Black cumin
Black cumin is twice as strong as the paler variety. Used frequently in Indian cuisine.

Celery seeds
An aromatic tiny brown seed with a bitter celery-like flavour, bought whole or ground. Added to fish, egg, and beef dishes. Celery salt is the ground seeds with added salt.

Coriander seeds
Beige small round seeds with a warm sweet spicy flavour with a hint of orange and a touch of sage. Bought whole or ground. Used in vegetable dishes, whole in pickling spice mixes and ground in curry powder.

Dill seeds

Flat ridged beige seeds, available ground or whole. Slightly bitter flavour, used for flavouring egg dishes, vegetables, fish and pickled cucumbers. The flavour deteriorates with prolonged cooking.

Fennel seeds

Small light brown ridged seed, with a sweet liquorice flavour. Used in marinades, sauces for oily fish or pork.

Onion seeds

Tiny, round black seeds.

Poppy seeds

Small, round, mild nutty-flavoured seeds. There are two types, the blue-grey used in Central European baking and the smaller creamy-yellow ones which are favoured in Indian cuisine. Both can be bought whole or ground.

Sesame seeds

Egg-shaped, small, flat seeds, differing from cream to black, the palest ones being the most common. Raw, they have a mild flavour, and when toasted a delicious nuttiness. Added to breakfast cereals and baked on top of breads.

Star anise

Small brown seeds in star-shaped brown pods. The seeds contain the oil anise which is its characteristic flavour. Used in Chinese cookery.

Saffron

Saffron is extremely expensive, the stigmas of over 75,000 crocuses are needed to produce 1 lb (½ kg) of saffron and these are harvested by hand. It has a pungent bitter flavour and only very small amounts are used. Intense yellow-gold colour.

Mustard seeds

Small pale brown round seeds. Used for pickling and chutney making.

HOT SPICES

Cardamom

Cardamon is a warm, pungent highly aromatic flavoured seed. It is a member of the ginger family, native of the humid forests of India, Sri Lanka and Guatemala. The pods are bleached to a pale creamy-green colour and contain numerous dark seeds. Used in Indian and Far Eastern cuisine.

Cumin

Thin yellow-brown seeds with a strong aromatic flavour. Bought whole or ground. Used in curries, rice dishes, chutneys and pickles.

Fenugreek

The seeds are small, flat and yellow-brown, with a bittersweet flavour. Dominant in curries, chutneys and spicy vegetable dishes. Essential in Indian cuisine.

Turmeric

Dried root belonging to the ginger family, normally bought powdered. Bright orange-yellow with a peppery smell and warm, slightly bitter flavour. Added to relishes, rice, egg, fish dishes and pickles. It can be used as a cheaper substitute for saffron.

Chilli

Red or green small pointed fruits, bought fresh, dried, whole, flaked or powdered. They are the hottest spice known to man and used extensively in South American cuisine. Blended in curry powder.

Chilli sauce & Tabasco
A liquid made from chillies, very hot.

Cayenne pepper
Cayenne pepper is made from pulverised red capsicums, it is hot, but not as fiery as chilli powder. Added to curry and traditional Mexican dishes. Traditionally served with smoked salmon and potted shrimps.

Paprika pepper
A scarlet powder made from dried sweet peppers. Chiefly produced in Hungary and widely used in Central Europe. It has a full, sweet, slightly smoky flavour and glowing colour. Traditional ingredient in goulash.

Garam masala
The Indian name for a special spice blend. A typical blend consists of three parts cardamon and cinnamon, one part clove, and one part cumin. Added towards the end of cooking to deepen the flavour.

Curry powder
A blend of spices used by Europeans. Not used in traditional Indian cuisine.

BREADS

Anthropologists have discovered that barley cakes were baked in Neolithic dwellings. Thousand of years ago early man discovered that grain when ground and mixed with liquid yeast and salt, produced a staple food.

The English produce **blommers, cottage, coburgs** and **baps**. The French specialise in **French stick, baguettes**, the solid round **pain de campagne**, flutted **brioches** and crescent shaped **croissants**. The Italians are famous for **Grissini** which are long dry bread sticks. The Jewish bread made from egg is **Challah** which is very rich. **Bagels** are small ring shaped breads which are boiled before being baked. **Pitta bread** from the Middle East is close textured, flat and oval shaped. San Francisco specialises in **sourdough** breads made from a fermented mixture of flour and water. **Soda bread** is traditional Irish bread raised with soda instead of yeast.

Bread sold to the public must, by law, contain added vitamin B and Nicotinic Acid. The milling of flour takes a large proportion of these out. Rye, barley, millet oats, corn rice and buckwheat are sometimes incorporated to increase nutritional content.

White Bread
White bread is made from 70% to 75% extraction flour, which is flour containing 70% to 75% original wheat. It is generally the least nutritious.

Wholemeal Bread
Wholemeal bread is made from 100% extraction flour, containing all the bran and wheatgerm of the wholemeal grain.

Stoneground Wholemeal Bread
Bread made from flour that has been ground between stone rollers. The bread is close textured and has a nutty flavour, it is baked having being sprinkled with cracked wheat.

Brown or Wheatmeal Bread
This is a bread baked from 85% extraction flour. Granary bread is made from a blend of wheatmeal and rye flour with malted grain incorporated.

Wheatgerm Bread
Bread made from white flour with added wheatgerm and bran.

Scoffa Bread
Scoffa bread is a corse brown bread which is usually presented in large wedges.

Rye Breads
These breads are popular in Central Europe and Scandinavia. Rye breads can be light or dark breads, with added ingredients such as caraway seeds, fennel or orange. A famous black German rye bread is called 'Pumpernickel'.

Garlic Bread
Spread garlic and herb butter onto the incisions in a French stick. Bake in a hot oven until crisp.

Tomato & Oil Bread
Soak slices of corse white bread in a little olive oil mixed with tomato pulp, crushed garlic, salt and freshly ground black pepper. Serve with aperitifs.

BUTTER & FATS

"Honest bread is very well - it's the butter that makes temptation."(The Catspaw)
DOUGLAS JERROLD

Fats are an essential source of energy and hold fat-soluble vitamins. All fats are high in calories. Monosaturated fats contain some cholesterol; polyunsaturated fats have little or no cholesterol. Fats are divided into two, unsaturated and saturated.

Unsaturated fats are soft or liquid and usually come from vegetables. These include margarine and low-calorie spreads, most oils and white vegetable fats.

Saturated fats are mostly of animal origin. They are solid at room temperature, these include lard, dripping, suet and hard margarine.

BUTTER

Indispensable in the kitchen, many recipes do not tolerate a substitute. Butter is made by churning cream until globules of fat form a mass. This mass is then pressed to extract any liquid.

Butter divides into two types, sweet cream and lactic, both may have salt added. Sweet cream butter is made from the cream of fresh cow's milk, it is delicately flavoured, golden yellow in colour, firm, waxy, smooth. It is used for pastry and biscuits. Butter produced in United Kingdom, Irish Republic, Australia, New Zealand, Canada and the United States of America is generally of this type.

Lactic butter is made with cream soured by the introduction of bacteria. The savour of this butter is full with a soft fine texture and pale colour. Because it creams easily, it is used for cake making. This butter is made in France, Germany, Denmark and the Netherlands.

Butter should be bought weekly, it will store in the refrigerator for two to three weeks. Keep it covered, to prevent loss of vitamin D. Butter can be frozen wrapped in foil.

TO CLARIFY BUTTER

Clarified butter has a lower risk of catching fire, whilst frying, than ordinary butter. The object of clarifying is to eliminate the salt in the butter. Unsalted butter should never be clarified as it would lose its fresh taste.

To clarify butter put it in a thick-bottomed saucepan and melt it over a very low heat. The butter will foam, and the foam will fall gently to the bottom of the pan, leaving the clear oil on the surface which is the clarified butter. Pour the butter into a bowl, being careful not to disturb the sediment. Clarified butter should be kept covered in the refrigerator.

SAVOURY BUTTERS

Maître d'Hôtel

1 oz (25 g) of butter　　　　　　　　　　*1 tsp of finely chopped parsley*
1 tsp of lemon juice　　　　　　　　　　*Salt & pepper*

Cream the butter with the lemon juice, parsley and seasoning. Wet a sheet of greaseproof paper and put the butter in the centre. Fold the paper in half and ease the butter to a sausage shape. Roll the paper up and then twist the end of the paper to form a neat sausage cracker shape. Put in the refrigerator to harden.

Anchovy Butter

1 oz (25 g) of butter   *Four fillets of anchovy*
Anchovy essence   *Half a clove of garlic*
Freshly ground black pepper

Cream the butter with the anchovy. Add the anchovy essence, pepper and garlic, add salt if desired and mix thoroughly. Excellent with boiled, grilled, fried, or poached fish.

Garlic Butter

1 clove of garlic   *1 oz (25 g) of butter*

Cream together and season to taste.

Chivry or Ravigot Butter

3 oz (75 g) of butter   *Tarragon & chive*
Parsley   *1 shallot*
Chervil

Blanch the herbs for a few minutes. Squeeze out the water, chop the shallot and pound all the ingredients together. Season to taste.

Shrimp Butter

2 oz (50 g) of butter   *Seasoning & lemon juice*
2 oz (50 g) of peeled shrimps

Pound the shrimps and add the butter and seasoning, blend well together.

Herb Butter

2 oz (50 g) of butter   *½ clove of crushed garlic (optional)*
Mixed finely chopped herbs   *Seasoning & lemon juice*

Pound all ingredients together until well mixed.

Mustard Butter

2 oz (50 g) of butter   *1½ tbs of French mustard*

Blend well together and keep in a cool place, excellent with grilled ham and fish.

Paprika Butter

2 oz (50 g) of butter   *1 dsp of paprika*
1 tbs of finely chopped onion

Work together to form a smooth paste.

Tarragon Butter

1 oz (25 g) of tarragon leaves   *2 oz (50 g) of butter*

Blanch the tarragon leaves for two minutes, drain, refresh and squeeze. Pound them with the butter.

Lobster Butter

1 oz (25 g) of butter   *Cooked coral from a lobster*

Pound together.

Orange Butter

Finely grated zest of one orange	*1½ oz (37 g) butter*
½ a tsp of paprika	*Seasoning*
1 tsp orange juice	

Cream the butter and add the other ingredients together. Leave to harden the same way and for Maître d'hôtel. Serve with grilled sole.

Montpellier Butter

1½ oz (37 g) butter	*2 fillets of anchovy*
1 hard-boiled egg yolk	*A small handful of parsley*
2 or 3 leaves of spinach	*Salt & pepper*
2 sprigs of tarragon	

Boil the herbs together for 5 minutes, sieve the yolk with the anchovy, work all the ingredients together. Season well. Use with grilled fish or meat.

WAYS TO SERVE BUTTER

Butter curls and balls are easy to make when the butter is firm, neither solid nor soft. With hard butter, cut into pretty shapes. Do not shy away from serving some of the butters listed above, they are an interesting addition to any dish.

MARGARINE

Made from vegetable oils, milk, salt and colourings. Contains fish oils or animal fats. Hydrogen is passed through margarine to harden it. Margarine is used in the same way as butter (the texture and flavour will of course be different). Soft margarines have been treated to render them easy to spread. Low-fat spreads contain more water than ordinary margarines, they are used in diet recipes. Margarine containing butter should be stored in the same way as butter, others can be stored for 2-3 months in the refrigerator. Low-fat spread can be stored for 1 month.

LARD

Lard is made by melting down pork fat. Lard can be stored in the refrigerator for approximately 6 weeks and deep frozen for up to 5 months. To make your own lard, mince or chop pork fat, place in a heavy-based pan with just enough water to prevent it sticking. Melt it very slowly, pouring off the fat as it melts. Store.

SUET

Suet is the hard fat around lamb's and beef's kidneys and liver. It is used for suet pastries, mincemeat and boiled puddings. Packet suet stores for approximately two months and fresh suet for 1 month.

DRIPPING

Is the fat that drips from beef and lamb whilst roasting. It can also be made from rendering down chunks of fat. To store the dripping from roast joints, leave it to get hard, then turn it out of the bowl and scrape off the jelly and sediment (use this to enrich any gravy). Do not mix drippings and never pour new dripping onto old.

GHEE

Used in Indian cookery. Ghee is excellent for frying as it can be heated to a very high temperature without burning.

GOOSE FAT

Is an extremely flavoursome fat, rich and oily. Goose fat was traditionally smeared onto patients' chests when they had a bronchial infection to cure their ailment!

CHICKEN FAT

Much used in Jewish cookery, as dietary laws prohibit the combination of meat and dairy products. It comes from the roasted bird and should be stored in the refrigerator as dripping. It will keep for up to 6 weeks.

SAUCES

Sauces were used during the Middle Ages to mask the flavour of meat inadequately cured and rancid. Today they are served to complement the dish.

There are five elementary techniques in sauce making, and mastering the essential principles will enable you to prepare most sauces.

- **ROUX:** Melt butter or margarine, add flour and cook until it stops forming bubbles.
- **BROWN ROUX:** Melt butter, add flour and cook until the flour takes on a light brown colour.
- **BROWN BASIC SAUCE:** Dilute the browned roux with stock or water.
- **WHITE SAUCE:** Dilute the white roux with liquid i.e. milk, vegetable, fish or meat stock.
- **BÉCHAMEL SAUCE:** Infuse milk with a bay leaf, onion and seasonings, and add it to the white roux in the usual manner.

THICKENING SAUCES

The Roux: The oldest method used to thicken liquids.

Cornflour or Cornstarch: Mix cornflour with a small amount of the liquid. Pour it in the pan with the sauce and bring to boil.

Beurre Manie (Flour & butter): Combine flour with butter in equal quantities to form a ball. Gradually whisk into the liquid until it thickens.

Egg Yolks: Take your sauce off the heat and gradually whisk the egg yolks into it. Never reboil the sauce as the egg will curdle.

Butter: Whisk softened butter into a much reduced liquid off the direct heat, and the sauce will thicken.

Cream or Soured Cream: Add the cream at the end of cooking and gently heat.

Purée: Simply add vegetable purée to the liquid, excellent if you are counting the calories!

SAUCE CONSISTENCIES	USES	INGREDIENTS BUTTER & FLOUR	MILK
Thin sauce	Basis for soups	½ oz (10 g) of each	½ pt (275 ml)
Pouring sauce (medium)	For accompanying sauces	¾ oz (20 g) of each	½ pt (275 ml)
Coating sauce (medium thick)	For coating	1 oz (25 g) of each	½ pt (275 ml)
Panada sauce (very thick)	For binding croquettes, & as a basis for soufflés	2 oz (50 g) of each	½ pt (275 ml)

BASIC WHITE SAUCE

❀ ☆☆☆
PREPARATION TIME: 10 MINUTES

Ingredients:

1 oz (25 g) of butter
1 oz (25 g) of flour

½ pt (275 ml) of milk
Salt & pepper

Method:

Melt the butter over a moderate heat, add the flour, stir until combined. Take off the heat and gradually whisk in the cold milk to a smooth consistency. Re-heat and season.

BÉCHAMEL SAUCE

❀ ☆☆☆
PREPARATION TIME: 30 MINUTES

Ingredients:

½ pt (275 ml) of milk
½ small bay leaf
Thyme
½ small onion
¼ level tsp of grated nutmeg

1 oz (25 g) of butter
1 oz (25 g) of plain flour
Salt & pepper
2-3 tbs of double cream (optional)

Method:

Infuse the milk with the bay leaf, thyme, onion and nutmeg in a pan, bring to the boil. Set aside for 15 minutes. Strain and continue as for white sauce.

BROWN SAUCES

ESPAGNOLE SAUCE

The basis of many compound brown sauces, the Espagnole is made from a brown roux.

❀ ☆☆☆
PREPARATION TIME: 10 MINUTES
COOKING TIME: 1 HOUR 15 MINUTES

Ingredients:

1 carrot, finely diced
1 onion, finely chopped
2 oz (50 g) of green streaky bacon, chopped
1 oz (25 g) of butter

1 oz (25 g) of plain flour
¾ pt (425 ml) of brown stock
Bouquet garni
2 level tbs of tomato paste
Salt & black pepper

Method:

Melt the butter in a pan and cook the vegetables and bacon over a low heat for 10 minutes until light brown. Add the flour and stir until brown. Gradually add the stock until a smooth sauce has been achieved. Cook thoroughly. Add the bouquet garni, cover with a lid and simmer for 30 minutes stirring frequently. Strain the sauce through a fine sieve, and skim off any fat. Season to taste.

To clear an Espagnole sauce, rapidly boil and as the scum forms skim it away. Whilst the sauce is boiling, throw a small amount of cold water into the liquid and quickly bring back to the boil, skim any scum off. Repeat this process 3 or 4 times until the sauce has a glossy appearance.

DEMI-GLACE SAUCE

❀ ☆☆☆
PREPARATION TIME: 40 MINUTES

Ingredients:

½ pt (275 ml) of Espagnole sauce   ¼ pt (150 ml) of jellied brown stock

Method:
Add the jellied stock to the Espagnole sauce, bring to the boil and cook until the sauce is shiny and thick enough to coat the back of a spoon.

Serving Suggestions: If serving with game, add 3 tablespoons of Madeira. For poultry add 4 oz (110 g) of sliced sautéed mushrooms and 1 tablespoon of Madeira.

DEVILLED SAUCE

❀ ☆☆☆
PREPARATION TIME: 40 MINUTES

Ingredients:

½ pt (275 ml) of Espagnole sauce   Sprig of thyme
½ pt (275 ml) of white wine   Small bay leaf
1 small onion, finely chopped   1 tbs of parsley
1 tbs of wine vinegar   Cayenne

Method:
Mix the wine, vinegar, onion, thyme and bay leaf in a pan, bring to the boil and reduce to half. Strain and add to the Espagnole sauce. Boil for a few minutes, and season with the chopped parsley and cayenne.

Serving Suggestion: Grilled chicken.

RED WINE SAUCE

❀ ☆☆☆
PREPARATION TIME: 40 MINUTES

Ingredients:

½ pt (275 ml) of Espagnole sauce   ½ pt (275 ml) of red wine
½ an onion, finely chopped   Bouquet garni

Method:

Sauté the onion in 1 oz (25 g) of butter until clear. Add wine and bouquet garni, and boil until it has reduced by half. Strain and add to the Espagnole sauce. Cook until it has reduced by one-third. Stir in 1 oz (25 g) of butter and serve immediately.

Serving Suggestion: Game or grilled red meats.

TOMATO SAUCE

❀ ☆☆☆
PREPARATION TIME: 30 MINUTES

Ingredients:

½ pt (275 ml) of Espagnole sauce made with tomato juice instead of brown stock

4 oz (110 g) of chopped ham

Method:

Dice the ham and add to the sauce.

Serving Suggestions: Grilled chicken or meat, pasta and meat patties.

GRAVIES FOR ROAST MEAT POULTRY & GAME.

Beef, Lamb, Pork or Poultry Gravy:

When you make gravy always use natural ingredients. Keep the juices from the roast joint, and any green or root vegetable water (not potato or leek water).

In the roasting tin or a saucepan thicken the joint juices with flour forming a roux, and gradually add the vegetable water making a smooth gravy.

Beef, lamb and mutton gravy should be thin, pork and poultry gravy is slightly thicker. The caramelised juices from the pan should give natural colour to your gravy (add a few drops of liquid gravy browning for extra colour if needed).

Game Gravy:

Fry some chopped bacon in a pan until crispy, and then add the juices from the roasting pan. Make a roux and add the vegetable water. Game gravy should be very thin with a glossy appearance.

How to make gravy without juices from the pan:

Always drain off excess fat from your roast joints and keep a little bowl for each kind in your refrigerator. When you make gravy, use the fat and follow the above instructions. To add any extra flavour, use a good quality stock cube.

CREAM SAUCE

❀ ☆☆☆
PREPARATION TIME: 15 MINUTES

Ingredients:

¼ pt (150 ml) of dry white wine

1 pt (570 ml) of double cream

1 tbs of butter

Salt & pepper

Method:
Pour the wine into a pan and reduce to half over a moderate heat. Add the double cream and whisk until it has reduced by half. Remove from the heat and whisk in the butter. Season to taste and serve immediately.

S I M P L E   W H I T E   S A U C E S

CAPER SAUCE

❀ ☆☆☆
PREPARATION TIME: 10 MINUTES

Ingredients:

1 oz (25 g) of butter	*¼ pt (150 ml) of fish or white stock*
1 oz (25 g) of flour	*1 tbs caper juice or lemon juice*
¼ pt (150 ml) of milk	

Method:
Mix the caper or lemon juice with the stock before making the sauce. Make a white sauce with ½ milk and ½ fish or white stock. Add the finely chopped capers to the sauce before serving.
Serving Suggestions: Serve with mutton or white fish.

CHEESE SAUCE

❀ ☆☆☆
PREPARATION TIME: 15 MINUTES

Ingredients:

½ pt (570 ml) of white sauce	*½ level tsp dry mustard*
2 oz (50 g) of mature Cheddar cheese, grated	*Pinch of cayenne*

Method:
Make a white sauce. Take it off the heat and stir in the grated cheese until smooth. Season with mustard and cayenne.
Serving Suggestion: Serve with egg, fish pasta or vegetable dishes.

EGG SAUCE

❀ ☆☆☆
PREPARATION TIME: 15 MINUTES

Ingredients:

½ pt (275 ml) of white sauce	*2 level tsp of chopped chives*
1 hard-boiled egg	

Method:
Chop the chives and the egg and add to the white sauce.

307

Serving Suggestion: Serve with poached or steamed fish.

FISH SAUCE

❀ ☆☆☆
PREPARATION TIME: 15 MINUTES

Ingredients:

½ pt (275 ml) of white sauce made with ½ milk & ½ fish stock

2 oz (50 g) of shrimps
1 tsp of anchovy essence

Method:

Peel and chop the shrimps, add it with anchovy essence to the sauce, and season to taste.

MUSHROOM SAUCE

❀ ☆☆☆
PREPARATION TIME: 15 MINUTES

Ingredients:

½ pt (275 ml) of white sauce
2 oz (50 g) of mushrooms

½ oz (10 g) of butter
Squeeze of lemon juice

Method:

Trim and slice the mushrooms. Sauté them in the butter and lemon juice until soft. Drain and stir into the sauce. Serve.

Serving Suggestion: Serve with fish, meat and poultry.

ONION SAUCE

❀ ☆☆☆
PREPARATION TIME: 40 MINUTES

Ingredients:

1 onion
4 whole cloves
¾ oz (20 g) of butter

¾ oz (20 g) of flour
½ pt (275 ml) of milk

Method:

Tub the onion with the cloves. Slowly cook the onion in the milk until tender, approximately 30 minutes and strain. Make a white sauce with the milk. Chop the cooked onion and add to the sauce. Season to taste.

Serving Suggestion: Serve with roast lamb, mutton or tripe.

PARSLEY SAUCE

❀ ☆☆☆
PREPARATION TIME: 10 MINUTES

Ingredients:

½ pt (570 ml) of white sauce   2 level tbs of parsley

Method:

Finely chop the parsley and add to the melted butter, make a roux and proceed as for white sauce. Season to taste.

Serving Suggestions:

Serve with boiled or steamed fish, bacon joints, vegetables.

C O M P O U N D   W H I T E   S A U C E S

VELOUTÉ SAUCE

❀ ☆☆☆
PREPARATION TIME: 5-10 MINUTES
COOKING TIME: 1 HOUR

Ingredients:

1 oz (25 g) of butter   Salt & black pepper
1 oz (25 g) of plain flour   1-2 tbs of single or double cream
1 pt (570 ml) of white stock   (optional)

Method:

Make the roux with the butter and flour, gradually stir in the stock until smooth. Bring to the boil and let the sauce simmer for 1 hour until reduced by half. Stir the sauce occasionally. Strain through a sieve, season to taste and stir in the cream.

CHAUDFROID SAUCE

❀ ☆☆☆
PREPARATION TIME: 1 HOUR + COOKING TIME

Ingredients:

½ pt (275 ml) of velouté sauce   4 tbs of single cream
¾ pt (425 ml) of jellied white stock

Method:

Add the cream and stock to the sauce. Cook over a gentle heat until reduced to a coating consistency. Season to taste. This sauce is mainly used cold for coating chicken, eggs and fish.

ALLEMANDE SAUCE

❀ ☆☆☆
PREPARATION TIME: 1 HOUR

Ingredients:

½ pt (275 ml) of velouté sauce   ¼ pt (150 ml) of white stock
2 egg yolks   1½ oz (40 g) of butter

Method:

Whisk the egg yolks with the stock and add to the velouté sauce. Simmer gently stirring until thick, and reduce by one third. Stir in the butter and adjust the seasoning.

MORNAY SAUCE

❋ ☆☆☆
PREPARATION TIME: 15 MINUTES

Ingredients:

2 oz (50 g) of grated Parmesan or   ½ pt (275 ml) of béchamel sauce
Gruyère cheese

Method:

Blend the cheese into the béchamel sauce, but do not re-heat.

SUPREME SAUCE

❋ ☆☆☆
PREPARATION TIME: 15 MINUTES

Ingredients:

½ pt (275 ml) of velouté sauce   2 tbs of double cream
2 egg yolks   1 oz (25 g) of butter

Method:

Make a velouté sauce. Take off the heat and beat in the egg yolks and heat without boiling. Turn off the heat, stir in the butter and cream.

HUNGARIAN SAUCE

❋ ☆☆☆
PREPARATION TIME: 20 MINUTES

Ingredients:

½ pt (275 ml) of velouté sauce   1 level tsp of paprika
1 onion, finely chopped   Pinch of salt
½ oz (10 g) of butter   6 tbs white wine
Bouquet garni

Method:

Sauté the onion in the butter until clear, add the rest of the ingredients except the velouté sauce and bring to the boil and reduce by half. Strain through a sieve before adding to the velouté sauce.

AURORA SAUCE

❋ ☆☆☆
PREPARATION TIME: 15 MINUTES

Ingredients:

½ pt (275 ml) of velouté sauce

4 tbs of tomato purée or

1 tbs concentrated tomato paste

1½ oz (40 g) of butter

Method:

Blend together the tomato purée and the velouté sauce, stir in the butter and season to taste.

BEURRE BLANC

A white butter sauce.

❀ ☆☆☆

PREPARATION TIME: 20 MINUTES

Ingredients:

5 shallots

½ pt (275 ml) of dry white wine

4 oz (110 g) of cold butter

Salt & pepper

Method:

Finely chop the shallots and put in a pan. Add the wine, and bring to the boil over a high heat. Reduce almost all of the wine leaving only the base of the pan moist. Take off the heat, add the cold butter in pieces and whisk in. Season to taste.

HOLLANDAISE SAUCE 1

❀❀ ☆☆☆

PREPARATION TIME: 20 MINUTES

Ingredients:

8 oz (225 g) of butter

2 egg yolks

4 tbs of white wine

Juice of ½ a lemon

Salt & white pepper

Method:

Heat the butter over a moderate heat, and spoon off the scum. Set aside. Tip the egg yolks and white wine into a metal bowl and whisk over a pan of hot water until frothy. Whisking continuously add the butter, a few drops at a time. Season with lemon juice, salt and pepper.

HOLLANDAISE SAUCE 2

❀❀ ☆☆☆☆

PREPARATION TIME: 20 MINUTES

Ingredients:

3 tbs of white wine vinegar

1 tbs water

6 whole black peppercorns

1 bay leaf

3 egg yolks

6 oz (175 g) of soft butter

Salt & black pepper

Method:

Boil together the vinegar, water, bay leaf and peppercorns in a small pan until reduced to 1 tablespoon. Leave to cool. Cream the egg yolks with ½ oz of butter and a pinch of salt. Strain the vinegar into the cream and set the bowl over a pan of boiling water. Turn off the heat and whisk in a small nut of butter at a time. When the sauce is shiny and has the consistency of thick cream, season to taste.

Hollandaise sauce may curdle during preparation. This is because the heat is too sudden or too high, or the butter has been added too quickly. Sometimes the sauce can be saved by removing it from the heat, and beating in 1 tablespoon of cold water.

BÉARNAISE SAUCE

Béarnaise sauce is similar to Hollandaise sauce but has a sharper flavour. It is served with grilled fish or meat.

❀❀ ☆☆☆☆
PREPARATION AND COOKING TIME: 20 MINUTES

Ingredients:

2 tbs of tarragon vinegar	*3-4 oz (75-100 g) of butter*
½ small onion, finely chopped	*Salt & black pepper*
2 egg yolks	

Method:
Put the vinegar and onion in a small pan and boil steadily to reduce to 1 tablespoon. Strain and set aside to cool. Then follow the instructions for Hollandaise sauce.

E G G - B A S E D   S A U C E S

MAYONNAISE

It is essential that all the ingredients are at room temperature.
Pitfall: Mayonnaise may curdle if the oil is too cold or added too quickly. To save it, whisk a fresh egg yolk in a clean bowl, and gradually whisk it in the curdled mayonnaise. Alternatively, whisk in a teaspoon of tepid water until the mayonnaise is thick and shiny. Mayonnaise is easier made in a liquidiser, food processor or using an electric whisk.

❀ ☆☆☆
PREPARATION TIME: 10 MINUTES

Ingredients:

2 egg yolks	*Black pepper*
½ level tsp of dry mustard	*2 tbs of white wine vinegar or lemon juice*
Pinch of caster sugar	*½ pt (275 ml) of olive oil or salad oil*
Pinch of salt	

Method:
Add together in a bowl or in your liquidiser the egg yolks, salt, sugar, mustard, pepper and vinegar, and mix well. Gradually add the oil in a steady fine stream until the mayonnaise has thickened to the desired consistency.

Note: The flavour of mayonnaise may be varied by using tarragon, garlic or chilli vinegars. Chopped herbs, parsley, chives or crushed garlic may be added to the mayonnaise when made.

TARTARE SAUCE

❀ ☆☆☆
PREPARATION TIME: 5 MINUTES

Ingredients:

1 tbs of parsley, finely chopped   *Chopped chives*
1 tbs of capers, finely chopped   *½ pt (300 ml) of mayonnaise*
1 tbs of gherkin, finely chopped

Method:
Mix all the ingredients together in a bowl, season to taste.

SEAFOOD DRESSING (MARIE ROSE DRESSING)

❀ ☆☆☆
PREPARATION TIME: 5 MINUTES

Ingredients:

½ pt (300 ml) of mayonnaise   *Dash of Worcester sauce*
¼ pt (150 ml) of tomato ketchup   *Dash of chilli sauce*
Dash of Tabasco

Method:
Mix all the ingredients together in a bowl, chill and serve.
Variation:
1-Add a drop of Whisky   *2-Add very finely chopped red pepper*

HORSERADISH MAYONNAISE

❀ ☆☆☆
PREPARATION TIME: 5 MINUTES

Ingredients:

¼ pt (150 ml) of mayonnaise   *Dash of Worcester sauce*
4 tbs of strong horseradish

Method:
Mix all the ingredients together in a bowl, chill and serve.

ALABAMA SAUCE

This sauce is used as an alternative dressing to seafood, but also makes a delicious dip for crudités.

❀ ☆☆☆
PREPARATION TIME: 15 MINUTES

Ingredients:

1 tbs of celery, finely chopped
1 tbs of green pepper, finely chopped
1 tbs of cucumber, finely chopped
¼ pt (150 ml) of mayonnaise

4 tbs hot horseradish
2 cloves of fresh garlic, crushed
4 tbs chilli sauce

Method:

Mix all the ingredients in a bowl, chill and serve.

MISCELLANEOUS SAUCES

GARLIC SAUCE

❀ ☆☆☆
PREPARATION TIME: 10 MINUTES

Ingredients:

6 cloves of garlic
12 walnuts
1 tsp of Armagnac

Salt & pepper
½ pt (275ml) of olive oil
Chopped herbs

Method:

In a mortar pound together the garlic, walnuts and Armagnac to form a smooth paste. Season with salt and pepper, then add the oil gradually. The amount of oil should be equal to the combined weight of the garlic and nuts. Add chopped herbs if you desire.

BREAD SAUCE

❀ ☆☆☆
PREPARATION TIME: 30 MINUTES

Ingredients:

8 oz (225 g) of breadcrumbs
½ pt (275 ml) of milk
1 onion

1 bay leaf
10 cloves
Pieces of carrot

Method:

Stud the onion with the cloves, and put in the milk with the bay leaf and carrot. Bring to the boil and then leave to steep for 30 minutes. Strain the milk over the bread and stir. Season to taste.

MINT SAUCE

❀ ☆☆☆
PREPARATION TIME: 10 MINUTES

Ingredients:

40 fresh mint leaves

1 tsp of caster sugar

4 tbs of boiling water or vegetable water

¼ pt (150 ml) of wine vinegar or lemon juice

Method:

Finely chop the mint leaves or pound with a pestle and mortar. Cover with the sugar, add just enough boiling liquid to dissolve the sugar. Sharpen the sauce with vinegar or lemon.

BLACK CHERRY SAUCE

❀ ☆☆☆☆
PREPARATION TIME: 20 MINUTES
COOKING TIME: 20 MINUTES
SERVE WITH: ROAST DUCK, BRAISED PIGEONS

Ingredients:

1 lb (450 g) of stoned fresh black cherries

½ pt (275 ml) of giblet stock, or brown stock

2 tbs of vinegar

Juice of ½ a lemon

Juice of ½ an orange

Arrowroot

Seasoning

Method:

Boil the vinegar until it has reduced by half, add the fruit juices and the stock, and boil for a further 10 minutes. Add the cherries. Thicken with the arrowroot, and season to taste. At this stage add a little Madeira or cherry brandy if you desire, it will give it a little zap.

D R E S S I N G S

BASIC FRENCH DRESSING

❀ ☆☆☆
PREPARATION TIME: 5 MINUTES

Ingredients:

¹/₃ of vinegar

²/₃ of oil

½ tsp of dry mustard

½ tsp of caster sugar

½ tsp of ground black pepper

¼ tsp of salt

Method:

Combine all the ingredients in a screw-top jar. Always give the dressing a good shake before serving.

Note: There are many variations to this recipe which can be achieved by adding a clove of crushed garlic, fresh or dried herbs, chopped nuts, crumbled cheeses, or by using different types of mustards, oil or vinegars.

ROQUEFORT SALAD DRESSING

A perfect dressing for tomato or cucumber salad, or a coleslaw.

✿ ☆☆☆

PREPARATION TIME: 8 MINUTES
CHILLING TIME: 2 HOURS

Ingredients:

1½ oz (40 g) of Roquefort cheese
4 fl oz (110 ml) soured cream
1 tbs of lemon juice

1 large spring onion, white part only
finely chopped

Method:

Sieve the cheese and work it in the soured cream and lemon until smooth. Add the chopped onion. Store in a screw top jar in the fridge. Shake well before use.

ROQUEFORT CHEESE DRESSING

✿ ☆☆☆☆

PREPARATION TIME: 10 MINUTES

Ingredients:

8 oz (225 g) of Roquefort

10 fl oz (300 ml) of single cream

Method:

Pound the cheese and add the cream until you have a smooth consistency which will coat the back of a spoon. The Roquefort can be substituted with Stilton cheese.

COLESLAW DRESSING

✿ ☆☆☆

PREPARATION TIME: 20 MINUTES

Ingredients:

1 dsp of sugar
1 dsp of flour
1 tsp of mustard
1 tsp of salt
Few grains of cayenne

1 tsp of butter
1 egg yolk
Vinegar
½ cup of single cream or top of milk

Method:

Mix all the dry ingredients together in a bowl, and then add the butter, vinegar and egg. Cook in a bowl over boiling water until it thickens. Cool, add the cream and beat thoroughly.

BRANDY CREAM

✽ ☆☆☆☆
PREPARATION TIME: 10 MINUTES

Ingredients:

10 fl oz (300 ml) of single cream   *4 tbs of brown sugar*
4 tbs of brandy

Method:

Put all the ingredients into a pan and cook gently over a moderate heat until the sugar has dissolved. Do not boil. Serve warm.

CREME A LA VANILLE (ENGLISH BOILED CUSTARD)

✽ ☆☆☆
PREPARATION TIME: 15 MINUTES

Ingredients:

2 yolks of egg   *1 tbs of sugar*
½ pt (275 ml) of milk   *½ vanilla pod or vanilla essence*

Method:

Beat the egg yolks. Put the sugar, milk and vanilla in a pan and bring slowly to the boil. Remove the pod and pour the milk over the yolks, mix and return to the pan. Stir over a moderate heat until scalding point, and the liquid coats the back of your spoon. Cool and serve.
Note: Custard curdles if it is boiled. It is best to thicken custard in a double saucepan to prevent boiling, or in a bowl over boiling water.

RICH CHOCOLATE SAUCE

✽ ☆☆☆
PREPARATION TIME: 5 MINUTES
COOKING TIME: 10-15 MINUTES

Ingredients:

6 oz (250 g) dessert bitter chocolate   *½ pt (275ml) water*
4 oz (200 g) granulated sugar

Method:

Melt the chocolate in the water over a gently heat until smooth. Add sugar and bring to the boil. Simmer with lid on pan for 10-15 minutes until the sauce is of a syrupy consistency. Serve hot or cold.

STAIN REMOVAL

"Unpleasant stains which cannot be removed are unhappy reminders of what may otherwise have been a very jolly party."
LADY ELIZABETH ANSON'S PARTY PLANNERS BOOK, 1986.

Treat a stain as soon as possible. If the surface requires professional treatment, leave it alone and seek advice.

Before treatment consider three things:
The stain.
The surface it has fallen on.
Is there any special dye, treatment or finish?

Some quick first aid treatments are:
- For a non-greasy stain sponge or rinse with cold water.
- For a greasy stain sprinkle talcum powder to stop it spreading.
- Sprinkle salt on wine, fruit or beetroot stains to stop them from spreading, but not onto carpets as it can affect colours and attract moisture.

Always test on a small hidden area. This is essential!
A golden rule is to go cautiously when treating, often milder methods used several times are better than a blast from a strong solvent which may damage the surface. When applying a solvent to an absorbed stain which has not responded to sponging or laundering, work from the underside of the stain, holding a dry white absorbent pad on the other side. A built-up stain should, if possible, be treated from the underside with a pad held on the top of the mark so that the deposit is not drawn through the fabric. If any stain is removed with this method, the absorbent pad should be moved around to stop the stain being re-deposited on the surface.

TACKLING STAINS

Treat a stain working from the outside to the middle to prevent the stain from spreading. Dab at a stain rather than rub, to prevent damaging the surface. After removing the stain launder or dry clean immediately. Use only white absorbent cotton cloth or cotton wool as a dabber for any solvent or treatment, as dye may be affected on coloured cloths and transfer onto the surface being treated.
Professional cleaning is a must if the stain has fallen on an expensive garment or soft furnishing. Specialists have numerous solvents not available on the market. Do not attempt home treatments as this may hamper professional cleaning. Always tell them if you have tried, and how.

Stains are divided into three groups:
Absorbed stains: Spilled liquids such as tea, coffee, milk or beer absorbed into the surface.

Built-up stains: Such as grease, nail varnish and paint. Generally these do not penetrate far into the surface. The quicker you treat them, the less likely they are to set and cause damage to the surface below.

Compound stains: i.e. blood. They penetrate the surface and leave some residue on the top. The deposit should be treated as a built-up stain, then the penetration should be attended to as an absorbed stain. Final sponging or laundering will also be necessary.

STAIN REMOVAL KIT FOR ALL OCCASIONS

Many solutions are poisonous and should be kept out of the reach of children and animals. Certain solvents are flammable and give off toxic vapours, these should be used in a ventilated room, when possible wear rubber gloves to protect your hands, and never smoke or use near an open flame.

Ammonia: Neutralises acid stains.

Enzyme (biological) washing powder: Used for protein stains, egg, milk, blood and perspiration, but should not be used on protein fibres such as wool, silk, non-colour-fast, flame-resistant or rubberised fabric.

Glycerine: Softens stains on fabric. Leave the items soaking in a solution of equal parts glycerine and warm water.

Grease solvents: Recommended solvents include Dabitoff, K2r aerosol, K2r paste, Boots dry cleaner and Goddards dry cleaner. Used on grease-and-oil-based stains, always following manufacturer's instructions.

Laundry or domestic borax: Works on acid stains. Used in solution (15 ml to 500 ml of warm water) for sponging and soaking washable fabrics. If the item is white, laundry borax can be sprinkled directly onto the dampened stain. It can be used safely on most fabrics.

Methylated spirit: Highly flammable and poisonous. It is an excellent solvent for stain removing. It is used neat and dabbed onto stains, but you must check for colour fastness first. Never use on acetate or triacetate fabrics, or on French-polished surfaces as it will dissolve the polish.

White vinegar or dilute acetic acid: Always protect your hands when using acetic acid, never use on acetate or triacetate fabrics. Always thoroughly rinse out of the fabric after use. Acetic acid may cause dye bleeding, so test beforehand.

Pre-wash aerosols: Use on heavily soiled, stained areas on washable colour-fast fabrics. Two examples are Friend and Shout. Read manufacturer's instructions before use.

Other solvents used are: liquid lighter fuel, non-oily nail polish remover, amyl acetate, white spirit and turpentine substitute.

G E N E R A L   R U L E S

Upholstery: Never overwet upholstery, blot with a towel as you proceed with removing the stain. Velvet, (other than acrylic) and any brocatelles should be handled professionally. Water-borne stains can usually be removed from Dralon velvet and non-removable flat-weave Dralon covers by immediate and thorough blotting, followed by sprinkling the stain with a weak warm solution of enzyme detergent, always wiping the way of the pile with a clean sponge.

Carpets: A soda siphon is excellent to flush out spilled liquids if used immediately on the spill. Water-soluble stains and dirty marks can usually be removed with carpet shampoo, (following manufacturer's instructions). If the stain persists seek professional advice. Never soak a carpet, if a carpet can be raised treat the back as well. Care must be taken when using solvents on rubber or foam-backed carpets. Always smooth carpet pile in the direction it lies and allow to dry naturally. A solution of 5 ml detergent + 5 ml white vinegar + 1 lt. of warm water can be used as a substitute for carpet cleaner.

When using any product always follow the manufacturer's instructions.

MISCELLANEOUS STAINS

Beer

Carpet: squirt with the soda siphon or sponge with clear warm water. Blot well. Treat any remaining stain or dried marks with a carpet shampoo, i.e. 1001 Dry-Foam.

Table linen and washable fabrics: Soak fresh stains in luke-warm water then launder. Dried stains on white cottons or linens can be bleached with a hydrogen peroxide solution (1 part of hydrogen peroxide to 6 parts cold water). On coloured fabrics, sponge with white vinegar solution (30 ml vinegar to 500 ml water). On acetate or triacetate sponge with a laundry borax solution then launder.

Upholstery and non-washable fabrics: Blot well and then wipe with a clean cloth wrung out in clear lukewarm water. Use K2r or Goddards dry cleaner for stubborn stains.

Beetroot juice

Linen: Rinse immediately in cold water. Use a solution of laundry borax for soaking coloureds (15 ml of borax to 500 ml of warm water) and for whites, sprinkle borax onto the dampened stain and pour boiling water through it, rinse and launder.

Blood

Washable fabrics: Sponge with cold salt water then soak in an enzyme detergent, launder as usual.

Carpets: Flush with the soda siphon or sponge with cold water. Bolt dry and then shampoo if necessary.

Non-washable fabrics and upholstery: Wipe and brush the stain lightly to remove any surface deposit. Sponge with cold water to which a few drops of ammonia (2.5 ml of ammonia per 1 lt. of water) has been added. Rinse with clear water and blot well.

Candle wax

Carpets: Scrape off as much deposit as possible from the pile with a spoon. Place a sheet of blotting or brown paper over the wax and gently apply the toe of a warm iron to the mark. Keep moving the paper around until all the wax is absorbed. Treat any remaining mark with liquid Dabitoff or methylated spirit.

Polished wood surfaces: Hold a plastic bag of ice over the wax to harden it thoroughly. Chip at it carefully with a plastic spatula or fingernail. When all the wax has been removed burnish with a duster to remove any film, polish as usual. If a heat mark is left rub hard along the grain of the wood with a cloth dipped in metal polish i.e. Brasso.

Table linen and washable fabrics: Remove surface deposit with your fingernail. Place clean blotting paper on both sides of the stain and iron to remove the remaining wax, keep moving the paper around for maximum absorbency. Launder as usual.

Upholstery: On closely woven fabrics absorb the wax onto blotting paper with a warm iron, any remaining colour mark can be removed by dabbing with methylated spirit (not on acetate or triacetate).

On loosely woven fabrics do not pull off the wax as you may pull threads. Absorb the wax onto blotting paper with a warm iron, remove any colour traces with methylated spirit. On pile fabrics remove deposit by lightly rubbing with a clean cloth, absorb the wax onto blotting paper with a warm iron being careful not to flatten the pile.

Coffee

Carpets: Spoon and blot up as much as you possibly can, then flush out with a soda siphon or warm water. Blot dry. Use a carpet shampoo if necessary.

Non-wash fabrics and upholstery: Sponge with laundry borax solution (15 ml of borax to 500 ml of water) then with clear water. Blot dry. If any stains remain use a stain remover i.e. K2r.

Dralon: Thoroughly blot, then sprinkle with a warm enzyme solution (15 ml of powder to 1 litre of water) and lightly rub in direction of pile. Blot well. Never overwet the stain. Old stains should be lubricated with glycerine before treatment.

Table linen and washable fabrics: Rinse in warm water, soak in an enzyme detergent or laundry borax solution. Launder as usual. If any stain remains use a stain remover such as liquid Dabitoff.

Fats, grease and oils

Carpets: Blot and scrape off any deposits. Apply a stain remover i.e. Boots dry cleaner. Use a carpet shampoo.

Leather shoes: Shoes are protected by regular polishing, so quickly wipe off any oils as they occur. Alternatively use Meltonian Mel on stubborn marks, and Meltonian stain remover on light ones. Clean both shoes to disguise any light patches.

Leather upholstery and handbags: Cover the stain with a thin layer of bicycle puncture repair adhesive to absorb the grease, leave for twenty four hours then roll off carefully. Treat the article with a good quality hide food i.e. Hidelife.

Non washable fabrics and upholstery: Spread French chalk, talcum powder or powdered starch over the mark, replace when it has absorbed the oil. Leave for several hours then brush clean. Alternatively use a stain remover i.e. Boots dry Cleaner.

Flat woven or velvet pile Dralon: Should be treated with liquid Dabitoff. On larger areas use a warm iron over clean blotting paper to absorb any deposits.

Table linen: Blot and scrape off deposit. Cotton and linen can be laundered at a high temperature. Other fabrics should be treated with a stain remover i.e. Beaucaire before laundering as usual.

Washable fabrics: Scrape off any deposit then launder in hot water.

Delicate fabrics and wool: Dab with eucalyptus oil, then launder or sponge.

Fruit juice

Carpets: Absorb as much as possible with paper towels and then shampoo the area. When dry treat any remaining traces stain with a cloth moistened with methylated spirit.

Table linen: Rinse in cold water then pour hot water over the stained area so that it goes through it. Lubricate any remaining stain with glycerine then launder as usual.

Spirits

Carpets: Blot, flush the area with a soda siphon and sponge. Sponge. Treat any remaining stain with carpet cleaner.

Non-washable fabrics and upholstery: Sponge with clear luke-warm water, then blot dry. Treat with an upholstery cleaner.

Grass stains

Washable clothes: Light stains should wash out, dab heavier stains with methylated spirit. Rinse in clear water before laundering.

Gravy

Carpets: Remove as much as possible with a dry cloth, then treat with a liquid stain remover such as Boots dry cleaner followed by a carpet shampoo.

Non-washable fabrics: Treat with a stain remover i.e. Beaucaire, wipe with a cloth wrung out in warm water.

Table linen and washable fabrics: Soak in cool water then launder in warm detergent. Any remaining mark should be treated with a stain remover i.e. liquid Dabitoff. Dried stains should be soaked in enzyme detergent before laundering.

Mayonnaise

Non-washable fabrics: Remove residue with a damp cloth, then use a dry fabric stain remover i.e. K2r.

Linen and washable fabrics: Sponge with warm water, soak in an enzyme detergent then launder as usual.

Milk

Carpets: Immediate treatment is vital to eradicate the smell. Use a soda siphon or lukewarm water to flush the area, then blot. Shampoo the carpet as the smell can penetrate.

Non-washable fabrics and upholstery: Sponge with lukewarm water, if the stain remains use a stain remover, i.e. Goddard's dry cleaner, when it is dry. Thawpit is recommended for Dralon.

Linen and washable fabrics: Rinse well in lukewarm water then launder. If the stain remains soak in an enzyme detergent.

Mud

Carpets: Allow to dry, then brush off with a stiff-bristled brush or vacuum. Use a carpet shampoo if a mark remains.

Mustard

Non-washable fabrics: Sponge with a mild synthetic detergent, rinse in clear water.

Delicate fabrics: Should be treated professionally.

Table linen and washable fabrics: Wash in a mild synthetic detergent as usual.

Tea

Carpets: Blot, flush with a soda siphon or sponge with luke warm water. When necessary use a carpet shampoo, especially if the tea contained milk. If the stain persists, use an aerosol stain remover such as Dabitoff.

Table linen: Rinse immediately under a cold tap and then soak and launder in an enzyme detergent. On white linen or cotton a bleach solution may be used to soak stubborn stains, then launder in the usual way.

Wine

Carpets: Flush the area with a soda siphon or sponge with lukewarm water. Blot, then rub the area with a carpet shampoo, and wipe with a cloth wrung out in clear water. Repeat until clean. A solution of glycerine and water can be left on the stain for up to one hour to clear any remaining traces, then rinsed and blotted.

Non-washable fabrics and upholstery: Blot as much as possible and sponge the area with clear warm water. If a mark remains, sprinkle with French chalk or talcum powder whilst it is still damp. Brush after a few minutes and keep repeating this process until it is clear. Dry stains can be soaked in glycerine solution of equal parts glycerine to warm water and left on for fifteen minutes then wiped with a damp cloth wrung out in a detergent solution, followed by clear water. An upholstery-spotting kit may also be used.

Linen: White wine poured over a fresh red wine stain will neutralise it and make the stain easier to remove. Pour hot water through the stain, rinse in warm water, soak in laundry borax solution or an enzyme detergent before laundering. Soak all dried stains in a similar fashion. On white cotton and linen a solution of household bleach can be used to soak the cloth, then it can be laundered in the usual way.

Washable fabrics: Rinse in warm water, and if the stain remains sponge with a laundry borax solution or enzyme detergent. Wash as usual.

CLEANING

Decanters and carafes: Fill with a warm solution of enzyme detergent and leave to soak. A mixture of vinegar and salt may also be poured into a decanter and shaken from time to time. After these methods rinse the decanter thoroughly in warm water, then leave to drain upside down.

Burns: If the burn has caused light discoloration in the wood surface rub the mark with a metal polish, i.e. Brasso, working in the direction of the grain. On waxed or oil-finished wood rub the burn with turpentine. If the burn is more serious we suggest that you seek professional advice.

Heat marks: Burnish the mark with turpentine, always rubbing in the direction of the grain of the wood.

Scratches: Scratches can be masked using a shoe polish or wax crayon of similar colour to the wood. Leave this for a while and then buff the area.

Water marks: Burnish with turpentine as for burn marks. If this does not work use Brasso and rub it along the grain of the wood. Then polish and buff.

If the furniture is valuable, always seek professional help before any home attempts to rectify it.